MW01037583

ADMIRED DISORDER

A Guide to Building Innovation Ecosystems

**Complex Systems,
Innovation,
Entrepreneurship,
And Economic
Development**

Alistair M. Brett

Admired Disorder: A Guide to Building Innovation Ecosystems
© Alistair M. Brett, 2019

ISBN (Print Edition): 978-1-54396-617-6
ISBN (eBook Edition): 978-1-54396-618-3

Contents

1. Introduction   1

2. Summary of book Sections: Applications   9

3. A Little Background   15

4. What is an Innovation Ecosystem?   23

5. What is a Complex Adaptive System?   29

6. The Science of Innovation Ecosystems: A Brief Introduction   40

7. The Rainforest Model Explained   47

8. Systems, Models, and Attractors   59

9. The Ties That Bind Us: Strong Links, Weak Links, and Relevant Links   74

10. Building Blocks for Innovation Ecosystems   81

11. Boundaries, Limits, and Connections   100

12. Boundary Spanners: Network Holes and How to Plug Them   109

13. Contextual Qualifiers: One Size Doesn't Fit All   117

14. Networks and Feedback   125

15. Wicked Problems are Everywhere   134

16. Hierarchy and Necessity   144

17. Cause, Effect, and Trying to Predict   153

18. Sowing the Seeds of Resilience: Shocks to the System   161

19. Indicators and Fallibility   166

20. Noise and Housekeeping   177

21. Reusing Knowledge: Create Early, Use Often   181

22. Should Everything be Optimized?   186

23. Thinking about Diffusion   203

24. Practical Reasoning: Decision Making and Solving the Right Problem   208

25. Strategies for Building Innovation Ecosystems: The Workbook   222

26. A Framework, Geometry, and Grammar for Rainforests   259

27. Beyond Metaphor   268

28. What Next?   272

1

Introduction

· ·

Innovation requires supportive innovation ecosystems. These have the character of what are known as complex adaptive systems.

This book is about explaining the statement above and applying it to building innovation ecosystems and improving existing ones. No previous knowledge of complexity is assumed. All concepts are explained as they occur. In most cases we shall introduce examples and the underlying science in whichever order better aids understanding. Examples have been chosen to illustrate widely applicable fundamentals. All cases and examples are real, suitably anonymized to respect privacy and proprietary results. Whether you are building ecosystems to support startups or mature businesses, coffee shops or corporations, this book supplies insights.

We know that new companies founded by entrepreneurs have the potential to create jobs and economic benefits. It is critical for new businesses to have a support network or 'ecosystem.' What we need to understand better is how to design and build effective local and distributed ecosystems. Our focus is on *building* innovation ecosystems engineered to support economic and technology development and commercialization, including those environments experiencing dislocation and transition. The book's methodologies and findings can be applied more generally to enhancing innovation in individual companies or organizations within innovation ecosystems or in other settings. The knowledge in this book can be applied to developed nations and regions as well as those less developed.

The book is not about new business incubators, accelerators, seed capital funds, proof of concept centers, or any of the functional components of innovation ecosystems *as such*. Knowledge of how to build these resources is readily available. The book is about how such component building blocks can function as an integrated whole – and why.

For whom is this book written?

- Builders of innovation and entrepreneurial ecosystems and policymakers because of their need to focus on 'solutions' to building innovation and technology-based economies for communities, cities, and countries.

- Businesses that want to build or improve internal ecosystems to support R&D and innovation.

- Those teaching innovation and entrepreneurship, creating technology commercialization programs, practitioners, consultants, government officials, and advisors, because of their need to understand the role of innovation ecosystems in supporting their efforts.

- International development banks, government agencies, and non-government organizations in the developing world because of their need to provide support services which are often absent.

- Social scientists who need to add to their knowledge of how to support innovation.

- Developers of incubators and accelerators because of their need to plan how these fit into the broader innovation ecosystem.

- Those who need to create strategic plans in uncertain or unpredictable environments.

What this book is about and is not about.

- The book draws on research into complexity, in a variety of disciplines, to analyze innovation ecosystems and bring research results to the more general reader. It is firmly research-based and extensively cites research results to support views expressed.

- Our role is not to send the reader to the research literature, although references are provided for the adventurous, but to bring selected results from research and practice which may not be easily accessible to the reader in a manageable form for practical application. All references can be found using your favorite search engine.

- Most importantly, the book uses the results of research and practice to provide *practical help in engineering supportive innovation ecosystems which are robust and highly scalable*. It also encourages new ways of thinking about innovation ecosystems. This is not a book about innovation as such[1] but *innovation ecosystems which support innovation*. Similarly, this book is not about entrepreneurship as such (there are many of these) but ecosystems that support entrepreneurship.[2]

Reading this book

Printed books are linear; our topic is not. Interconnectivity poses some difficulties in writing separate Sections for this book. A consequence is that some necessary repetition results to reduce flipping back and forth between Sections. While it is recommended that the Sections be read in sequence, some readers may want to go to the capstone Section 25 first to see how concepts are applied and then work backwards. Others may want to jump to Section 7 to understand the Rainforest concept or preview Section 10 which is the core of the book. Still others may wish to review a Section where a topic of particular interest is discussed. Each Section begins with a brief summary.

· ·

[1] There are hundreds of books and thousands of articles and blogs on innovation. A useful source for different innovation models over the years is Maxim Kotsemir, Dirk Meissner "Conceptualizing the Innovation Process – Trends and Outlook, and Innovation Models.... What Determines the Capacity for Continuous Innovation in Social Sector Organizations?" *Rockefeller Foundation Report* by Christian Seelos and Johanna Mair January 31, 2012.

Also, "Innovation Models," Tanaka Business School, Imperial College, London (2006) is an excellent review.

[2] Social Entrepreneurship 1.0 focuses on individual heroic social entrepreneurs, Social Entrepreneurship 2.0 focuses on creating institutions to bring about social change, and Social Entrepreneurship 3.0 which recognizes social change requires a whole ecosystem consisting of the potential of all people and their interactions.

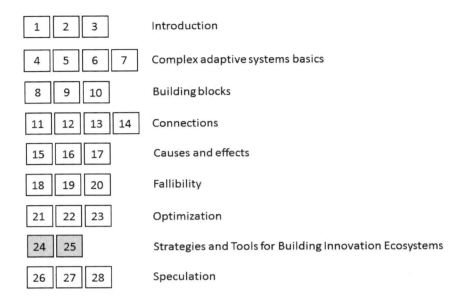

1	2	3		Introduction
4	5	6	7	Complex adaptive systems basics
8	9	10		Building blocks
11	12	13	14	Connections
15	16	17		Causes and effects
18	19	20		Fallibility
21	22	23		Optimization
24	25			Strategies and Tools for Building Innovation Ecosystems
26	27	28		Speculation

Figure 1. Section sequences.

How this book came about

The genesis is the publication by my colleagues Victor W. Hwang and Greg Horowitt in 2012 of **The Rainforest: The Secret to Building the Next Silicon Valley**.[3] The theme of the Rainforest work is summarized in Section 7. It will not be assumed dear reader that you have read Victor and Greg's book, although I recommend doing so for the new perspective it gives on innovation.

The investigations described here began with the realization that Rainforests *are complex adaptive systems* (defined in Section 5). Rainforests are often described by useful metaphors (Section 26) which may imply this is the only possible description. It is not. There is a science of Rainforests – the science and philosophy of complexity. I started to think about what features of the complex adaptive systems model might both explain Rainforests systems but also display Rainforests in a new light, especially

3   Victor W. Hwang and Greg Horowitt, "The Rainforest: The Secret to Building the Next Silicon Valley," *Los Altos Hills: Regenwald* (2012).

helping to explain their more mysterious characteristics, or make predictions about the behavior of innovation ecosystems.

We shall further see that understanding such complex adaptive innovation ecosystems helps deliver economic and social benefits, achieve competitive advantage, and create a robust innovation culture through new business opportunities, workforce utilization, exports, investment, quality of life, prosperity, and more in a holistic, positive manner. This new book extends the Rainforest concept and aims to provide:

The science behind stories of innovation ecosystems.

1. Practical applications for engineering high potential innovation ecosystems.

2. An understanding of complex adaptive innovation ecosystems to help create an innovation culture.

3. Explanations of the behavior of Rainforest systems which can only be understood by treating Rainforests as complex adaptive systems.

4. Where possible, prediction of a complex innovation ecosystem's future behavior given certain kinds of knowledge about present conditions.

5. Ways to intervene in complex innovation ecosystems to influence present and future behavior and sustainability.

To use an analogy: architects design buildings and draw their visions. These drawings are converted into detailed construction plans by engineers so a building can be built and function. Rainforest principles have to be converted into applications, which is where knowledge of the science comes in. Not everything in these principles is new but Rainforest science pulls them together into a system of thought.

Introducing 'science' will put off some readers perhaps because it was an indigestible subject in school. Applying science does not mean intuition and experience not important; throughout history the best scientists have relied on these capabilities. It does not mean human behavior is not important, so, don't worry.

A complex adaptive system does not have a single concise definition. However, the systems we are about to study will be systems of people. For now, let's just think of such a system as having unpredictable behavior, although parts of the system may be predictable, and one in which the whole is more than, or different from, the sum of its parts (just as our bodies are more than the sum of individual cells). Unpredictable does not mean inexplicable. Detailed properties of complex adaptive systems will be described in Section 5 where the term 'adaptive' will also be explained.

How *does* knowledge of complex systems help us make decisions about, and help to solve, real world problems?

- By analyzing a situation and recognizing complex systems features of the kind to be discussed.
- By using knowledge of these features to help make predictions and decisions for the intelligent application of resources to support innovation.

These real world systems may not have familiar cause and effect connections. We may have to adjust or abandon our preference for intuition or our mental models on the evidence or explanatory theory from science and observation.

Note that any theory must (i) explain observed results, and (ii) make predictions where possible. If not, we must be prepared to walk away. At this stage we might ask "have the theories found in this book been tested by collecting and analyzing empirical data?" Where there are data and case examples these will be referenced. Because many ideas presented here are new there is a need for much more empirical evidence to support or question these theories. In collecting and examining data and cases it is important to remember that to verify a proposition we must be able to understand what the proposition means.

Speaking in terms of 'problems' might seem a gloomy way of looking at the world but in the sciences it is a standard learning process. Scientists, engineers, and many others, rejoice in wrestling with problems until they find a solution; in the challenge of knowing there is a solution 'somewhere out there' – we just need to find it. A problem is not, as we frequently use the word in everyday speech, something to worry us or be a burden on our lives (there is a similar situation with the word 'complex' noted in Section 6). In the sense used in this book, a problem is something not completely understood. It's a challenge to be overcome, to solve it, to resolve it, and move on to the next one. As one writer out it "No one descends with such fury and in so great a number as a pack of hungry physicists, adrenalized by the scent of a new problem." [4]

This book focuses on the building blocks of innovation ecosystems and the connections among them. The world is seen as a series of relationships rather than things. Supporting new business creation, commercialization, and economic development requires supportive innovation ecosystems (an often neglected fact). An innovation ecosystem requires building blocks. Building blocks have to be assembled to optimize overall innovation ecosystem fitness.

Tools are needed. There is a shortage of science-based tools to analyze and engineer innovation ecosystems. This book introduces some tools and tips for application. It is hoped that readers will be encouraged to develop more tools for complex innovation ecosystems.

A 2010 IBM Global CEO Study [5] based on face-to-face conversations with more than 1,500 chief executive officers worldwide identified the Complexity Gap: the difference between expected complexity and the extent to which CEOs feel prepared to manage complexity was the single biggest area of concern about their businesses. CEO's expressed the need for more tools.

Innovation ecosystem examples are drawn from the author's three decades of experience in developing innovation ecosystems and technology commercialization in the USA, UK, Western, Central, and Eastern Europe, Central Asia, and Latin America. Evidence is from experience with developing new businesses and enhancing existing ones long before the term 'innovation ecosystems' was coined. If you are reading this book in a developing/middle-income country my wish is that you will apply much of what is described here. If you are in a more developed country there is much of value that can be applied to your situation.

Finally, it's of little use knowing about the complex nature of innovation ecosystems unless we can understand and resolve issues with which we are confronted, such as how to improve the flow of innovation, how to

. . . .

4   D. Watts. "Small Worlds: The dynamics of networks between order and randomness." *Princeton University Press* (1999).

5   "Capitalizing on Complexity: Insights from the Global Chief Executive Officer Study." *IBM* (2010). Complexity was the 2010 theme of IBM's annual survey.

anticipate disruptions, how to optimize leadership, and many others. If we cannot do this then knowledge of complex systems may be an interesting intellectual exercise, but not much more.

Therefore, a test for readers is to ask of every Section and its content "how does this knowledge help me to build an innovation ecosystem, understand the operation of an existing innovation ecosystem, correct its faults, and improve its efficiency – and what new knowledge have I acquired?"

2

Summary of book Sections: Applications

· ·

Applications of the concepts described in this book to engineering innovation ecosystems are provided in each section. They are summarized here to give you a general idea of the scope for reference. For details, see the appropriate Section. Here are just a few examples:

Q: *What elements constitute innovation ecosystems?*

See Section 4. What is an Innovation Ecosystem?

Q: *How to apply what is known about complex adaptive system concepts to develop high performance innovation ecosystems. Why these concepts are not mysterious or difficult to understand and use.*

See Section 5. What is a Complex Adaptive System?

Q: *Why understanding the science of innovation ecosystems which investigates building blocks, strong and weak links, cause and effect, optimization, networks and feedback, and many other characteristics found in this book, is the fundamental basis for engineering real-world innovation ecosystems.*

See Section 6. The Science of Innovation Ecosystems: A Brief Introduction.

Q: *How to recognize when regions of complex adaptive innovation ecosystems (Rainforests) behave as if they were almost linear and where cause and effect relationships may be assumed.*

See Section 7. The Rainforest Model Explained.

See Section 25. Strategies for Building Innovation Ecosystems: The Workbook.

See Section 27. Beyond Metaphor.

Q: *How to recognize where regions of stability (attractors or 'farms') are embedded in complex adaptive innovation ecosystems (Rainforests) and how to take advantage of these attractors in creating stability in innovation ecosystems.*

See Section 8. Systems, Models, and Attractors.

Q: *How to recognizing innovation ecosystems characteristics such as autonomous components or agents; exchanging signals across boundaries; autonomously self-organization; and being more than, or different from, the sum of its parts.*

Q: *How ecosystem behavior emerges from a myriad of interconnected local behaviors of constituent components apparently spontaneously and in mostly unpredictable ways.*

See Section 10. Building Blocks for Innovation Ecosystems.

See Section 9. The Ties that Bind us: Strong Links, Weak Links, and Relevant Links.

See Section 11. Boundaries, Limits, and Connections.

Q: *How to encourage emergence which leads to innovation.*

See Section 5. What is a Complex Adaptive System?

See Section 10. Building Blocks for Innovation Ecosystems.

See Section 25. Strategies for Building Innovation Ecosystems: The Workbook.

Q: *How to cultivate links within innovation ecosystems and with their external environment to stabilize the ecosystem, improve transaction efficiency, optimize the use of resources, and open the innovation ecosystem up to new ideas and different ways of thinking.*

See Section 9. The Ties That Bind Us: Strong Links, Weak Links, and Relevant Links.

See Section 10. Building Blocks for Innovation Ecosystems.

Q: *How to recognize what critical building blocks are needed when engineering an innovation ecosystem.*

Q: *How to arrange and rearrange the basic building blocks of an innovation ecosystem to encourage emergent innovation.*

Q: *How, and under what conditions, may innovation ecosystems may be subdivided with the possibility of reusing these components as building blocks for other systems.*

Q: *How to benefit from degrees of interdependence within an innovation ecosystem.*

Q: *How to create innovation ecosystem components to support agility.*

Q: *How to set up standard interfaces to reduce transaction costs between innovation ecosystem building blocks.*

See Section10. Building Blocks for Innovation Ecosystems.

Q: *How to assure innovation ecosystems are directed by objective rather than methods.*

See Section 14. Networks and Feedback.

Q: *How to recognize areas of within innovation ecosystem space where picking 'low hanging fruit' and making small early stage investments can yield quick results.*

See Section 5. What is a Complex Adaptive System?

Q: *How to create cultural alignment within an innovation ecosystem.*

See Section 11. Boundaries, Limits, and Connections.

See Section 13. Contextual Qualifiers: One Size Doesn't Fit All.

Q: *How to connecting networks of entrepreneurs with their own strong, weak, and relevant links by bridging structural holes in innovation ecosystems.*

Q: *How to provide access to valuable new ideas, alternative opinion and practice, and an ability to move ideas between groups where there is an advantage in doing so.*

Q: *How a broker or boundary spanner who bridges the hole could gain competitive advantage by engaging in information arbitrage.*

See Section 12. Boundary Spanners: Network Holes and How to Plug Them.

Q: *How to assess whether a given policy or practice, implemented elsewhere, is truly relevant or applicable to the user's environment.*

Q: *How to assess the influence of contextual factors when making decisions and taking actions.*

See Section 13. Contextual Qualifiers: One Size Doesn't Fit All.

Q: *How to use positive feedback to encourage deviation from the existing state of affairs and thus enable innovation to emerge.*

Q: *How to use negative feedback as a stabilizing force to reduce deviations from an existing state, and to keep needed minor changes and adjustments from becoming too large by re-stabilizing the system post-changes.*

See Section 14. Networks and Feedback.

Q: *How to recognize the need to create higher level supportive policies when planning an innovation ecosystem.*

Q: *How to assess when an innovation ecosystem has a lower level of hierarchy made up of subsystems say, training programs, mentors, an innovation culture, an early stage investment fund, research centers, and policies.*

Q: *How to assess when, and why, why these characteristics may not be sufficient to create a fully functioning ecosystem without bringing in upper level contextual issues which policymakers may not be aware of.*

See Section 17. Cause, Effect, and Trying to Predict.

See Section 16. Hierarchy and Necessity.

See Section 13. Contextual Qualifiers: One Size Doesn't Fit All.

Q: *How to engineer innovation ecosystems to be sustainable and resilient to internal and external shocks.*

Q: *How to engineer an innovation ecosystem to recover from a disruptive event such as a bifurcation, inflection, or a tipping point.*

See Section 18. Sowing the Seeds of Resilience: Shocks to the System.

Q: *How to develop leading indicators for the development paths of innovation ecosystems.*

Q: *How to understand the degree of fallibility of an indicator, and guard against cognitive traps.*

See Section 19. Indicators and Fallibility.

Q: *How to prevent innovation ecosystems from falling into a non-productive, non-innovative, static equilibrium state.*

Q: *Why innovation ecosystems need a constant input of energy in the form of new knowledge, challenges, and so forth, to maintain innovation.*

See Section 20. Noise and Housekeeping.

Q: *How to determine conditions under which knowledge may be re-used to reduce re-invention in engineering and maintaining innovation ecosystems.*

See Section 21. Knowledge Reuse: Create Early, Use Often.

Q: *How to determine when trying to optimize all the elements of an innovation ecosystem is not necessary, or always desirable to do so.*

Q: *How to make cost/benefit decisions to help decide which building blocks to optimize.*

See Section 22. Does Everything Have to be Optimized?

See Section 16. Hierarchy and Necessity.

Q: *How to enabling rapid diffusion and social learning in innovation ecosystems.*

See Section 23. Thinking about Diffusion.

Q: *How to apply non-deductive reasoning in innovation ecosystems for dealing with wicked problems – those problems having an unclear cause and effect connection.*

Q: *How to avoid jumping to 'obvious solutions.'*

See Section 24. Practical Reasoning: Decision Making and Solving the Right Problem.

See Section 15. Wicked Problems are Everywhere.

Q: *How a framework may help identify phenomena not previously understood.*

See Section 26. A Framework, Geometry, Grammar.

Q: *How to develop innovation ecosystem strategies for uncertain and unpredictable environments.*

See Section 25. Strategies for Building Innovation Ecosystems: The Workbook

In Section 25 **Strategies for Building Innovation Ecosystems** which is the capstone for the entire book each 'How-to' is incorporated into designing and building a model innovation ecosystem.

3
A Little Background

....

Every innovation ecosystem is a complex adaptive system with shifting regions of non-complexity embedded within it.

A community intent of becoming a vibrant technology hub developed an innovation ecosystem system designed to support the creation and expansion of high growth companies. The ecosystem apparently has all the right pieces: an incubator, an accelerator, a seed capital fund, and an umbrella management organization. There was only one problem; it isn't working. In another part of the globe, in spite of government policies tediously agreed with international aid organizations, generous funding, and several training programs, attempts to move university research to market are not working. In a third location, attempts to find a consensus on what is required to build an ecosystem to support regional entrepreneurship could not be achieved even by eagerly absorbing so-called 'best practices know-how' from elsewhere.

This book is about answering the question "why isn't it working" and, more impactfully, about how to build innovation in companies, communities, science parks, and smart cities, by engineering supportive innovation ecosystems? The CEO of the Aga Khan Foundation, USA, recently expressed the opinion that "We need more than 'know-how' to solve complex development problems; we need 'do-how.' We need to find people who have relevant experience and learn from them." [6] This book attempts to provide both know-how and do-how.

Stepping back further, we can ask "why does innovation need an ecosystem?" There is plenty of evidence from the experience of communities and indeed entire nations being disappointed by, for instance, insipid economic

....

6   Aleem Walji, "Innovation for International Development Navigating the Paths and Pitfalls," Eds. Ben Ramalingam and Kirsten Bound, *Nesta* (April 2016).

development through new business creation, poorer than expected conversion of R&D from universities to markets, and weak competitiveness, among other outcomes. It is frequently not recognized that the missing, or existing but malfunctioning, factor is a true innovation ecosystem – an answer to the "why isn't it working" question.

'Innovation' is a mid-15 century term, 'restoration, renewal,' from Latin *innovationem*. Innovate (verb) 'introduce as new,' is from the Latin *innovatus*, 'to renew, restore; to change,' meaning 'make changes in something established.'

The term 'Ecosystem' was introduced in 1935 by ecologist Arthur Tansley (1871-1955) to draw attention to the importance of transfers of materials between organisms and their environment. He described an ecosystem as "The whole system, ... including not only the organism-complex, but also the whole complex of physical factors that form what we call the environment." [7]

As the name implies, innovation ecosystems are systems; systems of people usually in organizations who behave as normal non-rational beings, making decisions, experiencing successes and failures, learning, and living. We shall see that an innovation ecosystem is a complex system of connections and relationships among people and their environment. For example, it will be shown how the concept of 'emergence' (emergence of innovations, ideas, and so forth) is connected to the ways in which the building blocks of innovation ecosystems are arranged and on hierarchies or levels in innovation ecosystems, these being necessary to demonstrate cause and effect and, in turn, how to make decisions in innovation ecosystems where there may not be any clear cause and effect.

I just used the term 'cause and effect.' We shall soon see that this is a slippery concept when trying to understand complex adaptive systems with shifting regions of non-complexity embedded within them. Seeking causes for observed effects or predicting effects from supposed causes and achieving better than random results is, in our everyday activities, important to us. In complex adaptive systems we have to think differently to avoid error.

. . . .

7   Christian Leveque, "Ecology: From Ecosystem to Biosphere," *CRC Press* (2003), p 27.

The science of innovation ecosystems which investigates building blocks, strong and weak links, hierarchies, optimization, networks and feedback, and many other characteristics found in this book may sometimes seem to be abstracting away the human element. To a degree it is, but only because an understanding of abstracted science enables us to explain and sometimes anticipate real world results of the behavior of individuals and organizations functioning in a complex world. Science does not displace humanity. Many of the problems and solutions discussed here will be pictured as systems and communications. The term system will be used in just the same way as we talk about school systems or systems of government. It's worth noting that geographical proximity is a factor in communicating but not necessarily a limiting one.

"The organization of components typically integrates then into an entity that has an identity of its own…. Accordingly, investigators who already understand in detail how the parts behave are often surprised by what happens when they are organized in particular ways…In virtue of being organized systems, mechanisms do things beyond what their components do. …" [8]

Brief examples may help. What is the reason an innovation ecosystem system designed to support the creation and expansion of high growth companies "isn't working?" Understanding the science of such systems (specifically emergence, building blocks, links, feedback loops, and downward causation – all to be explained here) was the basis for discovering the problem: weak communications and misunderstandings between elements of the ecosystem and cultural misalignment among these elements.

You might say "this is obvious" when you know the solution. It was *not* obvious to participants before applying innovation ecosystems science.

Another case: in order to initiate some program, for example commercializing technologies from universities, the term "let's pick the low hanging fruit first" [9] is often heard. The meaning is to look for cases where a technology may be commercialized without too much effort or expense

. . . .

8   William Bechtel, a philosopher of neuroscience, quoted in William Jaworski, "Why Materialism is False," *Philosophy* Vol 91, No 356 (2016), p 194.

9   There can be a downside. Incentives to focus on 'low hanging fruits' may result in encouraging a risk-averse approach. However, doing so may require assuming that a problem which is actually a complex one is not complex and an invalid solution is proposed.

but will yield quick and visible results. Innovation ecosystems science tells us we are making use of a feature of nonlinear complex systems, namely small changes in certain parts may cause large changes in the system's overall behavior due to cross-coupling among building blocks. This feature is sometimes called a tipping point or nudge effect and can be used for advantage. For example, making small amounts of money available at the very early stage of commercializing a technology can produce large changes in the likelihood of successful transition to market.

A final representative case which can only be explained and made use of by an understanding of complexity is how does innovation occur in systems? What is special about the systems of people and organizations from which innovation emerges? There is no helpful brief answer. The explanation is the theme of this book and will lead us through a journey where we shall meet such curiosities as self-organization without a guiding hand, adaptation to change, feedback loops, housekeeping heat, beneficial noise, helpful disputes, a little painless physics and biology, and even metaphysics, together with insights from a variety of thinkers and writers from Francis Bacon and Niccolo Machiavelli to Anne Bronte and Facebook users. Not all problems will be solved or phenomena explained – there remains much that is still unknown about complex systems – but enough to guide the engineering of innovation ecosystems.

A Harvard business school alumnus responding to an intra-Harvard debate between a historian and a business school professor, about theories of disruptive technologies is quoted as saying "We don't learn laws of business. We learned stories." [10] Stories can be valuable learning aids, however, we must be careful to ensure that first, the learning from an individual story can be validly generalized and second, that there is an underlying basis of science in the story. I always find myself looking beneath a story for the explanatory science.

To emphasize: in a world where knowledge, creativity, and smart capital are the key drivers to producing extraordinary economic, social, or environmental outcomes we find it necessary to engineer innovation ecosystems. We call these Rainforests. We shall see that Rainforests *are complex adaptive systems.*

....

10   John McDermott, "Career Advice from Marina Keegan," *Financial Times* (June 26, 2014).

The US Department of Commerce, Economic Development Administration's definition of economic development reads "improved quality of life by expanding the capacity of individuals, firms, and communities to maximize the use of their talents and skills to support innovation, lower transaction costs, and responsibly produce and trade valuable goods and services." This is what innovation ecosystems support. Henry Doss, in his series of Forbes blogs on leadership, put the issue well "We live and work in a world that wants specificity and predictability, but we live and work in systems that defy predictability... A strong leader of complex systems knows this truth about systems, and understands that oftentimes judgment, intuition and commitment are more important than measurements, projections and predictions. Knowing that systems are resistant to predictive models, and are rich in unforeseen, often positive, outcomes is a powerful foundation for effective leadership. And it's an awareness that will make for more informed and nuanced decision-making." [11]

Complexity is about the formation and re-formation of patterns and structures whether in companies, research and development teams, communities, or cities and nations. Complexity is fascinating for its ability to enlighten and surprise. Complexity generates innovation and innovation systems by upsetting equilibrium. Stable equilibrium does not generate innovation.

This book talks about linear and complex systems. Many of you will have read about the next stage of the sequence – a state of chaos. We will not discuss chaos as such, although the 'edge of chaos' may be approached. Incidentally, a simple demonstration of these phases is with a kitchen faucet. Turn it on so the water flows in a steady stream (linear flow), increase the flow and you will see regular pulsations in the flow (complex flow), turn the flow up further and the water will gush out splashing about in all directions (chaotic flow).

An innovation ecosystem consists of a large variety of people and organizations as well as attitudes, culture, and a physical environment, functioning together as a unit. An innovation ecosystem is self-sustaining and accelerates innovation because it is 'borderless' composed of diversified constituents cohesively networked together.

. . . .

11   Henry Doss, "Does Synergy Really Mean Anything?" *Forbes blog* (2014), http://www.forbes.
com/sites/henrydoss/2014/03/24/does-synergy-really-mean-anything/

Victor W. Hwang in his 2013 book **The Rainforest Blueprint: How to Design Your Own Silicon Valley** [12], notes that "Humans are biological animals, so our society is a biological system. Biological systems, like natural rainforests, thrive because of the unplanned, uncontrolled results of countless interactions among flora and fauna. As a result they adapt, they evolve. It's similar for human beings. Our societies, our networks, are a type of ecosystem too… Innovation is basically the opposite of mass production. We don't want predictable crops. We want weeds." This Rainforest concept is described more completely in Section 7 of this book.

The building blocks of innovation ecosystems are constructed of other building blocks, strongly or weakly connected. Furthermore, as we shall see, re-arrangement and re-packaging of such building blocks can create emergence of new ideas – innovation.[13] [14] One example is how technologies tend to build on each other. A smart phone is built from a series of technologies stretching back to the fundamental equations of James Clark Maxwell describing electric and magnetic fields published in 1861.

These building blocks are more than just physical objects or organizations; they are attitudes, experience, feelings, and culture. We have to be careful to allow emotions, to encourage feedback, to enable small changes to have a large impact, and not to over-plan which may restrict emotions.

Research and practice are described and interpreted in order to explain complex adaptive innovation ecosystems, and, where possible, steer them to support innovation and predict a limited number of possible behaviors. Innovation ecosystems have not been extensively investigated from a complexity viewpoint. What is also new about this book's content is that it rests on the Rainforest concept.

. . . .

12 Victor W. Hwang, "The Rainforest Blueprint: How to Design Your Own Silicon Valley," *Los Altos Hills: Regenwald* (2013).

13 This is not a new idea. In 1939 Joseph Schumpeter observed that "innovation combines components in a new way, or that it consists in carrying out new combinations." J. Schumpeter, "Business Cycles," *New York: McGraw-Hill Book Company, Inc.* (1939).

14 Many of us will have experienced the opposite result, how re-arrangement of units within an organization can stifle innovation by creating poorly connected silos. The danger of organizational rigidity is discussed later.

Do we need to try and fit everything about innovation ecosystems, or innovation, into a complex adaptive systems framework? No. As we shall see the world is a mix of complex and non-complex parts.

It was noted earlier that innovation ecosystem building blocks may be individuals or organizations which are brought together to discuss or brainstorm. In a Latin American city, my colleagues and I brought people together from universities and businesses in an informal neutral setting to have, as it turned out, a heated argument about how universities don't understand the time pressures of business and how businesses do not appreciate what universities can offer them; a classic dispute. After setting out the problem of existing poor university-industry relations there was no moderator for the meeting. The result was an example of complex system emergence; the arguments produced practical agreements for specific cooperation. Of course, we don't need any formal knowledge of complexity to understanding this result. Neither should this result necessarily be attributed to some underlying complex systems framework. However, I *do* suggest that an understanding of such a complexity science framework can provide novel insights into the dynamics, context, and environmental constraints which produced the outcome. This understanding enables the practitioner to either replicate similar stimuli for emergence or, as we shall see, generate insights into other situations for which a complexity explanation is the only illuminating one.

There have been many books and articles written about complexity from the viewpoint of biology, mathematics, physics, economics, sociology, and philosophy, with applications to economics, social sciences, entrepreneurship, small business, and some recently about international development, which have been researched in depth – and which break down barriers between these disciplines. This book is not a general introduction to complexity and complex systems. Applications of complexity in general, not covered in this book, are legion ranging from traffic flow engineering, to cell biology, to identifying terrorist groups. Ilya Prigogine and Murray Gell-Mann have each been awarded Nobel prizes for their discoveries in complexity.

Not surprisingly, there is no complete agreement and certainty nor any simple definition of a complex adaptive system among researchers and practitioners. Whatever definitions we give in explaining such systems there will be something missing. Occasionally, we cannot answer the question "it works in practice but will it work in theory?"

We will usually give a working definition and build on it as we progress through the book. Keep in mind that we need to be elastic about definitions; more important is that we understand the behavior and characteristics of the entity being defined. As someone once said "definitions are like belts. The shorter they are, the more they need to stretch."

I recognize that some readers may have an urge to get quickly to "what works," what are the "10 secrets to building successful innovation ecosystems" or "just give me the formula." Doing so will result in only being able to understand and apply a narrowly limited set of results to applications restricted to very limited contexts, and producing very limited predictive capabilities. Better to invest effort into understanding how complex adaptive innovation ecosystems function and use this knowledge in a broad set of practical applications. Before we can anticipate what a system may do we need to have a thorough understanding it how it works.

Furthermore, "A prevailing expectation among practitioners is that smart research on successful organizations can unearth the underlying factors or recipes by which 'success' or intended and desired outcomes can be generated more predictably." [15] As a result, practitioner research frequently assumes a low complexity in the systems it investigates rather than the actual higher complexity of real world systems and ignores important factors (such as context). It's an issue of surface knowledge versus deep knowledge. We should not practice medicine without a thorough grounding in the medical sciences, or financial management without an understanding of economic sciences. Innovation is not always seen always seen as having a corresponding science base and the need to understand it.

---

15   Christian Seelos and Johanna Mair, "What Determines the Capacity for Continuous Innovation in Social Sector Organizations?" Rockefeller Foundation Report, *Stanford Center for Philanthropy and Civil Society* (2012) p 11.

4

What is an Innovation Ecosystem?

. . . .

Section Summary: Innovation ecosystems support innovation. They are systems of people usually in organizations behaving as normal non-rational beings, making decisions, experiencing successes and failure, learning, and living. An innovation ecosystem is a complex system of connections and relationships among people and their environment. We call these Rainforests or complex adaptive systems. Understanding such systems helps deliver economic and social benefits: new business opportunities, workforce utilization, exports, investment, quality of life, prosperity, and more in a holistic, positive manner; and, most importantly, a robust innovation culture. The building blocks of innovation ecosystems are constructed of other building blocks, strongly or weakly connected, and these of still other building blocks. If this was not the case and the ultimate building blocks were simple linear systems then stasis would result and there could be no innovation.

"The biological ecosystem is a system that includes all living organisms (biotic factors) in an area as well as its physical environments (abiotic factors) functioning together as a unit. It is characterized by one or more equilibrium states, where a relatively stable set of conditions exist to maintain a population or nutrient exchange at desirable levels.... Because the energy dynamics are a complex function, an ecosystem can only be considered as a whole, not piecemeal, as every part of the ecosystem has a functional effect on another. In summary, a biological ecosystem is a complex set of relationships among the living resources, habitats, and residents of an area, whose functional goal is to maintain an equilibrium sustaining state."

— Dr. Deborah Jackson, US National Science Foundation, What is an innovation ecosystem?

We can imagine an ideal world where everyone has all the information needed to make rational decisions, where we are all perfectly rational beings thinking deductively and where causes have logical and linear connections to their effects….. or, we can try and deal with the world as it is, messy, confusing, unpredictable where we behave as real people subject to the stresses of existence, who make illogical, irrational, decisions influenced by emotions and the culture and norms in which we live our lives. The latter choice means engineering and optimizing innovation ecosystems under such real world conditions.

Innovation ecosystems support innovation. In this Section and the next set out the foundations of innovation ecosystems that function in the real world. *We claim that all the principles and their applications in this book hold true for all innovation ecosystems – regardless of the ecosystem's constituent parts.* Furthermore, the same principles apply to all sizes of innovation ecosystems. Such universal applicability is the strength of the principles described herein.

Typical examples of ecosystems designed to support innovation are:

- An innovation ecosystem within a community, region, or country
- An innovation ecosystem within a company or other organization
- An innovation ecosystem within a cluster of organizations
- A distributed or cross border innovation ecosystem

Consider the common case of an innovation ecosystem within a community, region, or country which has been engineered to support new business creation, entrepreneurship, and commercializing research from universities and research institutes; that is, moving technologies from research to market.

Such an innovation ecosystem may have a wide variety of building blocks (to be introduced in Section 10); its 'hardware' and 'software.'[16] Hardware building blocks typically include companies, universities and colleges, a new business incubator, an accelerator, an early stage investment fund,

---

16   At this stage the terms are being used rather vaguely and the distinction between each is not precise. These definitions will be tighten up later (Section 7) and are discussed in detail in: Victor W. Hwang and Greg Horowitt, "The Rainforest: The Secret to Building the Next Silicon Valley," *Los Altos Hills: Regenwald* (2012).

grants to support proof of concept and prototype development, economic development organizations, a contract research organization, and perhaps a science and technology park together with miscellaneous organizations which were formed for different times but are still functioning. Software building blocks may include mentors to coach new businesses, leaders and role models, a culture of innovation, respect for intellectual property, and trusted cooperation among all building blocks and the ecosystem's external environment.

We shall see as we proceed that a collection of building blocks such as these do not in themselves constitute an innovation ecosystem. A community or organization which has companies, universities, leadership, a culture of innovation, and so forth may believe they have an innovation ecosystem. Maybe yes, maybe no. There is undoubtedly an ecosystem, but is it an innovation ecosystem? An innovation ecosystem is created by how the building blocks are connected and interact among themselves and with their environment to support innovation within it. Better fit among building blocks correlates with better innovation ecosystem performance.

Building blocks are not static but will change over time. Therefore, an innovation ecosystem is not a fixed scaffolding to support innovative activities. It must be adaptable; changing as the needs of what it supports change. It must be sustainable, scalable, and resilient to internal and external shocks.

The activities supported by the ecosystem may be in some way bounded within a domain (sometimes called the 'unit of analysis') or extend its influence beyond what is usually a very ill-defined and permeable boundary. For example, an innovation ecosystem engineered to support efficient manufacturing within a company may be replicated, in whole or in part, by other organizations. A policy developed within one ecosystem may influence policies developed by others.

Innovation ecosystems do not have to be engineered to be complete. It is better to build a 'minimum viable product' rather than to over-engineer and end up with unneeded building blocks. Many new business incubators stand idle because they were built before there was sufficient need or before their own ecosystem of mentors and seed capital was in place.

This book will look into the questions below, among others. A better understanding of these questions will enable tools to be developed which will create, improve, and sustain innovation ecosystems.

Some questions to guide our understanding of supportive innovation ecosystems:

1. *How can innovation ecosystems be engineered to have emergent properties and what different kinds of emergence are there?*

    'Emergence' is a fundamental feature of complex adaptive systems. For example, emergence may create a new business with capabilities that are not reflected in the properties of, or interactions between, each component within the system. Emergent organizations are typically very robust and able to survive perturbations, and self-repair following substantial damage from shocks. Emergence of innovation occurs incrementally, or in leaps as in disruptive innovation. In a corporation innovative products may emerge from internal transactions, discussions, arguments, and trial and error; in the way human society works in general. Emergence in complex systems enables small changes which may give rise to disproportionally large consequences.

2. *When engineering innovation ecosystems how can building blocks such as people, ideas, physical resources, and culture, among others, be combined to create ecosystems which support innovation?*

    A complex adaptive system can be expressed as a set of building blocks with varying degrees of connectedness meaning they cannot be completely 'decomposed' into independent units with clear boundaries. For example, technologies tend to build on each other – except where there is a new radical disruptive idea (another case of emergence). These building blocks are themselves complex systems with degrees of connectedness. Re-arrangement of such building blocks can create emergence.

3. *What are ways in which an innovation ecosystem be measured?*

    What does it mean to measure an innovation ecosystem? What features or properties of an innovation ecosystem can be measured? Can different levels and perspectives of innovation ecosystems be measured? Questionnaires, interviews, and capturing narratives can measure peoples' opinions. Some form of objective scoring is a necessary initial step to begin the process of cultural change in organizations and communities. The scale, scope, and level of detail which may be reached in completing this process will vary from organization to organization and is a function of available time and resources. Some properties will remain challenging to measure.

4. *Can the behavior of innovation ecosystems be predicted through cause and effect relations?*

A notion of causality based on regularities can only be meaningfully defined for systems with linear interactions among their variables. This implies that we cannot understand causation in complex systems by a process of analysis of variables because complex systems have emergent properties, and a change in one variable will probably affect all the other variables. This further implies that a notion of causation can only be meaningful for regions in which the behavior of a nonlinear system is topologically equivalent to that of a linear system. However, it may be possible to track cause and effect by studying cases which take different paths to the same results. This approach puts emphasis on cases and trajectories rather than variables. Knowledge of how complex adaptive systems behave enables some leading indicators to be developed. Another way of expressing this is that because complex systems are adaptable and can self-repair it is sometimes possible to assume linearity – until the next disruption arrives.

5. *What is the role of context in engineering innovation ecosystems?*

The context in which complex innovative ecosystems are being engineered is critical. What works in one context will not necessarily work in another. The concept of 'contextual qualifiers' needs to be defined. Contextual qualifiers are those pieces of knowledge that allow a user to assess whether a given policy or practice, either new or implemented elsewhere, is truly relevant or applicable to the user's environment. Contextual qualifiers are statements which 'qualify' the knowledge presented as being dependent on certain conditions.

6. *How are seemingly intractable problems solved and decisions made in complex adaptive systems?*

The search for non-deductive ways of reasoning and decision making in environments where there is an abundance of 'wicked problems' – which is almost everywhere – needs to be better understood. A 'tame problem' can be clearly written down. The problem can be stated as a gap between what is and what ought to be, and where there is clear agreement about the problem definition. A wicked problem has an unclear cause and effect connection and is difficult to define. Many possible explanations may exist. Different individuals perceive the issue differently. Depending on the explanation, the solution takes on a different form.

7. *How can shocks and disruptions to innovation ecosystems be managed?*

Shocks and disruptions can damage organizations but can also trigger innovations, especially when some threshold is reached. Shocks and disruptions can maintain or strengthen some properties while constraining others. Weak links in the system's network may provide new paths to recover from shocks. Adaptation in complex systems allows systems to be more resilient to internal confusion or external disturbances, subject to the always present constraints of finite time and resources. In natural ecosystems, shocks and disruptions will sometimes produce mutations. These mutations may be beneficial or they may limit ecosystem fitness. Disturbances can also increase the speed at which an innovation moves through a network. Conversely, tightly controlled, not so agile, systems designed to operate efficiently under prevailing conditions, with too many strong links and too few weak ones, reduce communications and become unresponsive to external shocks leading to instability or even collapse.

5

What is a Complex Adaptive System?

· ·

Section Summary: A complex system is defined by its typical characteristics such as autonomous components or agents; exchange of signals across boundaries; autonomous self-organization; and being more than, or different from, than the sum of its parts. Its behavior emerges from a myriad of interconnected local behaviors of constituent components apparently spontaneously and in mostly unpredictable ways. Emergence leads to invention and innovation. Positive feedback encourages deviation from the existing state of affairs and adaptation. It also helps to keep small adaptations localized. Emergence may create a new business with capabilities that are not reflected in the interactions of each agent within the system. Emergent organizations are typically very robust and able to survive and self-repair substantial perturbations or damage. Ten basic characteristics of complex systems are described.

"Today the network of relationships linking the human race to itself and to the rest of the biosphere is so complex that all aspects affect all others to an extraordinary degree. Someone should be studying the whole system, however crudely that has to be done, because no gluing together of partial studies of a complex nonlinear system can give a good idea of the behavior of the whole."

— Murray Gell-Mann, Noble Prize winner physicist.

Perhaps the easiest way to get a feel for what complex adaptive systems are is to look around at our lives, conditions, and environment. For many of us, life is a mix of predictable and unpredictable events. We walk down the street keeping away from traffic, passing familiar landmarks, purchasing from stores open at predictable hours, and for some people working hours are predictable, as is sunrise each morning. Within this certain world lurks unpredictability; a car swerves and dangerously mounts the sidewalk, we lose our job, or a new unexpected opportunity arises. For those living in fragile conditions such as poverty or conflict, this balance of predictable and unpredictable events is tipped towards one extreme. All the cases explained in this book are similar mixtures of the predictable and unpredictable. Next, it is necessary to become more precise and formal.

There are many definitions of a complex system but no single concise one, which reflects the fact that we have an incomplete understanding of such systems. Before going into cases in subsequent Sections, we can say a complex system typically has these basic characteristics: [17]

1. It consists of a large variety of *autonomous components* (also called *agents* and *building blocks*), which may have *conflicting goals*, and which *interact* (frequently at short range) with each other and their environment, may be arranged in a hierarchical structure, and where there is no centralized control. This and other features make it difficult to predict cause and effect relationships. Agents, which may be individuals, groups, or organizations, influenced by local conditions, create higher level structures which become the basis for other structures (e.g. coalescing groups and groups of groups). Each agent has a *program* that guides its interactions with other agents and its environment.

   Example: the global market, in which massive numbers of different suppliers, customers, intermediaries, investors and administrators, each with individual declared or undeclared objectives, produce, sell, purchase, borrow, invest, exchange information, and communicate, are woven together.

2. Its components have adaptable and permeable *boundaries* and exchange signals across these boundaries. Boundaries have different *degrees* of connectedness.

---

17   Adapted from Christian Leveque, "Ecology: From Ecosystem to Biosphere," *CRC Press* (2003) and other sources.

Example: in an innovation ecosystem, organizational components such as incubators, accelerators, and investment funds, are all closely interconnected and communications between them influence their behavior. Efficient connections between the components making up the innovation ecosystems may be more important than the properties of the individual components themselves.

3. It is capable of autonomously self-organizing, that is, changing its behavior or structure in response to unpredictable events to produce an increase of order, and is therefore *adaptive* [18] to changes and resilient to attacks. It does this by having active internal elements of sufficient variety to enable the system to survive as it adapts to unforeseen circumstances. Adaptive agents co-evolve over time. Such adaptive behavior may be continuously changing. It can create a degree of predictability within an unpredictable system. This process is not directed or controlled by any agent or sub-system inside or outside of the system.

    Example: Shocks and disruptions can trigger innovations, especially when some threshold is reached. Competition maintains or strengthens some properties while constraining others. Intervention and re-organization of system components may mitigate the effects of shocks.

4. It is more than, or different from, the sum of its parts. It is not a *reductionist* system – meaning it cannot be *decomposed* into a set of independent non-interacting parts. However, some systems may be nearly decomposable, that is can be separated with little resultant effect on each other (see Section 10). The system is constructed from a set of components that when joined together produce results not obtainable by the components alone.

    Example: Combining R&D knowledge, market intelligence, and marketing skills produce more effective results than when separated. Even R&D budget sources which might appear to be

. . . .

18 Adaptation is assisted by positive-feedback which is characteristic of complex systems. Adaptation is also enabled by groups of people within the complex system acting collectively. These and other features lead to the development of adaptive capacity in systems. It will be seen later that emergence and self-organization are necessary for systems to be adaptable. More on feedback in Section 14.

independent can influence each other. This also results in agents converting and recycling resources for new uses.

5. Its behavior *emerges* [19] from a myriad of interconnected local behaviors of constituent components apparently spontaneously and in mostly unpredictable ways. Emergence and self-organization are ways in which organizations adapt. Emergence leads to invention and innovation. For example, the emergent properties of a network come from the *interaction* of the network's components and are not necessarily inherent in any of the network's individual components. That is, emergence is the situation in which it is generally not possible to predict the behavior of the systems from the properties or activities of its individual parts.[20]

Emergence is an outcome of self-organization in the form of a new level of order in the system that comes into being as novel structures and patterns which maintain themselves over some period of time. Innovation springs from emergence. Self-organization and emergence are manifestations of adaptability, aided by the absorption of information and the formation of knowledge structures. Structural changes tend to be followed by long periods of more incremental variations.[21]

"Emergence in this format comes from patterns or properties that appear under the constraints imposed by the rules of combination of building blocks. Emergent properties often occur when co-evolving signals and boundaries generate new levels of organization. Newer signals and boundaries can then emerge from combinations of building blocks at this new level of organization. Some

. . . .

19   The concept of emergence can be traced back to the philosophy of John Stuart Mill (1843) and is still being actively debated by supporters and detractors.

20   Emergence is perhaps the most important feature of complex adaptive systems. We will see later that emergence can be stimulated by positive feedback and re-organization of building blocks. We shall also meet self-organization in problem solving (Section 24).

21   "In scientific practice, reductive, phenomenological, and functional explanations are typically interwoven. Consequently reduction and emergence are *matters of degree*: the more complete the reduction, the less significant the emergence; the more complete the emergence, the less significant the reduction." Lawrence Cahoone, "Towards A New Metaphysics of Natural Complexes," *Charlotte, NC: Society for the Advancement of American Philosophy* (March 2010) p 8.

properties can emerge only when the system reaches a high enough level of organization."

"Emergence in this sense occurs through the interactions across a group of agents – individual members and managers, networks, and organizations – rather than only through the behaviors of a formal manager."[22]

Example: Emergence may create a new business with capabilities that are not reflected in the interactions of each agent within the system (there would be no IT industry without the re-organization of sand and copper). Emergent organizations are typically very robust and able to survive and self-repair substantial damage or recover from perturbations. Emergence of innovation occurs incrementally or in leaps as in disruptive innovation. In a corporation innovative products may emerge from internal transactions, discussions, arguments, and trial and error; in the way human society works in general. Technologies build on each other. Components may be reused and re-organized.[23]

6. It functions in a *far from equilibrium* or *at the edge of chaos* state, because it is frequently disturbed and has no time to settle down in the intervals between events that cause disruptions. Complex systems may settle into *local* equilibria – basins of local equilibrium known as 'attractor' states – but these may be easily disrupted and change over time. It is this recombining into new patterns of interaction or moving from one basin of stability to another in an innovation ecosystem that allows us to build, if not complete ecosystem models, then at least some predictability around these stable regions.

Example: Rapid changes in the competitive context of firms with others taking market share with competitive products do not allow sufficient time to reach extended equilibria seen in classical economics or physics.

. . . .

22 John H. Holland, "Signals and Boundaries: Building Blocks for Complex Adaptive Systems," *MIT Press* (2012) p 50.

23 How emergence is produced by re-organizing components is a topic disputed by some researchers.

7. It has *feedback* loops. If new emergent order is creating value it will stabilize itself, finding variables and parameters that best increase its overall sustainability in an ecosystem. [24] Stability results by slowing the non-linear process that led to the amplification of emergence in the first place. Because complex systems exist in far-from-equilibrium states, small actions and events, fluctuations in the system, can be amplified through positive feedback and a cycle of self-reinforcement. This process creates a dynamic which increases the likelihood that other similar events will emerge. Positive feedback encourages deviation from the existing state of affairs and adaptation. Negative feedback reduces deviations from an existing state and acts as a stabilizing force.

    Example: Feedback from customers or potential customers provides essential guidance in new product or service development. It can reduce the risk of creating products or services for which there is no market. It can encourage bold moves or encourage incremental innovation.

    Positive feedback can lead to instability such as driving an investment system above its long-run sustainable level with too much cash chasing too few quality deals. During the downturn in investment which will follow, positive feedback can further exacerbate the situation.

8. Its behavior is *non-linear*. Non-linear change occurs when a response is neither directly nor inversely proportional to its cause; thus, small changes or disturbances may cause large changes in the system's behavior. Conversely, large changes or disturbances may result in small changes to the overall system. This characteristic of a complex system will be beneficial if the resultant change is positive; a large payoff for a small investment of effort. If the resultant change is negative, an event which is not wanted, then this characteristic of complex systems will be something to avoid. Carefully planned small interventions can enable small changes to have large consequences. This occurs by moving a system from one attractor to another (Section 8). Another feature of non-linear systems is

---

24   The meaning of 'parameters' which show this statement to be oversimplified is discussed in Section 8.

that what happens in one part of a system may not be replicated in another part.

Example: Small changes having large impact are the basis of the 'nudge' concept in which small policy changes have been found to create, for example, significant savings in applications of policies. Non-linear changes are thresholds or tipping points. Tipping points in complex systems are where a small change in the underlying parameters or the presence of perturbations can make a very large difference to outcomes. Changes in the ownership of IP from Government funded research in the USA during the 1980s, whilst being a small part of vast annual legislation, had a lasting impact and have been replicated around the world. Another case is where a role model may completely change someone's career path.

A practical problem for many developing countries in negotiating financing agreements to either acquire a technology or out-license IP is that someone has to 'put money on the table' meaning make a commitment to get started. Someone has to take the first step and agree to provide initial funding which could be matched later by others. Sometimes this can be in the form of a grant for early stage development. But, if these grants take too long to be approved, as is often the case, the deal may be lost. In other business transactions, such as real estate purchases, this takes the form of 'earnest money' – a small amount paid upfront to demonstrate good faith. The ability to provide such small sums quickly at a very early stage should be built into other forms of early stage technology development or technology translation funding.

9. It is an open [25] system which communicates (exchanges energy) with its environment. Therefore it is affected by *context, in time and space,* such as changes in the external environment, which is

25 Self-organization is a potential property of open systems. Closed systems do not exchange any energy with their surroundings.

itself a complex system composed of other complex systems. Thus *contextualized knowledge* is important. [26]

Example: A solution to a problem may work in one external environment (context) but not another (different context). However, complex systems can adapt (property #3), learn, and anticipate changes in context.

10. Its state depends on its *trajectory or history*. Complex adaptive systems are sensitive to initial conditions (starting points), and self-organizing networks are development path-dependent.

Example: An innovation ecosystem may be malfunctioning due to missing elements in its growth trajectory such as a lack of experience with IP management.

In subsequent Sections, each of these characteristics are expanded upon and used as the basis for explaining features of innovation ecosystems and applying them to building innovation ecosystems.

The complexity science model seeks to explain several issues, but especially addresses:

1. Innovation variables and parameters or constraints responsible for the evolution of complex systems into systems of greater innovation and adaptability.

2. The mechanisms by which improved social impact can be generated.

3. How to benefit from change that occurs both in continuous as well as discontinuous ways.

4. How to achieve equilibrium states within systems which are far from equilibrium.

. . . .

26 Some argue that contextualized knowledge is too strongly tied to specific cases. "The benefit of greater contextualization occurs because people often initially conceptualize a system in terms of its physically separable elements, when, in fact, these elements often interact strongly enough that the system is more felicitously viewed from a broader, more macroscopic perspective. It is easy to isolate single birds from a flock, but it is more useful and predictive to ask where the flock is going, not where the birds individually considered are going." Robert L. Goldstone, "The Complex Systems See-Change in Education," *Indiana University*, p 5.

The role of emergence in building innovation ecosystems

For building innovation ecosystems one of the most important features of a complex adaptive system is emergence. Emergence may be stimulated in unexpected ways. It's a warm cloudless summer morning in Central Asia as a glum looking group slides slowly but resolutely into the conference room to be appraised of new government initiatives to support R&D and new business creation. Several in the front rows sit, arms severely folded, questioning, *sans* words, the veracity of my explanation of these plans, and by extension that of the government's sincerity.

A 'presentation' was clearly not going to impress. Let's have a debate instead I thought – with not entirely flawless logic – had not Frederick Engels, co-revolutionary with Karl Marx whose philosophy had once dominated this land, believed in the negation of the negation to deliver the future? A noisy dispute among audience members follows, with me intervening only when the volume exceeded a decibel level sufficient to attract the visits of those in adjoining offices. One scientist becomes especially upset but is restrained by his colleagues from walking out in high dudgeon.

However, during the course of the bruising arguments which followed something exciting *emerges* out of the session's flotsam; new thinking and agreements among the previously hostile audience which takes the opportunity to vent against the government and their foreign consultants, but then moves on to a constructive deliberation. Oh yes, what happens at the end of the session? Standing applause and the person who seemed most pleased with what emerged is the scientist who has been the most negatively voluble. Naturally, new thinking and changes in a person's position and mental model will only occur if they are willing to accept change.

By definition, many components of a complex system or network tend to be connected to each other. Complex systems are 'open' [27] meaning these components will also be connected to the environment outside the system itself. This can result in a cascade of knowledge needs. For example, can we learn from knowledge networks that certain types of links in the network are important for the network's growth and stability? We should always remember that, although occasionally complex systems may appear to be mysterious, we are dealing with social systems – individuals or groups of *people*.

Stability and equilibrium

Now I need to define what is meant by stability. Evidence from studying complex adaptive systems shows that stability may depend on factors such as emergence. So, this means now I need to know more about emergence. I then find that emergence depends on other factors, so I now need to know about these ... and so on. Well, I think you get the picture. In this book we will set some reasonable boundaries to prevent the cascade becoming unmanageable.

The concept of equilibrium is fundamental to the physics of Isaac Newton, neoclassical economics, and much of social organization theory. In physics, equilibrium refers to a body or physical system at rest or in steady, un-accelerated, motion. The ball bearing on the rim of a bowl is a classic example of equilibrium; when released it swings around for a while and quickly settles at the bottom of the bowl and that is that. In economics, equilibrium is a point of rest from which there is no external cause creating a tendency for any individual, firm, or market to change. Organizations or social systems are said to be in equilibrium when all influences on the

....

27   Damian G. Stephen James A. Dixon, "The Self-Organization of Insight: Entropy and Power Laws in Problem Solving," *The Journal of Problem Solving*, Vol 2, no. 1 (Spring 2009) notes "An open system exchanges energy with its surrounding environment. As energy enters into the system, some of it is consumed to do work for the system. But energy flow also must produce fluctuations in the system, leading to a more disordered state at the microscopic scale. Thus, the influx of energy produces an increase in entropy. Unlike closed systems, however, open systems are not required to bottle up this entropy. Instead, open systems can self-organize macroscopic structure for the purposes of offloading entropy into the environment. By doing so, they regulate energy flow and promote the emergence of macroscopic structure. The offloading of entropy is closely tied to the emergence of structure." The greater these flows the more the system moves away from equilibrium.

system are canceled or balanced by others, resulting in an unchanging state of affairs. Nonlinearity, by contrast, is exhibited by systems that are far from equilibrium. If I try to balance a pencil on its point on my finger I must continually make small adjustments to keep the pencil balanced. The pencil is in a state of unstable equilibrium (also called dynamic equilibrium). We will return to these ideas later, but next the basic science of innovation ecosystems will be explored.

6

The Science of Innovation Ecosystems: A Brief Introduction

· ·

Section Summary: Several generations of innovation theory and practice have been proposed since 1900. Early versions followed a linear model that funded technological research and then attempted to 'push' the results of research and inventions into commercialization to serve a market need that was only a guess and never validated until the end of the innovation process. Innovation ecosystems are predominantly systems of people and organizations of people managing human and physical resources. The shared culture of such people is the foundation for innovative ecosystems and will ultimately determine the success of innovative initiatives. Differences between complex and complicated systems are described. What is meant by a theory is described.

"A scientist has "a healthy skepticism, suspended judgment, and disciplined imagination"—not only about other people's ideas but also about his or her own."

— Astronomer Edwin Hubble, speaking at Caltech's
1938 commencement.

Atul Gawande, an American surgeon, writer, and public health researcher, giving the California Institute of Technology commencement address in June 2016 said "Science is …. a commitment to a systematic way of thinking, an allegiance to a way of building knowledge and explaining the universe through testing and factual observation. The thing is, that isn't a normal way of thinking. It is unnatural and counterintuitive. It has to be learned. Scientific explanation stands in contrast to the wisdom of divinity and experience and common sense." Dr. Gawande went on to note that scientific explanation may not fit our mental models, but asserting true facts is what good science stands for "And including the narrative that explains them is even better."

"But you also hope to accept that nothing is ever completely settled, that all knowledge is just probable knowledge. A contradictory piece of evidence can always emerge. Hubble said it best when he said, "The scientist explains the world by successive approximations." "

Dr. Gawande's view of science is the one taken here. Some results will seem counterintuitive; others may be changed if new evidence makes them no longer plausible.

Pierre-Simon, Marquis de Laplace (1749 –1827) was a brilliant French scientist and mathematician who believed that nature's laws are deterministic and where we see apparent randomness in nature is only because the boundary conditions of nature's laws are not completely known. "Nature used to be perceived as a predictable entity, which was governed by numerous sets of laws and equations. There was an age, no longer, when scientists believed that with the knowledge gained from enough data, the future of the universe could be predicted considering that the universe can be reduced to a set of physical laws." [28] Although we shall see that concepts of boundaries and connectivity will still be important in engineering complex adaptive innovation ecosystems, we now understand that nature is not easily reducible to its separate component parts. "There is more and more evidence that the future is best characterized by disorder, instability, diversity, disequilibrium, and nonlinearity" [29] It is just this disorder which generates innovation.

Most of what you will find in a web search for 'the science of innovation' or similar will describe cases of successful innovations or the careers of well-known entrepreneurial scientists. What this book means by the science of innovation is the basic science that underpins innovation and particularly innovation ecosystems. The science of innovation is present but often

. . . .

28   Quoted in Truong Pham, "Thermodynamics of Far-from-Equilibrium Systems: A Shift in Perception of Nature," AME 36099; Directed Readings (2011) p 1.

29   Bill McKelvey, "Toward a complexity science of entrepreneurship," *Journal of Business Venturing* 19 (2004) p 37.

hidden. This is parallel to recognizing that the science of biology underpins the practice of medicine or physics supports engineering.

Millions of words have been written about innovation and continue to pour forth, so much so that the word has been debased; the kind of event that James J. Kilpatrick [30] called "fatally wounded" and "wordnapped." The Wall Street Journal in 2011 published an article: **You Call That Innovation?** [31] about abuse of the word. Another article written by former astronaut Buzz Aldrin in the MIT Technology Review about innovation's promise lost was entitled: **You promised me Mars colonies. Instead I got Facebook.** [32]

The Scottish philosopher David Hume (1711 –1776) said: "All men of sound reason are disgusted with verbal disputes …it is found that the only remedy for this abuse must arise from clear definitions." The language of innovation culture is usually considered to be the language of narrative and stories. Most of the language of *complex* innovation ecosystems cannot be mathematical for reasons we shall discover. This fact requires that we must not be sloppy with narrative but amplify it with clear definitions of words making which make up the narrative.

Complex or complicated?

On the subject of words, it's unfortunate that 'complex' used in the scientific and philosophical sense in this book is the word used colloquially, if incorrectly, by many of us to describe something which we find difficult to understand or which seems highly intricate or complicated. There is an important difference between identifying something as complex and something as complicated. The term complex comes from the Latin *complexus*, which means intertwined. This suggests that a complex system has many components which are interconnected, although with different strengths and degrees of relevance, and difficult to separate. In spite of this interconnectivity, we will see that it is possible, to a certain degree,

· ·

30   James J. Kilpatrick "The Writer's Art," *Kansas City: Andres McMeel Parker* (1984), p 184.

31   "You Call That Innovation?" http://www.wsj.com/articles/SB100014240527023047917045774182509023099144

32   Buzz Aldrin, "You promised me Mars colonies. Instead I got Facebook" http://buzzaldrin.com/mit-technology-review-the-imperative-to-explore/

to identify individual building blocks of complex systems. Thus, building blocks may be re-used and re-organized to produce complex systems with new properties and behaviors. The building block picture sees design as being bottom-up not top-down. One significant factor of this image will become apparent when we look into top-down assumptions in strategic planning (Section 25). Building blocks don't have to be physical objects but, as noted earlier, can be ideas for example (details in Section 10). To re-emphasize: "The whole is greater (or less) than the sum of its parts." [33] An economy is complex. Innovation ecosystems are complex. You, dear reader, and I are complex.

Complicated systems, on the other, hand may be broken down into smaller and smaller constituent parts, called the reductionist principle (details in Section 10). In a complicated system the whole is the sum of its parts, nothing more and nothing less, and its behavior is completely predictable from knowing the behavior of its parts.

Details about systems are given in Section 8, but to summarize: both complex and complicated systems are composed of system *elements* connected in a system *structure*. Both kinds of systems perform specific system *functions* in its system *environment*. Both systems have *boundaries* allowing *inputs* from, and *outputs* to, the external environment. Again, we must be clear about language. For example in Section 10, the concept of 'modular' systems and 'decomposable' systems will be introduced. Both are composed of subsystems but in the former these subsystems are connected via interface standards while in the latter subsystems are completely isolated. Right now, this is just a question of getting the language right. The significance of the frequently misused term modular will be considered in Section 10.

A recent documentary movie described the Airbus A380 with its approximately 4 million parts as "the world's most *complex* aircraft." If it is, then I will never board it. It may indeed be the most *complicated* aircraft. A critical difference is that complicated systems such as a passenger aircraft

. . . .

33   Lee A. Green, "The Implications of Measuring Complexity" The implications of measuring complexity. *Ann Fam Med; 8(4) (2010), pp 291-2,* "... a complicated system produces rich behavior by having many elements behaving linearly, while a complex system produces rich behavior from a few elements that interact in highly nonlinear fashion." Because of this interaction one cannot, as is often the fashion in science, just change one variable at a time while holding others constant.

can be fully modeled, that is, we can deduce the behavior of the whole aircraft from its parts, whereas complex systems are inherently resistant to modeling; as we have noted more than once, a study of the parts may not tell us how the whole will behave. Many of us get this distinction between complex and complicated wrong in our everyday speech.

People and theories

Innovation ecosystems are predominantly systems of people and organizations of people managing human and physical resources. The shared culture of such people is the foundation for innovative ecosystems and will ultimately determine the success of innovative initiatives. So how do cultural factors appear in innovation ecosystems? They define boundaries of an organization and sub-units within organizations. They affect how communication occurs between units within an organization, and with the outside environment (e.g. determined by national culture), both formally and informally, and how news networks are created. Other factors influenced, or driven, by culture include: leadership; sustainability; responses to external shocks; emergence, or not, of new ideas, products or services; transaction costs [34] and transaction efficiency; and ethical norms, among others. Thus we see that culture is embedded in innovation ecosystems.

Several generations of innovation methodology have been proposed since the early 1900s. Early versions followed a linear model that funded technological research and then attempted to 'push' the results of research, as inventions, into commercialization to serve a market need that was only a guess and never properly validated until the end of the innovation process. More will be covered in Section 10 when discussing new product development. [35] The linear model never worked well. Economist Paul Romer, who first explained the role of technology in an economy, said the following

....

34   Transaction costs are those costs that are not from the actual production of goods traded, but activities to complete the exchange. The higher the transaction cost, the less efficient is the transaction.

35   Technology push versus market pull is a continuing debate. Market pull may seem to make sense. However, think of many products and services we use for which there was no market pull. The telephone for example; in the 19th century the telegraph was considered perfectly satisfactory.

about the linear model. "If this (linear) model were correct, physicists would have developed the basic science of thermodynamics and used it to show that, in principle, heat could be converted into motion. Applied scientists would then have used the laws of thermodynamics to highlight the factors that determined the efficiency of this conversion process. Engineers and product designers would have used these results to solve practical problems in the marketplace and developed the steam engine first. This did not happen. As engineers studied the efficiency of different engines the basic science of thermodynamics was discovered." [36] The science of complexity is developing similarly. Two Nobel prizes have been awarded, to Ilya Prigogine (chemistry) and Murray Gell-Mann (physics), for pioneering contributions to complexity. The Rainforest metaphor has led to more discoveries of the science behind it.

Romer's explanation tells us how science has worked, at least since around the 17th century when Francis Bacon, Viscount St. Albans, an English philosopher and Lord Chancellor of England, helped move science from an abstract thinking mode to experimental one when, in 1626, he wanted to know if stuffing a dead chicken with snow would preserve it. The chicken was preserved but, unfortunately, Bacon was not so lucky he – caught pneumonia and died. We can come up, somehow, with a possible theory and then proceed to test the theory, which, if found wanting, must be rejected as false. Some theories, for example in astronomy, may take decades to determine if they are true or false. A theory which ultimately turns out to be false may make predictions which are true. We must be ready to dump a theory which is falsified. I said the theory is created 'somehow.' Most theories are not plucked out of the air but are based on observations, however limited, and the theory with its principles and axioms uncovered as for thermodynamics. We observe the world around us, collect and package what we have seen, then deduce conclusions about these behaviors and about what appears to work. The pieces we collect and package may have been visible for a long time, just never assembled.

We should have some common ground as to what is a theory. Thomas Kuhn, a philosopher of science, set out criteria, although not necessarily

. . . .

36   Paul Romer, http://www.econlib.org/library/Enc/EconomicGrowth.html

precise ones, to help chose a theory or chose from competing theories. [37]
He stated that a theory should be:

1. Accurate, in that it is empirically adequate with experimentation and observation.

2. Consistent, namely internally consistent, but also externally consistent with other theories.

3. Broad Scope, with consequences extending beyond the phenomena it was initially designed to explain.

4. Simple, using the principle that the simplest explanation is usually the best one.

5. Fruitful, in that any theory should predict new phenomena or new relationships among phenomena.

Let's turn next to describing how complex innovation systems behave.

. . . .

37   Thomas Kuhn, https://en.wikipedia.org/wiki/Thomas_Kuhn

7
The Rainforest Model Explained

Section Summary: A company that seeks to manufacture cheaper, better, more profitable products would run operations like an agricultural farm. The 'traditional' model is the agriculture farm where crops are grown for example in neat rows and any weeds which appear are eliminated; the perfectly reasonable goal being rational cultivation to maximize output. However, it's not a model that produces innovation. The Rainforest with its clutter and confusion is the optimal environment for the emergence and spread of new species. Many systems, including innovation ecosystems, are a mixture of 'farms' and 'Rainforests'– a farm may be embedded in a Rainforest for example – and there may be switching between the two.

What would the world be, once bereft

Of wet and of wildness? Let them be left.

O let them be left, wildness and wet;

Long live the weeds and the wilderness yet.

— Inversnaid, Gerard Manley Hopkins (1844–89).

Neoclassical versus Complex Innovation Ecosystems have been summarized as:

"Humans are biological animals, so our society is a biological system. Biological systems, like natural rainforests, thrive because of the unplanned, uncontrolled results of countless interactions among flora and fauna.

As a result they adapt. They evolve. It's similar for human beings. Our societies, our networks, are a type of ecosystem too.

They are Rainforests, but made of people. Our World depends on the interactions of people who possess talent, capital, and ideas.

That means everyone.

Innovation is basically the opposite of mass production. We don't want predictable crops. We want weeds.

Weeds are birthed from uncontrolled environments. We call such places, – like Silicon Valley – Rainforests." [38]

The rainforest metaphor

The rainforest *metaphor* as described by Hwang and Horowitt connects rainforests (the original object) to companies (the object for which the symbol now stands). "A company that seeks to manufacture cheaper, better, more profitable products would run operations like an agricultural farm. However, the community that seeks to generate high levels of innovation throughout the whole system would do the opposite ... not controlling the specific processes but instead helping to set the right environmental variables that foster the unpredictable creation of new weeds."

"To explain the difference between highly productive systems such as Silicon Valley and most other places in the world, what is most important are not the ingredients of economic production, but the recipe – the way in which the ingredients are combined together. Human systems become more productive the faster that the key ingredients of innovation – talent, ideas, and capital – are allowed to flow throughout the system."

"The Rainforest model is more than a metaphor. Innovation ecosystems are not merely like biological systems; they are biological systems. Talent, ideas, and capital are like nutrients moving in a biological system. Measuring the velocity of such nutrients can provide us with tools to measure the health of an innovation ecosystem by observing dynamic activity over time, rather than static points in time. When particular social behaviors allow the movement of talent, ideas, and capital to be even freer

38   Victor W. Hwang, "The Rainforest Blueprint: How to Design Your Own Silicon Valley" *Los Altos Hills: Regenwald* (2013), p 12.

– as they are in Rainforests – we find that human networks can generate extraordinary patterns of self-organization." [39]

The 'traditional' model is the agriculture farm where crops are grown in neat rows and any weeds which appear are eliminated, the perfectly reasonable goal being rational cultivation to maximize output. It's not a model that produces innovation. The Rainforest with its clutter and confusion is the optimal environment for the emergence and spread of new species. Many systems, including innovation ecosystems, are a mixture of 'farms' and 'Rainforests' – a farm may be embedded in a Rainforest for example.

Applying the metaphor

The linguistic philosopher Wilbur Urban [40] believed that a metaphor has (1) reference to the original object – a rainforest in our case – and (2) reference to the object for which the symbol now stands – a complex adaptive innovation ecosystem in our case.

Switching between farms and rainforests may also occur due to factors such as emergence and feedback, among others. Switching will occur as uncertainty enters or leaves the context. For example, a country or region has a program to provide phased financing for early stage companies,- frequently modeled on the US Small Business Innovation (SBIR) program. There is uncertainty in whether an individual proposal will meet published requirements and standards (Rainforest environment) but no uncertainty, it is hoped, in the transparent selection procedure that a submission meeting these conditions, subject to money being available, will be funded (farm environment). Post-funding, uncertainty as to whether the business will be successful re-enters (see Section 25 for more).

There is no control operating in the Rainforest, or in a highly innovative and disruptive culture, however, there are powerful principles at work. If we understand better how a Rainforest might operate to be more

. . . .

39   Victor W. Hwang and Greg Horowitt, "The Rainforest: The Secret to Building the Next Silicon Valley," *Los Altos Hills: Regenwald* (2012).

40   Warren A Shibles, "Analysis of Metaphor in the Light of W. M. Urban's Theories," *Mouton: Paris* (1971).

innovative, then we can take those principles and embed them into any organization at any scale and the result will be a culture that tends more and more toward innovation. Each mode – weeds and crops – has its own recognizable set of principles and values.

When an organization is in innovation mode, whether by design or by chance, it is very likely that the Rules of the Rainforest [41] will be dominant. When it's more in command and control mode, the Rules of the Farm will be more dominant.

What these principles are is one focus of this book and especially Section 25 where everything is pulled together.

In practice, there are no "pure" Rainforests or "pure" farms. Every system is a mix, a hybrid, of both. Farms are embedded in Rainforests and *vice versa*. Fuzzy, permeable, boundaries exist for both. This realization helps in our understanding of practical applications of Rainforest knowledge. Another way to view the picture is as a continuum with pure farms at one extreme and pure Rainforests at the other. Later, we shall see how both rainforest and farms are needed and how they function in the innovation ecosystem (clue: businesses want to be constantly innovative *and* employees want to know they will be paid next month, and we *don't* need bookkeepers to become 'innovative' in their accounts).

Readers should at least be beginning to see how the Rainforest metaphor expands our thinking and leads us to understand that Rainforest ecosystems not only have much in common with complex adaptive systems but that rainforest innovation ecosystems *are* complex adaptive systems. The rainforest symbolism has acquired a new and different interpretation as a complex adaptive system. This realization opens up the large volume of knowledge about complex adaptive systems to be used to understand, analyze, and predict the behavior of innovation ecosystems. Having grabbed our attention the metaphor remains as a comfort blanket as we enter the sometimes insecure world of complexity.

....

41   Rules of the Rainforest, Victor W. Hwang and Greg Horowitt, "The Rainforest: The Secret to Building the Next Silicon Valley," *Los Altos Hills: Regenwald* (2012) p 156.

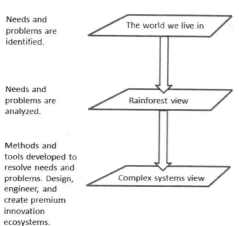

Needs and problems are identified.

Needs and problems are analyzed.

Methods and tools developed to resolve needs and problems. Design, engineer, and create premium innovation ecosystems.

The world we live in.
We live and work in a world that wants specificity and predictability, but we live and work in systems that defy predictability.

Rainforest view.
The Rainforest concept recognizes that innovation is chaotic, serendipitous, and uncontrollable, so processes that are linear and controlled are rarely self-sustaining. Blending of soft and hard components is essential to creating higher returns, more socially conscientious entrepreneurs, and a **culture** of sustainable innovation ecosystems.

Complex systems view.
Rainforests are non-linear complex adaptive systems. The behavior of such systems *emerges* from a myriad of interconnected local behaviors. Complex systems are more than the sum of their parts, and operate in far from equilibrium states.

Figure 2. Rainforest Layers: Visualizing the world.

The Rainforest concept recognizes that innovation is chaotic, serendipitous, and uncontrollable, so processes that are linear and controlled are rarely self-sustaining. [42]

"The Rainforest is a very powerful, all-encompassing concept with many very useful behavioral and policy concepts. The concepts are relevant for all country categories. From this point of view, there is surprisingly little difference between the construct of a Rainforest in one category or another. All Rainforests will look generically similar and be filled with similar actors behaving in more or less similar ways. But how you use these concepts to build an economy may differ substantially from country to country. We've only begun to think about all this." [43]

It may not always be easy to see the practical nature of Rainforest fundamentals so the purpose of this book is to apply some of these concepts

. . . .

42   Victor W. Hwang and Greg Horowitt, "The Rainforest: The Secret to Building the Next Silicon Valley," *Los Altos Hills: Regenwald* (2012).

43   Private communication, Alfred J. Watkins.

to issues, questions, and problems in innovation ecosystems using concrete examples.

It's not just the ingredients of economic production, but the way they are combined which is important in Rainforests. Rainforests are able to reduce transaction costs, increase transaction efficiency, and enable talent, ideas, and capital to flow throughout the system, thus improving social impact. Rainforests are examples of complex adaptive systems in far from equilibrium states compared to neoclassical models which assume equilibrium conditions. To sum up:

1. Innovation variables and parameters are responsible for the evolution of complex systems into systems of greater innovation and adaptability, trust, self-organization, networks, and emergence.

2. Trust reduces transaction costs, improves transaction efficiency, and supports self-organization.

3. Self-organization creates some predictability within unpredictable systems.

4. Networks with weak links make complex systems more stable, but not too stable so as to avoid echo chambers.

5. Emergence produces a new level of order in complex systems; innovation springs from emergence.

Axioms of the Rainforest

The Rainforest is considered to have guiding Axioms showing how different disciplines, such as biology, neuroscience, psychology, economics, law, and others, are necessary to explain the mechanisms of innovation ecosystems [44]. These Axioms can be compared with the properties of complex adaptive systems introduced in this book as shown here.

. . . .

44   These Axioms are from Victor W. Hwang and Greg Horowitt, "The Rainforest: The Secret to Building the Next Silicon Valley," *Los Altos Hills: Regenwald* (2012) pp 136-7. 'Axiom' is not used in the strict sense as in the axioms of geometry for example, i.e. statements that cannot be proved by reduction, but as fundamental supportive statements.

Axiom 1

"While plants are harvested most efficiently on farms, weeds grow best in Rainforests."

Properties of Complex Adaptive Systems (CAS)

It is more than the sum of its parts. It is not a *reductionist* system – cannot be *decomposed* into a set of independent non-interacting parts. Rainforests have intertwined components. However, for practical purposes some systems may be nearly decomposable. Farms are fully decomposable. Innovation emerges from non-reductionist systems.

Axiom 2

"Rainforests are built from the bottom up, where irrational behavior reigns."

It consists of a large variety of *autonomous components* (also called *agents*), which may have *conflicting goals*, and *interact* (frequently at short range) with each other and their environment, may be arranged in a hierarchical structure, and where there is no centralized control. This and other features make it difficult to predict cause and effect relationships. Agents, which may be individuals, groups, or organizations, influenced by local conditions, create higher level structures which become the basis for other structures (e.g. coalescing groups and groups of groups).

Axiom 3

"What we typically think of as free markets are not actually that free."

Attractors are islands of stability in complex, unpredictable, systems. Such systems can settle down into one of a number of possible steady states. These steady states are called 'attractor basins' caused by dynamic complex systems switching between attractor basins enabling control to be exercised.

Actions and interventions of individuals may move a system to an attractor, or, move from one less desirable attractor (a fitness state) to another more desirable attractor (a higher fitness state).

Axiom 4

"Social barriers – caused by geography, networks, culture, language, and distrust – create transaction costs that stifle valuable relationships before they can be born."

If an ecosystem is complex and full of conflicting constraints, it may be sub-divided into a number of non-overlapping but interacting self-optimizing parts called patches, like a patchwork quilt. Enabling each patch to optimize its behavior enables all patches to co-evolve with one another.

Patching may support decentralized leadership and decision making which are otherwise prevented by social barriers. Improved interfaces between sub-systems improve trust and lower transaction costs.

Axiom 5

"The vibrancy of a Rainforest correlates to the number of people in a network and their ability to connect with one another."

Self-organization is a process where some form of order or coordination arises out of the local interactions between the components of an initially disordered system. It can create a degree of predictability within an unpredictable system. This process is not directed or controlled by any agent or subsystem inside or outside of the system. The resulting organization is wholly decentralized or distributed over all the system's components.

Self-organization leads to decentralized leadership models, the importance of role models and trust. Self-organization is a process where some form of order or coordination arises out of the local interactions between the components of an initially disordered system. It can create a degree of predictability within an unpredictable system. This process is not directed or controlled by any agent or subsystem inside or outside of the system. The resulting organization is wholly decentralized or distributed over all the system's components.

Self-organization leads to decentralized leadership models, the importance of role models and trust.

Axiom 6

"High social barriers outside of closed circles of families and friends are the norm in the world."

Carefully targeted interventions enable communities to unlock their complex system dynamics and frequently enable small changes to have large consequences. Effective intervention points may, for example, be at self-organization, amplifying action, and stabilizing feedback stages.

Interventions may be applied through changing the system's parameters, such as bridging network holes by boundary spanning individuals.

Axiom 7

"Rainforests depend on people who actively bridge social distances and actively connect disparate parties together."

Structural holes develop when two separate networked clusters possess non-redundant information. This suggests that a broker or boundary spanner – such as an entrepreneur – who bridges the hole could gain competitive advantage by engaging in information arbitrage. Connecting networks of entrepreneurs with their own strong and weak links by bridging structural holes may provide access to valuable new ideas, alternative opinions and practices, early access to new opinions, and an ability to move ideas between groups where there is an advantage in doing so.

Complex systems exist in a far-from-equilibrium state where small actions and events, fluctuations in the system, can be amplified through positive feedback and a cycle of self-reinforcement.

This process creates a dynamic which increases the likelihood that other similar events will emerge. Amplifying actions can be enhanced by boundary spanners who bridge network holes, by group social entrepreneurship, and non-rational behavior.

Axiom 8

"People in Rainforests are motivated by reasons that defy traditional economic notions of 'rational' behavior."

It functions in a *far from equilibrium* or *at the edge of chaos* state, because it is frequently disturbed and has no time to settle down in intervals between events that cause disruptions. Complex systems may settle into *local* equilibria – basins of local equilibrium attraction known as 'attractor' states, but these may be easily disrupted and change over time.

It is this recombining into new patterns of interaction or moving from one 'basin of stability' to another in an innovation ecosystem that allows us to build, if not complete ecosystem models, then at least some predictability around these stable regions.

All this is completely different from traditional economic equilibrium.

Axiom 9

"Innovation and human emotion are intertwined."

Positive feedback produces deviations and innovation. Negative feedback acts as a stabilizing force.

Axiom 10

"The greater the diversity in human specialization, the greater the potential value of exchanges in a system."

Ecosystem behavior emerges from self- organization of interconnected components.

Emergence may be created by behaviors such as disputes and friction within systems or by re-organizing a system's building blocks. Emergence is more effective if the system has networks of strong, weak, and relevant links. Emergence is an outcome of self-organization in the form of a new level of order in the system that comes into being as novel structures and patterns which maintain themselves over some period of time.

Emergence may create a new entity with qualities that are not reflected in the interactions of each agent within the system.

Emergent organizations are typically very robust and able to survive and self-repair substantial damage or perturbations.

Axiom 11

"The instincts that once helped our ancestors survive are hurting our ability to maximize innovation today."

Interactions between the boundaries of innovation ecosystem building blocks help build ecosystems. Disconnections damage ecosystems.

Axiom 12

"Rainforests have replaced tribalism with a culture of informal rules that allow strangers to together efficiently on temporary projects."

Emergence may be created through a recombination of resources; a re-aggregation of some kind that increases the capacity of the overall system to operate. Recombination may include knowledge re-use and be supported by social contracts.

Recombination expands opportunities for all the agents in the ecosystem.

Hierarchies can be damaging or beneficial in enabling communications.

Axiom 13

"The informal rules that govern Rainforests cause people to restrain their short-term self-interest for long-term mutual gains."

If new emergent order is creating value it will stabilize or legitimize itself, finding parameters that best increase its overall sustainability in the ecosystem. Stability results by slowing the non-linear process that led to the amplification of emergence in the first place. Stabilizing feedback can increase trust and reduce transaction costs. Complex systems can maximize the effectiveness of a system even though its individual components may be operating sub-optimally.

Axiom 14

"Rainforests function when the combined value of social norms and extra-rational motivations outweigh the human instincts to fear."

The variety in a control system must be equal to or larger than the variety of the perturbations experienced by the system.

This law means that a flexible system with many options is better able to cope with change. One that is tightly optimized for an initial set of conditions might be more efficient whilst those conditions prevail but fail totally should conditions change.

8

Systems, Models, and Attractors

· ·

Section Summary: A *system* is anything that is composed of elements connected in a characteristic system structure. Innovation ecosystems, as complex adaptive systems, also exhibit the property of nonlinearity; the same input may not always yield the same output. This means the system cannot be broken down into individual components to see how each works and therefore how the whole system functions. Because a simplified model of a system seems to reproduce the behavior of the real system being modeled it cannot be assumed that this model will work in all circumstances or conditions. Different contexts may require different models. Attractors are islands of stability or niches in complex, unpredictable, possibly chaotic, systems. In the language of complexity these steady states, regions of quasi-stability or system-level order. In Rainforest language attractors are 'farms' although the metaphor begins to fail us. It is by intervening and causing dynamic complex systems to switch between attractor basins that development can be exercised.

One's got to change the system or one changes nothing. One can't put things right in a hole-and-corner way, if you take my meaning."

— George Orwell, *Keep the Aspidistra Flying* 1936.

We have been using the word 'system' so we had better define it and how it will be applied. A *system* is anything that is composed of system *elements* connected in a characteristic system *structure*. This configuration of system elements allows a system to perform specific system *functions* in its system *environment*. These functions can be interpreted as serving a distinct system *purpose*. The system *boundary* is permeable for *inputs* from, and *outputs* to, the environment. It defines the system's *identity* and *autonomy.*[45] The term system will be used in just the same way as we talk about school systems or systems of government.

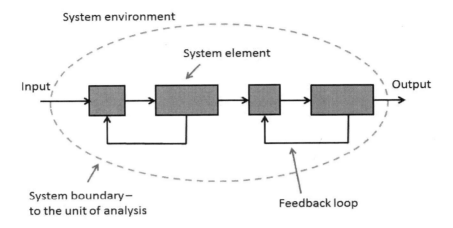

Figure 3. Basic system representation.

Systems and people

In the Introduction it was stated that, as the name implies, innovation ecosystems are systems of people usually in organizations behaving as normal non-rational beings, making decisions, experiencing successes and failures, learning, and making mistakes.

In Section 10 and elsewhere these system elements, or building blocks as we will rename them, and the way they are connected will be discussed in detail. To make it clear at this stage, these building blocks are not static elements but people and organizations of people working with and communicating with each other to create a culture of innovation.

It is the intangibles [46] of human relationships (trust, loyalty, misgivings, motivations, actions, mistakes, and so forth) that cause the uncertainties in the reality in which we live. Uncertainties will reappear frequently

45   Hartmut Bossel "Systems and Models: Complexity Dynamics Evolution Stability," *Books on Demand GmbH, Germany* (2007) p 1.

46   Section 7 states "The Rainforest model is more than a metaphor. Innovation ecosystems are not merely like biological systems; they are biological systems."

and dominate Section 25 when we address the question of how to do strategic planning in the face of such uncertainties and unpredictable environments.

It is the recognition of building blocks and sub-building blocks that make up an innovation culture. They are dynamic subcultures interacting with each other; agreeing, disagreeing, compromising, and dividing or coalescing in the usual human way, and developing relationships.

In some ways innovation culture may seem like a contradiction. 'Culture' suggests the existence of certain agreed behavioral or societal norms [47] and conformity to these norms. Might not such conformity establish boundaries which constrain innovation? Innovation is frequently generated by those who are motivated to actions which break rules, producing a culture which allows and expects innovation.

We can't *demand* that an organization or community have an innovation culture; it can't be imposed, it must emerge. Innovation culture is not a monolith; it is made up of sub-cultures which are the building blocks for the dynamic whole. 'Dynamic' because the re-arrangement of these building blocks create emergence over time. Thus, while there must be cultural norms within a culture of innovation they need not constrain because new sub-cultures are constantly emerging.

Many of the problems and solutions discussed in this book will be pictured as systems and communications within systems and with the system's environment. We also noted earlier, but worth repeating here, that the science of innovation ecosystems which investigates building blocks, strong and weak links, cause and effect, optimization, networks and feedback, and many other characteristics found in this book may sometimes seem to be abstracting away the human element. To a degree it is. But only because an understanding of abstracted science enables us to explain, and sometimes anticipate, real world results of the behavior of individuals and organizations functioning in a complex world. We may know many of the people within a system, but to understand the system we also need to know how these people are formally organized in a reporting structure. Of course, how individuals within these formal structures *actually*

. . . .

47   'Norms' is used here to describe how people believe things *should* be.

communicate may be different from an official organogram and this needs to be evident – as well as reasons for the differences.

Linear and nonlinear systems

Innovation ecosystems, as complex adaptive systems, exhibit the property of nonlinearity, namely, one where the same input may not always yield the same output. To understand a complex system we have to study the system as a whole. We already know that the system cannot be broken down into individual components to see how each works as a way of determining how the whole system functions.

Linear and nonlinear systems are familiar to us. A freshly served bowl of soup may be too hot to eat but cools down quickly and stays lukewarm for a long time. If cooling were linear this graph of temperature versus time would be a downward sloping straight line, not a curved one. If I throw a ball at 20 mph while running at 10 mph the ball has an initial speed of 30 miles per hour – a linear system (20+10 = 30). Linear systems have one equilibrium point at the origin. Think of a clock pendulum coming to rest. Nonlinear systems may have many equilibrium points, as we shall see.

Linear Systems	Nonlinear Systems
The amplitude of the system response is proportional to the amplitude of the input signal. This makes the mathematics straightforward.	The amplitude of the system response is not, in general, proportional to the amplitude of the input signal. The mathematics gets tricky.
The superposition principle holds. The system response to input signals can be computed by adding up input signals.	The superposition principle does not hold.
The equilibrium state is independent of initial conditions.	The equilibrium state depends on initial conditions.
System behavior is highly predictable with low adaptability.	Systems behavior is difficult to predict, except in sub-regions where the system behaves more like a linear system and has higher adaptability.

Table 1. Key characteristics of linear and nonlinear systems. [48]

. . . .

48   Adapted from Hartmut Bossel "Systems and Models: Complexity Dynamics Evolution Stability" *Books on Demand GmbH, Germany* (2007).

Models

Because complex systems are, well – complex, we need to construct *models* to try and simplify our picture of them. These can be computer simulation models known as 'agent based models,' verbal models, or even models built out of cardboard and glue, but all will contain simplifying assumptions. It's important to not forget what these assumptions are when drawing conclusions from manipulating models.

Therefore, it may be stating the obvious, although obviousness is sometimes overlooked, that all models are incomplete. A completely accurate model of the system would be the system itself; a model of you would be another you. Therefore any model is going to be a reduced or simplified version of the real thing. What we leave out may be important, but we can't be sure if it is important or not. However, as someone once noted: all models are wrong, but some are useful. Models and modeling are useful because there is no alternative. Some other dangers of wrong or 'false' models include: [49]

1. A model may be only locally applicable.

2. A model may be an idealization whose conditions of applicability are never found in nature.

3. A model may be incomplete with important elements missing.

4. A model may fail to describe or predict data correctly.

5. A system may have hidden factors which consequently cannot be modeled.

Models may be used and applied correctly but still be the wrong model. However, there is an upside; they can help to create better models including: [50]

1. An oversimplified model may be a starting point to produce more complex ones.

2. An incorrect model may suggest new predictive tests or refinements of an existing model.

. . . .

49 Condensed from William C. Wimsatt, "Re-Engineering Philosophy for Limited Beings," *Harvard University Press* (2007) pp 101-107.

50 *ibid* pp 104-105.

3. An oversimplified model may help explain properties of more complex cases which also appear in simpler situations.

"To *fully* understand a complex system, we need to understand it in all its complexity. Furthermore, because complex systems are open systems, we need to understand the system's complete environment before we can understand the system, and, of course, the environment is complex in itself. There is no human way of doing this. The knowledge we have of complex systems is based on the models we make of these systems, but in order to function as models – and not merely as a *repetition* of the system – they have to *reduce* the complexity of the system. This means that some aspects of the system are always left out of consideration. The problem is compounded by the fact that that which is left out interacts with the rest of the system in a non-linear way, therefore we cannot predict what the effects of our reduction of the complexity will be, especially as the system and its environment develop and transform in time." [51] Please, dear reader, do not be depressed by this statement; it's just the way it is.

We must be careful not to assume that because a simplified model of a system seems to reproduce the behavior of the real system being modeled that this model will work in all circumstances or conditions. Different contexts may require different models. A universal model of complex adaptive systems has not been constructed and may never be. 'Contextual Qualifiers' (Section 13) can be used to help handle different contexts.

System State and State Space

To understand the theory behind systems of Rainforests and farms we need to introduce the concept of a *state space* (also called *system space* or *phase space*). The term phase space was originally used about substances which can exist in several phases or states. For example, water can exist in solid (ice), liquid, or vapor (steam) phases. In this book, *state space* will be used. The formal definition is "a multidimensional space in which each axis corresponds to one of the coordinates required to specify the state of a physical system, all the coordinates being thus represented

- -

51   Rika Preiser, Paul Cilliers and Oliver Human, "Deconstruction and complexity: a critical economy," *South African Journal of Philosophy* (2013) p 262.

so that a point in the space corresponds to a state of the system." [52] As an example, when you are riding your bicycle the physical space you inhabit is the familiar 3-dimensional space. However, your state space is a 2-dimension one whose axes are position and velocity (remember velocity = speed *and* direction, such as 5 miles/hour due north). In economic systems, examples of state space variables are commonly the inflation rate, the interest rate, the national debt, and the unemployment rate. The **Rainforest Scorecard** [53] (Section 10) variables make up the Scorecard's state space which has 6 dimensions, or axes, on for each of the 6 variables of Leadership; Frameworks, Infrastructure, Policies; Resources; Activities and Engagement; Role Models; and Culture.

A system state describes where the state is – its present condition, its 'state of being,' to help understand its state of present or potential innovation. State space is a convenient 'term of use' to help describe and explain many complex system features such as the presence of farms within Rainforests and observed features such as discontinuous innovation. Actually, we live in multiple, sometimes overlapping or coalescing, state spaces. A state space is a state of being, necessary to inhabit and lead an innovative organization and create and maintain an innovation culture. Rainforests and farms constitute our state space; they *are* our state space. If you are having difficulty with all this, don't worry; it's useful but by no means essential to fully grasp the state space idea to understand how to *build* an innovation ecosystem.

One traditional view of systems introduces *state variables* and *parameters*. There can be any number of these variables. For example, the **Rainforest Scorecard** has 6 state variables just listed (Leadership; Frameworks, Infrastructure, Policies; Resources; Activities and Engagement; Role Models; and Culture). Many more could be identified. These variables are considered to be indicators to measure innovation *potential* in a 'unit of analysis.' As we shall see potential and actual innovation may emerge in different ways.

Parameters are usually fixed quantities or have controlled values and which describe the attributes of a system. In algebra the quadratic equation

. . . .

52   'Phase space,' Oxford Living Dictionaries.

53   Henry Doss & Alistair Brett, "The Rainforest Scorecard. A Practical Framework for Growing Innovation Potential," *Los Altos: Regenwald* (2015).

$y = ax^2+bx+c$ has x and y as variables and a, b, and c as parameters. For example, an innovation system's leadership could be said to be affected by parameters such as motivation, trust, communication, and so forth. The ability of entrepreneurs to act in networks and generate innovations is affected by variables and parameters. The performance of innovation ecosystems is determined by its variables and parameters, although not always in predictable ways.

Each variable has a set of parameters associated with each question in each **Rainforest Scorecard** category. A change to these parameters changes the measurement of variables for the unit of analysis being assessed. For example, the Culture variable is changed if the parameter measuring the level of individual motivation in the system changes. Overall, the Categories represent a basic set of elements of a knowledge structure, and serve as the vehicle to capture knowledge. New learning is accommodated via specific changes in Category sub-structure parameters. For an instrument such as the **Rainforest Scorecard**, the difficulty is how to measure the 6 variables. The Scorecard chooses, among other possibilities, to solicit the opinions of people within the unit of analysis through a survey questionnaire. Thus, practitioners can learn from their own experience and that of others what changes occurred as a result of parameter adjustments. Remember also that in some cases small parameter adjustments may lead to large impacts (large changes, for better or worse, in one or more variables). For example, a small increase in the level of trust (a parameter) within the unit of analysis can significantly affect a person's assessment about the level of Culture (a variable).

The description above is actually over-simplified because it does not take into account sufficiently the effect of connections between the building blocks of innovation ecosystems. In fact, parameters, like variables, are also influenced by other factors. For example, communication may be affected by organizational politics, and trust may be influenced by levels of communication. Some of these factors may be outside the unit of analysis. So, a more complete picture is that variables depend on other variables, which in turn depend on other variables, and so forth. In complex systems these parameters are in fact also variable, which clearly makes measurement more difficult. These variables behave as sub-complex systems – made up other complex systems, and so forth. But there is no need to panic. We shall see that this situation can not only be handled but yields valuable insights into how innovation ecosystems should be designed. [54]

Attractors

Imagining state space is a helpful way to explain attractors. Attractors or 'attractor basins' are islands of stability in complex, unpredictable, possibly chaotic, systems (characteristics of complex systems #6, Section 5). Such systems can settle down into one of a number of possible steady states. In the language of complexity these steady states, regions of quasi-stability or system-level order, are called 'attractors' or 'attractor basins.' Attractors are best described by seeing them as being in state space. An attractor can be describe an as a "stable pattern adopted by a system because of its routines, norms, and objectives, and highlight when stable these internal dynamics appear linear and proportional which enables linear thinking, predictability, and control to be undertaken" [55]

It is by intervening and causing dynamic complex systems to switch between attractor basins that control can be exercised. Once the system enters the attractor basin, variables are determined by ranges of values permitted by the attractor set. [56]

If I drop this book onto the floor it will stay there (please don't do this is you are reading on an electronic device), when a pendulum clock winds down it stays hanging in a stable position unless provided energy to move it when the clock is wound up. Both are in their most basic attractor basin static equilibrium states.

. . . .

54   A general way of writing the $y = ax^2+bx+c$ example is to say that y is a function of x, or f(x) = ax^2+bx+c. In linear systems the parameters a, b, and c are fixed. When parameters are themselves variable the equation has to be written showing the function is itself a function of some other function, or F[f(x)]. The mathematics gets tricky when there are variable parameters which are themselves sub-complexes.

55   Jeffrey Goldstein, J.K. Hazy, & B.B. & Lichtenstein, "Complexity and the Nexus of Leadership: Leveraging Nonlinear Science to Create Ecologies of Innovation," *New York: Palgrave Macmillan* (2010) p. 55.

56   James K. Hazy, Jeffery Goldstein, "Generative Conditions for Entrepreneurship: A Complexity Science Model" *Adelphi University School of Business Working Paper Series*: SB-WP-2010-05 (2010) p 9.

We *can* measure factors or variables as the basis for decision making because of these basins of stability – which are steady state (not static) systems maintained by the feeding in of external energy. For corporations and innovation ecosystems this equilibrium is a kind of order. Empirical research has shown that in large complex systems such as communities and corporations, these attractors maintain conditions required for emergent self-organization, adaptive capability, *and measurement.*

In Rainforest language attractors are 'farms.' An example of having a 'farm' and a Rainforest (an attractor basin embedded in a complex space) is a company which needs rules of operation to carry out its business – within an attractor – but also allows employees an agreed amount of time to pursue their own ideas in a more unstructured, unpredictable, non-linear, environment. In another example, a consulting organization wants to collection data about existing employee attitudes and opinions at a company. This it did by deploying a structured set of questions to be answered in a fixed time period by groups of employees. But there is also a need to have employees think more innovatively which could not be done in a closely structured, time constrained setting. Therefore time is allowed for a general discussion and even argument. Closely related to this experience is that organizational and regional or national culture is an attractor. Within this attractor people share accepted beliefs, norms, and customs which influence their opinions.

In the previous Section it was stated that in practice, there are no 'pure' Rainforests or 'pure' farms. Every system is a mix, a hybrid, of both. In fact, this is where the farm metaphor is an insufficient description. A pure farm would be a completely static system. More realistically an attractor is at least in part in a state of dynamic equilibrium. It needs to be noted that this is where the farm part of the Rainforest metaphor fails us; it does not distinguish between a static equilibrium and a dynamic equilibrium.

A steady state system is not the same as a system in *static equilibrium.* In A and B the level of water in the container is the same, However, in A the level is maintained in a *steady state* as water flows out is balanced by water coming in. Even if a business need does not want to grow it needs new sales and new clients to replace those no longer active. In B the water is in equilibrium; nothing interesting is happening.

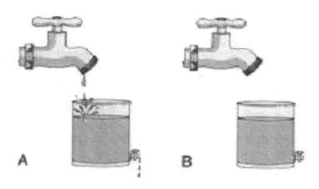

Figure 4. An example of steady state equilibrium and static equilibrium.

In non-equilibrium thermodynamics, which is the name for the study of heat flow and chemical reactions found in most systems of nature, external heat energy to keep a reaction going goes under the quaint name of 'housekeeping heat.' Think about heat needed to keep a kettle of water simmering. The need for permanent noise to continuously restructure networks resembles such housekeeping heat (see more on this in Section 20).

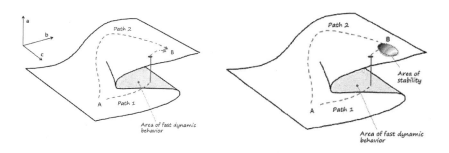

Figure 5. Moving around state space. [57]

Changes in parameters move the ecosystem to a new point in its state space. We can imagine, but cannot draw, a phase space diagram with more than three variables so let's just consider three ecosystem variables a, b, and c, represented along the horizontal and vertical axes in the illustrative

. . . .

57   Diagrams adapted from J. Goldstein *et al* "A Complexity Science Model of Social Innovation in Social Enterprise." *Journal of Social Entrepreneurship*, Vol 1, No 1 (2010) p.109

three dimensional state space diagram below. Path 1 represents, for example, a big jump to a new business model, or a new set of resources, or possibly some disruptive innovation, whereas Path 2 represents continuous transformation; maybe a gradual culture change, or breaking down a problem or opportunity into manageable pieces and sequentially tackling each one.

The above state space representation is of a dynamic innovation ecosystem which exhibits both self-organization and which may have leaders within or outside the self-organized groups with basins or regions of steady state equilibria. Some degree of direction may be needed, for example by those who have knowledge of constraining conditions such as available resources or the need to protect intellectual property.

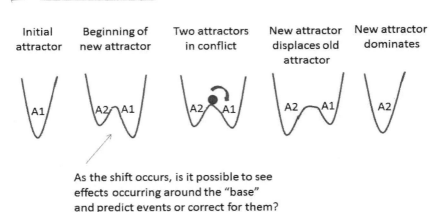

Initial attractor	Beginning of new attractor	Two attractors in conflict	New attractor displaces old attractor	New attractor dominates

As the shift occurs, is it possible to see effects occurring around the "base" and predict events or correct for them?

Figure 6. A representational two-dimensional slice of the state space attractors. [58]

The representation in Figure 6 illustrates how system parameters may change abruptly resulting in discontinuous shifts in equilibria from one attractor to another in the state space.

A market niche, for example, is an attractor where recirculation and reuse of resources occurs. Furthermore, in stable attractors if individuals behave differently from established operating rules or accepted norms, negative

. . . .

58   Diagram adapted from Sharon Zivkovic, "Government's role in social innovation: Balancing unplanned exploration and planned exploitation," *4th International Social Innovation Research Conference* (2012), p 2.

feedback reduces deviations from an existing state and acts as a stabilizing force – making innovation less likely.

Within an attractor, knowledge resources can be reused, building blocks can be rearranged, with standard interfaces supporting building block connectivity (Section 10) so that the space within attractors behaves as a nearly decomposable, near autonomous, sub-system. Most of the time most of us live in attractor basins; to live constantly under conditions of complexity would be intolerable. We want the bank holding our money and our government and legal system be stable, and the trains to run on time. Not all businesses want too much internal innovation.

The predictable and the unpredictable

As was noted in Section 5, for most of us life is a mix of predictable and unpredictable events. Novelist Paul Auster in a Financial Times interview expressed his opinion that the "mechanics of reality are far stranger than we think, that unexpected things are happening all the time and that we ought to embrace that and try to understand the world as an unstable, unpredictable, place, not insist that it's an exception every time we see it happen. This is how things work." [59]

How are we to describe such an environment? No, not describe it – how do we analyze it, and why is this important? How can you cultivate a Rainforest inside a farm, without killing one or the other? How can a farm manage a Rainforest? How can you grow innovative capacity without losing control of your business? How can you control your business to the degree necessary without stifling innovation? The answer to such questions is to have leadership with a clear understanding of attractors and complexity.

Typically, a business supported by an innovation ecosystem has control over how the business is structured and roles of its staff within its structure, its capabilities (including technological developments), the markets it serves, and its strategy for whatever its competitive environment may be. If the future external environment is uncertain a business's (and an innovation ecosystem's) assumptions, and its strategy, based on these

. . . .

59   *Financial Times*, Jan 27, 2017.

assumptions may be wrong; the higher the level of uncertainty the greater the risk of being wrong. Not necessarily under control of a business (and an innovation ecosystem) are factors such as customer needs, economic trends, and regulatory changes, among others.

Emergence of innovation can occur when an existing state of an attractor, which represents a stable pattern in a complex system, is disrupted by internal or external factors such as a falling out among the company's leaders over its direction, loss of an existing or anticipated customer or market, or the rise of a competitor. 'Criticalization' refers to such major transition periods. [60] A system may bifurcate (see Section 19) splitting into two attractors; one which continues the old way of working and a second one which operates in new ways. In this new attractor, re-combinations occur and new capacity is built. When an attractor is in an unstable state it will be extra sensitive to small changes or disturbances which may cause large changes in the system's behavior. Conversely, large changes or disturbances may result in small changes to the overall system (characteristics of complex systems #8, Section 5).

However, there is a potential downside. A comfortable life inside an attractor basin can lead to complacency. When a disruption or shock to the system occurs (Section 18) a community or organization may not be prepared for change. We need the right amount of stimulus (housekeeping heat) to keep us on our toes.

Examples of being stuck in an attractor, or a niche, are similar to those ecosystems with too many strong links leading to an echo chamber effect (Section 9). From the network perspective (Section 14) we will see that attractor basins appear as communities or organizations having a large number of internal connections but relatively few external connections. [61] These features, while making it possible for the niche community to behave autonomously and recirculate and reuse existing resources, can also trap it. For example, a community or regional economic development organization (e.g. a chamber of commerce) whose behaviors and actions

. . . .

60 Goldstein, J., Hazy, J.K., & Lichtenstein, B.B. "Complexity and the Nexus of Leadership: Leveraging Nonlinear Science to Create Ecologies of Innovation," *New York: Palgrave Macmillan* (2010), p. 55.

61 John H. Holland, "Signals and Boundaries: Building Blocks for Complex Adaptive Systems," *MIT Press* (2012), p 159.

are dictated by strong links of membership sometimes serve the immediate interests of members and fail to achieve true development as a result.

Another example is where a system of government research institutes has a large number of links among themselves but few with the corporate sector because the government had been their main client. When the government decides that these institutes should be partially privatized, only a minority which had encouraged working with the private sector are able to shift to this new attractor.

Once a complex system, of individuals in this case, is pushed to a far from equilibrium state, the more its leaders and members surface conflict and create controversy, the more likely that the system will generate novel opportunities and solutions. The more that leaders and members encourage rich interactions, the more likely that amplifying actions will be present in the system.

On the subject of leadership, Henry Doss, has written about organization's which mistakenly focus on training leaders to lead people, rather than training leaders to build and lead *systems*. He introduced the Innovation Syllogism:

Innovation is a product of culture (not individuals).

Culture is an emergent factor of systems (not individuals).

Therefore, systems drive innovation (not individuals).

"If the logic and assumptions of this syllogism hold, then you may find that the most critical aspect of building an innovative organization – systems – is absent from your training and development planning." [62]

Thus, practitioners can learn from their own experience, and that of others, what changes occurred as a result of parameter adjustments. This leads us into the next Section.

---

62   Henry H. Doss, "Why Your Innovation Leadership Training Will Fail," http://www.forbes.com/sites/henrydoss/2013/06/06/why-your-innovation-leadership-training-will-fail/

9

The Ties That Bind Us: Strong Links, Weak Links, and Relevant Links

Section Summary: If we only talk to people we know well, that is, strongly linked to, it's likely that discussions will proceed along familiar lines and new thinking or new information will not emerge. Strong links contribute to network stability, and if a strong link is lost the networks will behave in a different ways. A weak link is defined as a link in a network if it's addition or removal does not significantly change the functioning of the network. Weak links stabilize complex system networks. Both kinds of links are necessary for stable networks and stable societies. In addition to strong and weak links there is another type of link which is important in the study of information flow. The relevant link between complex systems, or their components, determines if one system is relevant to the other or not.

"The ties that bind us to life are tougher than you imagine, or than anyone can who has not felt how roughly they may be pulled without breaking."

— *Agnes Grey* by Anne Brontë, 1847.

Before discussing building blocks of innovation ecosystems and linkages between building blocks we will say something about what we mean by 'links.'

Anne Brontë (1820-1849) gives us a useful introduction to the concept of weak and strong links and the stability, resilience to external perturbations, of our professional networks. Think of a network's ability to roll with the punches as being like the shock absorbers and springs on a car as it rides over potholes in the road.

In fact it was not Anne, perhaps the least well known of the literary Brontë sisters, but Mark Granovetter, a Harvard graduate student in the 1960's, who began much of the contemporary discussion of networks in his now classic study [63] which investigated how job seekers found employment. To cut a long story short, he found that rather than by relying on their close friends most found their jobs through contacts they knew less well, such as friends of friends. The analogous situation is to consider how we find new ideas or gather information. When we talk about links and linking, it's assumed that some information, a message or signal, is being diffused through a network. If we only talk to the people we know well it's likely that discussions will proceed along familiar lines and new thinking or new information will not emerge. Granovetter noted in his follow up study [64] "that individuals with few weak ties [what are now usually called links] will be deprived of information from distant parts of the social system and will be confined to the provincial news and views of their close friends. This deprivation will ... insulate them from the latest ideas." Think of this as being in an echo chamber. Granovetter's insight was that network diffusion will reach the largest number of people (network nodes) when traveling through weak links and avoid echo chambers.

An analogy to the problem of too many strong links versus weaker ones is that of a diamond cutter who needs to cleave a stone in precisely the right spot or it will shatter. This is because the strong lattice structure links in a diamond cannot relax in the presence of a perturbation – the shock of the cleaver – except in certain planes.

The LinkedIn professional network and other social media are examples of the power of weak links. In addition to its main purpose of job seeking, LinkedIn can be an effective network to expand our thinking and absorb new ideas from participation in a multitude of LinkedIn Groups with people whom we either don't know well or don't know at all. InnoCentive [65] the online marketplace referenced in Section 10 which seeks solutions to problems posted on its website recognizes that diversity of potential

. . . .

63 Mark Granovetter, "The Strength of Weak Ties," *The American Journal of Sociology* (1973). http://sociology.stanford.edu/people/mgranovetter/documents/granstrengthweakties.pdf

64 "The Strength of Weak Ties: A Network Theory Revisited," Mark Granovetter (1983) http://www.soc.ucsb.edu/faculty/friedkin/Syllabi/Soc148/Granovetter%201983.pdf

65 InnoCentive http://www.innocentive.com/

scientific approaches to a problem – that is, many weak links in their network – was a significant predictor of problem solving success.

A negative example is the case of a national innovation fund in a rapidly developing nation where a government fund established to stimulate investment in small technology-based companies, was having problems making investments that would yield expected rates of return. Not enough promising investment opportunities were being found. The networks of the fund managers had many strong professional links, mostly in banking. But 'banking-thinking' was not what was needed for a venture capital type fund, and the fund personnel had insufficient weak links to open them up to new ideas and different ways of investment thinking.

But, you might point out that in a complex adaptive system functioning in *a far from equilibrium* state much is made of the need to reduce transaction costs by building trust. Surely, strong links imply a higher level of trust than weak ones? To understand this apparent paradox, once again context needs to be taken into account. In Section 7 it is noted that if new a emergent order is creating value it will stabilize or legitimize itself, thus finding functions and parameters that best increase its overall sustainability in the ecosystem, typically through negative and positive feedback loops. This process depends on the context in which it is embedded. The presence of strong links as one of the traits of one of the system's building blocks (the national innovation fund in the example above) may be a minor factor in the overall mix of traits and contextual factors influencing transaction costs and efficiency for the whole unit of analysis.

Weak links transfer knowledge, for example, through informal contacts or happenstance. We read something of value in social media, happen to notice something in a book or report, overhear a conversation, or chat with a fellow passenger on a train. Transferring knowledge, including tacit knowledge (knowledge in peoples' heads and not necessarily recorded anywhere), requires trust because knowledge transfer always opens up the possibility of error, especially if the knowledge is obtained through social media. A high level of trust is needed for low-error knowledge transfer.

We have been talking about weak links, so we should define them more carefully. A weak link is defined as a link in a network if it's addition or removal does not significantly change the functioning of the network. In our own professional networks, weak links are formed and also disappear all the time. Much more about weak links can be found in the fascinating book **Weak Links** by Peter Csermely. [66] Weak links stabilize complex system networks, although as Csermely states a general mathematical proof for weak links and network stabilization is lacking. Not a surprise.

Strong links also contribute to network stability, but if a strong link is lost the networks will be affected and behave differently. Both kinds of links are necessary for stable networks and stable societies. However, as we saw from the national innovation fund example, if the system becomes too stable it cannot change or develop and new ideas will not form. That is why networks need to be managed to preserve the 'right' combination of links. [67] Strong and weak links form and then disappear, some after only a short existence; others may be stable for longer periods. This dynamic behavior is more likely with weak links – by definition.

As an analogy, strong and weak links can be thought of as words in a sentence. Removing some words may make the sentence meaningless (strong links), others may be removed, for example, to simplify the sentence, and make no fundamental change in the sentence's meaning (weak links).

Network has many weak links	Network has few weak links
Communication is good in the network, relaxation goes smoothly.	Communication is restricted to the network, relaxation is disturbed.
Noise is easily dissipated or absorbed in the network.	Network is noisy and noise stays in segments of the network.
Network is integrated and behaves as a whole.	Network is segregated and behaves as an assembly of its constituent elements.
Changes are dissipated and occasional errors are isolated so that the network is stable.	Changes and noise persist; the network is error prone and unstable.
The network is plastic.	The network is rigid.
Elements are efficiently connected.	Elements are sparsely connected.

Table 2. Adapted from Peter Csermely, "Weak Links: Stabilizers of Complex Systems from Proteins to Social Networks" page 96.

· ·

66   Peter Csermely, "Weak Links: Stabilizers of Complex Systems from Proteins to Social Networks," *Berlin: Springer* (2006).

67   Noise may be good noise or bad noise depending on how it is defined (Section 20).

The 'relevant link' introduced by the philosopher Justus Buchler [68] is not usually defined in the literature on links, but is worthy of its own place. We shall meet other important ideas from Buchler as we progress. As he describes it [69] if two complex systems (what Buchler call 'complexes') are related, "then each is relevant to the other. But each may be relevant to the other in either of two ways. ... To say that a complex is strongly relevant to another, then, is to say that it is a condition of the others integrity,[70] that it either reinforces and sustains or modifies and perhaps destroys the integrity (a given integrity) of the other."

"Consider the two complexes, rainy weather and the growth of wheat. They are related, it makes no sense to say that rain is related to the growth of the wheat, but that the growth of the wheat is not related to rain. What we can say, given the typical agricultural order in which the complex known as the growth of wheat is located, is that the rain is strongly relevant to the growth of wheat, whereas the growth of wheat is weekly relevant to the rain. The wheat typically would not grow if there were no rain, but there would still be rain if the wheat did not grow or there were no wheat. In this order, the rain is strongly relevant to the wheat in the sense that it is a condition of the integrity of the complex other than itself."

Buchler continues "The city of New York may be strongly relevant to an individual taken at random," it provides services such as police, roads, hospitals, that the individual uses "while that individual would be weakly relevant to the city" – one addition to the populations of the city makes little difference. "But an extraordinary or historic individual might be strongly relevant to a city, as a source of major alescence [71] in it. The class of all individuals in a city would have to be strongly relevant – indispensable to the prevalence (maintenance) of the city." [72]

Another example is a researcher at a university, which is not especially well known, believes the results of her investigations are of value to industry.

. . . .

68   Justus Buchler, "Metaphysics of Natural Complexes," *Columbia University Press* (1966), p 108ff.

69   *ibid* page 107.

70   *ibid* defines 'integrity' as the constitution of a complex and the relations it has.

71   Alescense is defined and described in more detail in Section 26. For now, think of alescense as growth.

72   *ibid* page 109.

R&D and new business development divisions in companies don't have the resources to trawl research at thousands of universities. And, at best, the researcher is weakly relevant to any company. If the company decides to fund the research then the company becomes relevant to the researcher and *vice versa*. When a researcher cannot easily become relevant to the company, a solution is to introduce an intermediary connector or boundary spanner (see Section 12) with existing relevant links to the business sector. 'Relevant' here means experience working with companies in the researcher's area of research and familiarity with current developments. Thus, the researcher/company link becomes relevant via the boundary spanner.

It is often recommended that to commercialize innovations in a complex global marketplace innovators must break free of regional constraints and ultimately become interconnected to today's globally distributed markets, sources of investment, partnership prospects, and talent. This certainly seems to make sense. So should we just go and create as many network links of all kinds as we can and just link to everyone? It may not be quite that simple as will be demonstrated later (Section 22). Neil Johnson in his 2007 highly readable book **Simply Complexity**[73] and a follow up, maybe not so easy to read, research paper with colleagues [74] describes populations which might, for example, be competing for business. Their research found that for populations with modest resources adding small amounts of connectivity between members of the population *increased* the disparity between successful and unsuccessful people and reduced the mean success rate. In higher resource populations they found that the levels of interconnectivity increase the mean success rate and enable most to be successful. At higher levels of interconnectivity, the overall population became fairer (smaller disparity in success rates) but less efficient (smaller mean success rate) irrespective of the global resource level.

Or, as stated by Justin Marlowe at the University of Kansas in a related 2007 study of public debt management "the consequences of 'wiring up' an additive population depends quite dramatically on the interplay

. . . .

73   "Simply Complexity" Neil Johnson, *Oneworld Publications* (2007).

74   "Dynamical Interplay Between Local Connectivity and Global Competition in a Networked Population" http://arxiv.org/pdf/cond-mat/0401527.pdf

between the local connectivity and the global resources."[75] This finding is consistent with a growing literature that suggests networks in general, and stable networks in particular, distribute resources in ways that may reinforce inequalities. With the increasing concern about global inequalities these findings require more research.

We are beginning to see that is it important to have the right mix of strong and weak links in a network and that also simply saying that we should link to everyone might not always be the right choice. Also, this mix of link types is certainly necessary, but what is really important is the ease with which information moves through networks, a subject addressed in Section 23.

75   Justin Marlowe, "Network Stability and Organization Performance: Does Context Matter"
      http://www2.ku.edu/~pmranet/conferences/AZU2007/ArizonaPapers/Marlowe_2007.pdf

10

Building Blocks for Innovation Ecosystems

· ·

Section Summary: A building block may be 'hardware' or 'software;' a new business incubator or a law or regulation frequently as part of a political context. Re-arrangement of such building blocks can create emergence of new ideas. A complex adaptive system is more than, or different from, the sum of its parts. It is not a reductionist system – that is, it cannot be decomposed into a set of independent non-interacting parts. However, some systems may be nearly decomposable. These principles have been observed in both natural and man-made highly adaptable systems and organizations. Building blocks are not static; they may change over time, traits are added or removed, they coalesce or split, they generate new building blocks. Lessons from agile manufacturing and business model innovations are described.

"Yes, science is a powerful tool.... But the humble and difficulty, I am sure, in distinguishing instances based on idle fancy or sheer ignorance from instances that cast some light on the ways in which complexity exhibits itself wherever it is found in nature. I shall leave to you the final judgment of relevance in your respective fields."

— Herbert A. Simon, recipient of the 1978 Nobel Prize in Economics, in a talk to the Society for General Systems Research.

The following anecdote is told of a philosopher who gave a lecture on the structure of the solar system. After his presentation the philosopher was accosted by a little old lady. "Your theory that the sun is the center of the solar system, and that the earth is a ball which rotates around it, has a very convincing ring to it, but it's wrong. I've got a better theory," announced the little old lady. "And what is that madam?" inquired the philosopher. "That we live on a crust of earth which is on the back of a giant turtle" was the reply.

Wishing to be polite and not cause offense the philosopher inquired "If your theory is correct, madam, what does this turtle stand on?" "You're a very clever man and that's a very good question," replied the lady, "but I have an answer to it. And it's this: the first turtle stands on the back of a second, far larger, turtle, which stands directly under him." "But what does this second turtle stand on?" persisted the philosopher. To this, the little old lady crowed triumphantly "it's no use, sir – turtles all the way down."

Turtles all the way down

"Turtles all the way down" has become a phrase used to describe any system that appears to have dependencies that never end. It sometimes looks as through innovation ecosystems are examples of such turtle stacking. *Innovation* ecosystems are whole systems built from a complex of components. These building blocks are more than just physical objects or organizations; they include attitudes, experience, culture, and feelings. These building blocks and the composite systems they create are 'complex systems' or 'Rainforests.'

A building block may be a law or regulation, frequently as part of a political context. During the 1990s when countries in Eastern and Central Europe and Central Asia were transitioning to independent nations, many were eager to learn how they could capitalize on what in some cases was their impressive science base. However, the view was frequently expressed that "we cannot make progress on commercializing science and technology to create new businesses until we have clear laws on intellectual property ownership and protection" or "we must wait until we have sufficient investment capital resources." This was a case where these two needs, seen as necessary building blocks, were thought to be critical, but were not. In several countries many individual scientists and research institutions began to develop procedures and support systems for technology commercialization, even though most of the needed mechanisms were not yet in place, or potentially dangerously unclear; might the government, sometime in the future, claim all rights and revenues from new products or new businesses created from government funded research?

We build innovation in companies, communities, science parks, smart cities, and so forth, by engineering supportive innovation ecosystems. But, the building blocks of innovation ecosystems may be constructed of other building blocks, strongly or weakly connected, and these of still other building blocks, and ... well, you get the idea. If this is not the case, and the ultimate building blocks are simple linear systems, then stasis would result and there could be no innovation; complex systems must have complex constituents.

Re-arranging building blocks

Furthermore, re-arranging such building blocks creates emergence of new ideas. For example, technologies tend to build on each other. What does such re-arranging mean in practice? InnoCentive [76] is an online marketplace that connects organizations seeking solutions to technical problems with freelance problem solvers in a multitude of scientific and technical fields. InnoCentive found that frequently problem solvers with experience far from the problem to be solved was a significant predictor of problem solving success. For example, an electrical engineer came up with a successful solution to a problem dealing with adhesives. Another example of re-arrangement is illustrated in Figure 7. Re-arranging those who are attempting to solve a problem by bringing in diverse knowledge may enable a solution to emerge, or, more generally, create actions which will produce the desired outcomes. Building blocks can be almost anything, found from sources near and far, with a massive variety of properties or *traits* as we shall call them (See Section 26) and multiple ways in which they can be combined.

Thus we see that emergence derives from the properties of a complex system's building blocks plus the way these are combined and arranged.

· ·

76   http://www.innocentive.com

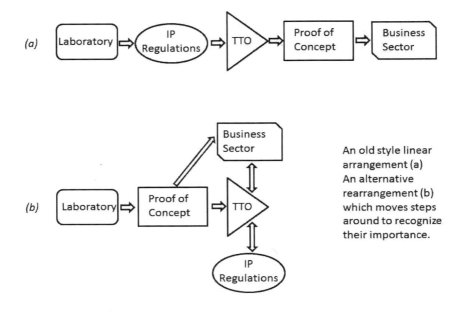

Figure 7. Rearranging Technology Commercialization Building Blocks

This idea of rearranging building blocks is not new. A book [77] written by the economist Joseph Schumpeter in 1911 defines economic development as innovation and continues "To produce means to combine materials and forces within our reach ... To produce other things, or the same things by a different method, means to combine these materials and forces differently. In so far as the 'new combination' may in time grow out of the old by continuous adjustment in small steps, there is certainly change, possibly growth, but neither a new phenomenon nor development in our sense. In so far as this is not the case, and the new combinations appear discontinuously, then the phenomenon characterizing development emerges. ... Development in our sense is then defined by the carrying out of new combinations."

Building blocks are sometimes referred to as 'generators.' Building blocks are not static; they may change over time, traits are added or removed, they coalesce or split, they generate new building blocks. So, it can be

77   "J. Schumpeter, "The Theory of Economic Development: An Inquiry into Profits, Capital, Credit, Interest, and the Business Cycle," *Transaction Publishers* (1911). Translated from the original German by John E. Elliott.

seen that it is crucial to engineering innovation and innovative products and services to break down innovation ecosystems into their component building blocks, even if they cannot be completely decomposed into independent units with clear boundaries, and building new innovation ecosystems from re-usable components.

But wait a moment, if re-arranging innovation ecosystem building blocks in each 'nested' layer generates more and more emergence with cause and effect relations possible between layers, it might seem we've got ourselves into a problematic 'turtles all the way down' situation.

Fortunately, there's a way around this scenario which may be explained by way of an analogy: the hardware and software of my smart phone is made up of many sub-technologies assembled to form the whole phone. However, I don't need to know details about these sub-divisions to productively use the phone. Likewise, in the practice of engineering innovation ecosystems, there are only a limited number of levels we need to know about. This is further discussed in Section 16. We may not need too many building blocks to construct a large variety of systems, just as words, sentences, and paragraphs are constructed from the limited number of letters in an alphabet.

Later in this Section, results from ways in which inventors may combine components are presented. Because of the massive number of ways in which the components of previous inventions may be combined, inventors focus on a limited set of components and combinations to use.

Another case: one version of **The Rainforest Scorecard: A Practical Framework for Growing Innovation Potential** provides a systematic, detailed strategy for assessing and quantifying building blocks of an organization's innovation potential by measuring six traits of an innovation ecosystem at one level. These are: Leadership; Frameworks, Infrastructure, Policies; Resources; Activities & Engagements; Role Models; Culture. Another version of **The Rainforest Scorecard** assesses and quantifies one hierarchical level below. These are sufficient for most applications, although drilling down to further levels may lead to additional insights; but it's not "turtles all the way down."

In the Introduction we noted that complex system components cannot just be added up as components in complicated systems can be. Additivity does not hold. ". .. by extracting building blocks and examining their combinations we acquire a new way to understand a wide spectrum of complex adaptive systems, ranging from biological cells and visual perception to games, computer programs, and inventions. In most complex adaptive systems, building blocks at one level of complexity are combined to get building blocks for structures at a higher level of complexity." [78] New technologies are constructed from existing components. [79] This process can be regarded as forming a network of elements where new elements are being created from existing ones. Some of these component building blocks will be enabling or platform technologies. In Section 16 the advantage of viewing these constituent elements as a hierarchy will be discussed; but first a quick look.

The watch builders

To describe how innovation ecosystems can be constructed from building blocks it's easier to begin with the reverse; how a complex system may be (nearly) decomposed into its constituent parts. In 1962 Herbert A. Simon, recipient of the1978 Nobel Prize in Economics, published a classic work **The Architecture of Complexity**. [80] In this very readable article he introduces the concept of *hierarchic systems*. Complex systems have been described as "messy" but they do have structure – frequently a hierarchy. As we have described, these systems are composed of interrelated sub-systems, which in turn are composed of hierarchic subsystems, and so forth. In most systems, some limit will be reached beyond which no further subdivision is possible or makes sense. In principle, such subdividing can continue indefinitely without reaching any non-divisible entity (what philosophers call a 'simple').

This Section describes 'almost decomposition' into sub-systems, what we can learn from it, and how and when complex systems may be subdivided with the possibility of reusing these components as building blocks for other systems. To demonstrate the complex relationship of sub-system building blocks and their larger wholes, Simon described the parable of

. . . .

78   John H. Holland,, "Signals and Boundaries: Building Blocks for Complex Adaptive Systems," *MIT Press* (2012), p 109.

79   W Brian Arthur, "Complexity and the Economy," *Oxford University Press* (2015), p 120 ff.

80   Herbert A. Simon, "The Architecture of Complexity," *Proceedings of the American Philosophical Society*, Vol. 106, No. 6 (1962), pp 467-482.

two makers of fine watches. Repeated here is the story in a simplified version. The full mathematical explanation is given in the referenced Simon article.

Once upon a time there once were two watchmakers, named Hora and Tempus. New customers were constantly calling them and the phones in their workshops rang frequently. However, Hora prospered while Tempus became poorer and poorer. In the end, Tempus lost his shop. What was the reason behind this?

The watches made by Hora and Tempus consisted of about 1,000 parts each. Tempus had so constructed his that if he had one partly assembled and had to put it down, say to answer the phone, it immediately fell to pieces and had to be reassembled from the elements. The better the customers liked his watches, the more they phoned him, the more difficult it became for him to find enough uninterrupted time to finish a watch.

The watches that Hora made were no less complicated than those of Tempus. But he had designed them so that he could put together subassemblies of about ten elements each. Ten of these subassemblies, again, could be put together into a larger subassembly; a system of ten of the latter subassemblies constituted the whole watch. Hence, when Hora had to put down a partly assembled watch in order to answer the phone, he lost only a small part of his work when the subassembly fell apart, and he assembled his watches in only a fraction of the hours it took Tempus.

It is rather easy to make a quantitative analysis of the relative difficulty of the tasks of Tempus and Hora by making a few assumptions about how frequent are the interruptions (their probability) which show that it will take Tempus, on the average, about four thousand times as long to assemble a watch as Hora.

Nearly decomposable systems

Recall characteristic #4 from Section 5. A complex adaptive system is more than, or different from, the sum of its parts. It is not a *reductionist* system – it cannot be *decomposed* into a set of independent non-interacting parts. However, as Simon proposed, some systems may be *nearly* decomposable. More later in this Section.

Hierarchies

Before going any further the concept of hierarchy need to be introduced. Simon also explained that the interacting units, what we are calling building blocks, constituting a complex adaptive system are typically arranged in a hierarchical structure as "sets of boxes nesting within sets of boxes." Hierarchical structure may also be visualized as a set of layers. We shall return to these ideas when causation is investigated in Section 17. Some agents may belong within a number of different boxes at the same hierarchical level. For example, a person may be a member of several organizations or families. Hierarchy does not necessarily mean that one sub-system is more important or influential than another one. It can be argued that hierarchic systems will evolve far more quickly than non-hierarchic systems of comparable size. Hierarchy and its importance in innovation ecosystem will be considered in more detail in Sections 16 and 17.

A simple example is when an organization has a hierarchical management structure. Policies and objectives are established at upper levels. These are implemented by staff at lower levels. More realistic cases are analyzed in Section 16. For example, when knowledge resides at lower levels where employees often have tacit knowledge, information, and implementation capacity that upper level management does not. We shall see that those at lower levels can sometimes address complex problems more effectively than those at upper levels in the hierarchy.

"[L]evels are pivotal parts of our hierarchical view of nature .... each new level of organization has characteristic emergent properties. Some systemic trends emerge with increasing size; higher-level interactions almost always take place more slowly, and levels become less well-defined as the increasing complexity leads to greater interpenetration of levels." [81] As boundaries between levels break down new kinds of emergence may appear. Boundaries are discussed in Section 11.

In hierarchical systems there are two types of interaction (1) within the boundaries of the subsystems and (2) among subsystems. Both are going to limit decomposability. Some kinds of hierarchic systems can be successfully approximated as nearly decomposable systems. To build innovation

81   William C. Wimsatt, "Re-Engineering Philosophy for Limited Beings," *Harvard University Press* (2007), p 165.

systems from building blocks, effective communication will be needed among the parts for the whole to function optimally. Poor connectivity is a common reason for innovation ecosystems malfunctioning.

Interactions

Two building blocks are said to interact if the value or behavior of one building block depends on the value or behavior of the other building block. Two building blocks are said to reinforce each other if the value of each building block is increased by the value or behavior of the other building block. This is a slight twist on the definition of a relevant link.

Section 9 explained much more about strong, weak, and relevant links. We cannot be too cavalier about assuming weak links are not important and assuming they don't exist. I am leaving aside for now how the complex system interacts with what is outside the system, namely its context (see Section 13), what kinds of interactions or linkages we're talking about (see Section 9), whether all sub-systems should function optimally (it turns out they don't need to – see Section 22), and whether too much, too strong, connectivity might cause difficulties (it can – see Section 9). These issues are all dealt with in the cited Sections.

Buchler noted that reduction and emergence are *matters of degree*: the more complete the reduction, the less significant the emergence; the more complete the emergence, the less significant the reduction. To put it another way, if there are few links between sub-systems the emergence of creativity will be low. A *nearly decomposable* system is one in which the interactions among the sub-systems are weak, but not negligible. In Section 9 which discussed weak, strong, and relevant links, we saw that too strong links may make it difficult to separate building blocks for re-use elsewhere.

Simon used the example of where in formal organizations there will generally be more interaction, on the average, between two employees who are members of the same department than between two employees from different departments. The analogy is with organic substances where intermolecular forces will generally be weaker than molecular forces within molecules. While the organization example may still be largely true, remember this was written before the emergence of social media, living in virtual space, or even the invention of the Internet. Unlike previous generations, we are comfortable living in a virtual space where ecosystem components are not physically proximate. Think of companies with R&D in one location, manufacturing in another, and sales and marketing in yet another. How support can be provided by an innovation ecosystem can be a challenge. Advancing communication technologies have also contributed to differences between an organization's formal organizational structures versus how people *actually* network.

In practice most innovation ecosystems are mixtures of decomposable and nearly decomposable subsystems. If, in fact, a system is completely decomposable, emergence is unlikely to occur because rearranging subsystems will make no difference (they are said to be invariant or aggregative [82]).

Stimulation of emergence in the form of entrepreneurship has been described [83] as 'new combinations' and 'new production recipes' thus:

Creating new combinations – Creating new production recipes – Entrepreneurship

Invention and Building Blocks

Some have suggested that invention, as well as innovation, is the recombining of elements within an environment of culture and knowledge. Earlier we quoted W Brian Arthur, who noted that new technologies are constructed from existing components. [84] In speaking of innovation we must not forget that the root of innovation, at some earlier stage, is invention. Invention is here defined as the creation of a product or process for the first time.

Hypotheses about invention that are *partially* verified from patent data are:

· ·

82 An aggregative system is one in which the system's properties do not depend on how its components are organized and is therefore the opposite of an emergent one. William C. Wimsatt, "Re-Engineering Philosophy for Limited Beings," *Harvard University Press* (2007), p 174.

83 Philip E. Auerswald, "Enabling Entrepreneurial Ecosystems: Insights from Ecology to Inform Effective Entrepreneurship Policy," *Ewing Marion Kauffman Foundation* (October 2015).

84 W Brian Arthur, "Complexity and the Economy," *Oxford University Press* (2015), p 120 ff.

Components degree of interdependence	Results of combining components (Hypotheses) [1]
High	Inventors' efforts become more varied in their usefulness as they combine components. Inventors' efforts become more varied in their usefulness as they *recombine* a greater number of components. Usefulness of inventors' efforts *declines* most rapidly when they combine a *small* number of components.
Intermediate	Usefulness of inventors' efforts increases.
Low	Inventors' efforts become *less* varied in their usefulness as they recombine a *greater* number of components.
	Usefulness of inventors' efforts *increases*, but at a decreasing rate, when they recombine a *larger* set of components.

Table 3. Combining invention components

Response Ability: learning from manufacturing

Before there were lean software startups there was lean manufacturing. Lean manufacturing, which seeks to eliminate all expenditures which do not support value for the customer, was developed by Toyota in the 1950s and was in part responsible for the Japanese auto industry becoming the US auto industry's fierce competitor two or so decades later. Agile software development, introduced in the 1990s was influenced by ideas and methods from lean manufacturing. Its purpose is to make software more usable, adaptable to changes, and allow people to excel according to their strengths, rather than according to a system. More recently, lean startup methodology has become popular as a way to shorten product development cycles by iteratively creating products and integrating user feedback.

Agility in manufacturing and software development is a well-known concept which we will meet again elsewhere in this book. Related is the concept of 'Response Ability' [85] in manufacturing systems and beyond which is especially relevant to our subject because it describes how 'response-able' components can be designed into enterprise ecosystems to support

85   Rick Dove, "Response Ability: The Language, Structure, and Culture of the Agile Enterprise," *John Wiley and Sons, Inc.* (2001).

agility. For example, how can analyzing agile manufacturing systems help us to build agile innovation ecosystems able to self-organize and respond effectively to external perturbations?

Let's see if 'response-able' component ideas illuminate how innovation ecosystems may become agile; able to adapt rapidly to system environment changes. After all, we have already introduced the idea of self-organization in a complex adaptive system, which implies agility.

Rick Dove notes about the response-able idea: "These principles have been observed in both natural and man-made highly adaptable systems and organizations. They can be employed effectively in both inanimate directed configurations and in thinking/deciding self-organizing configurations. These are synergistic design guidelines which accommodate innovative interpretation and have greatly amplified value when employed as a complete set. Much more can be successfully understood about all principles than that which is contained in the table [summarized below], most especially about components and frameworks – the fundamental system structural elements." [86]

Why should we make comparisons between systems? What new understanding might be gained? Comparisons only make sense if we can learn more about system B by comparing it with system A, and then only if any similarities are more than just coincidences. A cloud in the sky may look like a face, but I doubt we will learn anything enlightening about how faces grow from studying how clouds form. History shows benefits of comparisons; some argue our understanding of economic systems has been improved by the study of thermodynamics, and innovation flow may be helpfully compared with biological flow. The results of Rick Dove's extensive research on systems such as the manufacturing cell indicate that principles of response-able systems include components with certain characteristics are a widely applicable model.

Dove's conclusions of relevance to engineering innovation ecosystems are in italics, with my relevancy to innovation ecosystems added.

1. *Components of response-able systems are distinct, separable, self-sufficient units cooperating towards a shared common purpose.*

. . . .

86   *ibid* p 140.

In innovation ecosystems the function and activities of each stakeholder and the strength of their cultural alignment (meaning: sharing a common purpose or cultural norms) should be clear to other stakeholders as well as all cross-functional and collaborative activities and existing supportive and incentive policies. This also applies to stakeholders outside the community. Without alignment towards common purposes 'friction' between components can be destructive.

2. *Components of response-able systems share defined interaction and interface standards; and they are easily inserted or removed.*

Interfaces are elements of a system that connect subsystems and make rearrangement, removal, insertion, and re-use more efficient. Examples of standard interfaces include: *a standard or express intellectual property license agreement between a university and company to minimize individual negotiations,* [87] *matching of results expectations, matching of cultures, matching of* hand-over conditions from an incubator to an accelerator (more details in Section 25). Building blocks with standard interfaces will tend to reinforce one another. Standard interfaces can reduce common disconnects (Figure 9).

3. *Components within a response-able system communicate directly on a peer-to-peer relationship; and parallel rather than sequential relationships are favored.*

Parallel execution is a way to accelerate projects. For example, the execution of a commercialization project supported by an innovation ecosystem will always consist of several stages similar to the StageGate™ new product development process (see Section 17). In many cases it is possible to begin a stage even with incomplete results (those which are not likely to change) from the previous stage. This parallel overlap of stages reduces time to project completion.

4. *Component relationships in a response-able system are transient when possible; decisions and fixed bindings are postponed until*

. . . .

87   An example of an express license agreement's standard interface is from the University of North Carolina, USA, http://research.unc.edu/files/2014/01/CarolinaExpressLicenseAgreement2.02011.pdf

immediately necessary; and relationships are scheduled and bound in real time.

This is not a recommendation for procrastination; rather an avoidance of decision making with insufficient information which may solidify an ecosystem component which later turns out to be a mistake (e.g. building a new business incubator before a reliable deal flow is apparent). Another example from Section 25 is creating strategic plans assuming a system is a farm (within an attractor basin) when it is actually a Rainforest (a complex system).

5. *Components in response-able systems are directed by objective rather than method; decisions are made at a point of maximum knowledge; information is associated locally, accessible globally, and freely disseminated.*

    Training programs often focus on methods, not the outcomes which these methods should produce. For example, many innovation ecosystems developers want the system to support technology commercialization. A training program's content may include basics of intellectual property, financing, market research, and so forth, but fail to show how this knowledge clearly leads to the expected outcome. See also Section 25 for more on objective rather than method.

6. *Component populations in response-able systems may be increased and decreased widely within the existing framework.*

    Standard interfaces and contextual qualifiers make this process easier.

7. *Duplicate components are employed in response-able systems to provide capacity right–sizing options and fail-soft tolerance; and diversity among similar components employing different methods is exploited.*
    Innovation ecosystems should incorporate some degree of redundancy in its building blocks to have a flexible capacity to react to perturbations. Redundancy can also isolate and help the repair of internal damage from internal and external perturbations that break pathways. See Section 18 for more on tolerance to system shocks.

8. *Component relationships in response-able systems are self-determined; and component interaction is self-adjusting or negotiated.*

Emergence in complex systems is an outcome of self-organization, without centralized control, in the form of a new level of order in the system that comes into being as novel structures and patterns which maintain themselves over some period of time. Innovation springs from emergence. Emergence may create a new entity with qualities that are not reflected in the interactions of each agent within the system. Emergent organizations are typically very robust and able to survive and self-repair substantial damage or perturbations. Although distinct from principle 7 above, these two principles may be highly correlated with regard to their respective functions in a system,

9. *Components of response-able systems are reusable/replicable; and responsibility for ready reuse/replication and for management, maintenance, and upgrade of component inventory are specifically designated.*

Modular systems can be re-used but under contextual qualifier restrictions (see Section 21 for more on knowledge re-use).

10. *Frameworks of response-able systems standardize into component communication and interaction; defined component compatibility; and are monitored/updated to accommodate old, current, and new components.*

Modular innovation ecosystems, which by definition (Section 22) have standard interfaces, enable updating and monitoring.

Many of these conclusions are a practical guide to building innovation ecosystems.

Business model innovation

The World Bank, whose mission is to reduce global poverty, set up a group to investigate business model innovation (BMI) and see how innovative business models can be broken down into component parts.

Nearly all respondents to a series of interviews with the organization's staff agreed with the statement that business models, in general, are capable of being broken down into components parts which may, under contextual constraints, be re-used. Such re-use should both avoid unnecessary re-invention, which frequently occurs in practice, but can also reduce the time and effort in creating BMI in new environments. The term 'nearly decomposable systems' was not used, but this was the identification. The driver of this work was the question: under what conditions is it reasonable to presume that lessons from project X in region or country A translate to country B?

A caveat to re-use is noted in a report on learning results from the World Bank. [88] "..BMI components must be sufficiently detailed or generalizable to be of operational significance. Insufficient detail is a common failing in business models." The report stressed "If a project involves tried and tested solutions that are not subject to immediate change, the project experience will likely be amenable to codification and distillation. If, however, the project involves solutions whose effectiveness in particular circumstances is not yet fully known or whose solutions vary significantly depending on the context, experimentation, iteration, flexibility, and adaptation will be key. In these cases, any written or electronic documentation of the project's experience would best be in the form of options considered, pros and cons of each option, the option chosen and why, what trade-offs were made, and what the preconditions of success were or why the project failed, while also identifying a series of questions to ask that help customization to the local context."

See Section 13 for 'contextual qualifiers' which are those knowledge fragments, sometimes called 'facets,' that allow a user to assess whether a given policy or practice, implemented elsewhere, is truly relevant or applicable to the user's environment. Acknowledgement of the complex nature of BMI was found in the studies when inflection points and possible perturbations (Section 18) were identified.

· ·

88   "Learning and Results in World Bank Operations: How the Bank Learns," (2014). https://ieg. worldbankgroup.org/Data/reports/chapters/learning_results_eval.pdf

The same report also poses the question "..under what conditions is it reasonable to presume that 'lessons' from project X in country Y translate to country Z? No one seems to have a really good answer to that question." p 32.

The above warning is of value when engineering innovation ecosystems. A proposed model to be implemented may indeed contain "solutions whose effectiveness in particular circumstances are not yet fully known or whose solutions vary significantly depending on the context." This is one reason to first build a minimum viable product rather than to over-engineer and end up with unneeded building blocks.

For business models in general and specifically those BMI's cited by me as the World Bank's external consultant, the following building blocks with the widest reuse appeared to be:

Financial	Replication/Scaling /Sustainability
Legal status	Second movers
State/public funds	Checklists for key features
Non-profit	Stage financing strategy
For-profit	Franchises, partnerships
Hybrid	
Maintenance & Upgrading	**Marketing**
Local technicians – distributed	Distributed team
Dedicated team – centralized	Partnerships
Identifying maintenance needs	Market intelligence methods
Product Manufacturing	**Management**
Local capacity, quality	Finding talent
Availability of, and ability to contract with,	Checklists for strategic partners
manufacturing partners	Local management
	Training
	Sources of employees/talent
Risk Assessment	**Monitoring/Evaluating**
Dealing with onerous checklist compliance	Measuring outcomes not outputs.
issues even for small grants and contracts.	
Local Business Services Providers	
Assessing capacity and quality	

Table 4. Reusable Business Model building blocks.

As an example, **Agastya** which brings innovative science education to disadvantaged students in rural India, and **Waterlife** providing sustainable and affordable safe drinking water solutions to underserved populations, both have hybrid – public and private – finance components in their respective business models.

As another example, some case examples of standard interfaces which match incubator and accelerator functions for an innovation ecosystem are:

1. The objective of the Incubator should be to incubate businesses during their first two years or so to help them get their first clients or customers and first sales.

2. The Accelerator will select those businesses which have been incubated and are ready to scale. Thus, the Incubator plus the Accelerator have the potential to become a powerful new business generator if (i) there are stable and sustainable funding sources, and (ii) funding for both is predictable over a three year period to support planning.

3. The Accelerator's focus is on the transition phase from incubation to acceleration for companies that already have around, as an example only, $2 million in sales and who need resources between $1 million and $3 million to accelerate their growth.

Matching of cultures:

Experience gained in working in different national cultures shows that communication breakdown between scientists at universities and research institutes and foreign (outside the country) business partners can cause projects with high potential to fail from the very beginning, or not even start. The most frequent reasons for communication problems are: (1) lack of trust between partners, (2) wrong expectations, (3) preconceptions and stereotypes, (4) language barriers, (5) lack of business communication skills, and (6) fear of recriminations for open communication of bad news (see Section 12 for an example of this). Recommendations for competencies required by R&D and new product development teams, and technology commercialization managers to support efficient and stable communication between scientists and business partners include: (1) international team-style communication skills; (2) social networking skills; (3) expectation management skills; (4) negotiation skills; (5) business communication etiquette.

Core building blocks

When identifying innovation system building blocks it's helpful to decide which ones are core building blocks. These are defined [89] as having (1) a high interdependency with other current organizational elements; that is interacting with many other building blocks, and (2) a large influence on future organizational elements; that is, changing a core element may not only affect most of the present building blocks and thus the behavior of the innovation ecosystem but its future development as well. Core building blocks are unlikely to change too much over time. Core building blocks may also be identified by having *relevant links*.

Core building blocks in an innovation ecosystem will certainly include a culture of innovation and whatever building blocks strongly support the primary purpose of the ecosystem. If the reason for building the ecosystem is, for example, developing alternative businesses after regional economic decline initiated by the closure of a large employer, then core building blocks will be those critical to that purpose. Some of these will be universities, technical colleges, and the brainpower, skills, and experience of those who previously worked for a departed company. [90]

A peripheral building block can be changed without causing much change in the overall functioning of the whole innovation ecosystem. If this definition sounds familiar it is because this is the equivalent of how weak links are defined in the network view of systems. Siggelkow introduces 'elaborating elements' which in the context of innovation ecosystems are building blocks which reinforce one or more core building blocks either directly or indirectly.

89   Nicolaj Siggelkow, "Evolution toward Fit," *Administrative Science Quarterly*, 47 (March 2002), pp 125 -159.

90   Many stories are in Antoine Van Agtmael and Fred Bakker, "The Smartest Places on Earth," *NY: Public Affairs* (2016).

11

Boundaries, Limits, and Connections

· ·

Section Summary: A boundary can define a particular 'unit of analysis' being studied. A boundary must separate what is inside and what is outside, but boundaries can be permeable. Every building block has a boundary which may change as a prevailing building block or entire innovation ecosystem is extended, enhanced, or reduced. Innovation ecosystems with apparently the right building blocks but where the inter-connections are not in place or broken are considered. Building blocks and signals exchanged between them are not only used to construct innovation ecosystems but also to analyze them. A group of building blocks of an innovation ecosystem which have a great number of internal connections but relatively low signal exchange via external connections are sometimes called niche communities. A connection/signal may be broken or never formed, or in place but not functioning optimally.

O God, I could be bounded in a nutshell, and count myself a king of infinite space...

— Shakespeare, *Hamlet Act 2, scene 2.*

The last Section discussed the importance of innovation ecosystem building blocks and how re-arranging building blocks can create emergent innovation. In the Introduction, a case was given where an innovation ecosystem has apparently the right building blocks but where the inter-connections are not in place or broken. This Section presents a deeper look at the role of signals passing back and forth across sub-system boundaries. Sometimes we have to define boundaries to delineate a particular 'unit of analysis' being studied. Building blocks have boundaries in order to recognize them. We are familiar with the boundary concept including physical boundary 'no admittance' or more subtle social boundaries. All complex adaptive systems have boundaries that divide the complex adaptive system into diverse sets of semi-autonomous sub-systems. Think of the membrane of the biological cell or sub-divisions into departments within a company. To define building blocks it is necessary for them to have constraining boundaries, even though these boundaries may be flexible and permeable, and sometimes hard to define exactly. Boundaries may overlap. Later in the book, 'wicked problems' will be discussed (Section 15). These are problems which are difficult to contain within boundaries because it seems that every problem is a symptom or cause of another problem.

In Section 6 we described the difference between a complicated and a complex system. In a complicated system the boundaries which define sub-systems are fixed and stable. In a complex system the boundaries defining sub-systems are emergent, temporary, and evolving. [91] Agents operate within a unit of analysis, with some prescribed boundary, which may be changed by augmentative alescence, spoliative alescence, or coalescence (these terms are summarized on the next page and described in more detail in Section 26). A boundary must separate what is inside and what is outside. This concept of inner and outer contexts is significant. In the reductionist view, boundaries are non-permeable, and sub-modules are decomposable, not connected. Innovation ecosystem building blocks are decomposable and permeable. Even more, they are differentially permeable, allowing certain signals to pass through, while other signals are prevented. Later in this section this effect will be modeled.

"As an example of this logic, think of the eardrum. It forms the boundary between the inner and the outer ear, but at the same time it exists in order to let the sound waves through. As a matter of fact, if it was not there, the sound waves would not be able to get through at all! If the boundary is seen as an interface participating in constituting the system, we will be more concerned with the margins of the system, and perhaps less with what appears to be central." [92] For innovation ecosystems being "concerned with the margins of the system" means, for example, identifying and repairing disconnects (Figure 9).

. . . .

91   Kurt A. Richardson & Michael R. Lissack, "On the Status of Boundaries, both Natural and Organizational: A Complex Systems Perspective." *EMERGENCE*, 3(4), (2001), pp 32–49.

92   Paul Cilliers, "Boundaries, Hierarchies and Networks in Complex Systems," *International Journal of Innovation Management*, Vol. 5, No. 2, (2001), pp 135–147.

The eardrum analogy tells us about the importance of 'signals' – communications – passing between boundaries. Signals are what networks describe when nodes communicate with each other through links. However, most network research has not focused on boundaries within networks (see Section 14). Boundaries separate sub-systems but more importantly boundaries connect a sub-system with its environment, just as in the eardrum example. The geometry of boundaries is explained in more detail in Section 26. The main points are repeated here: [93]

Every complex system has a boundary which is the limit of a system, the conditions under which these limits are formed, and where these limits are located. The limits of a complex, like every other aspect of it, may be emergent or more precisely – alescent (the term coined by Buchler as more encompassing than emergence, or growth). That is, boundaries will change, for example, as a complex system grows by adding properties or traits.

"Identical conglomerates can have distinct individual histories because of conditional reactions to different local environments and agents. The agent's boundary encapsulates this history so that propagation of the boundary propagates the effects of that history." [94] The effect of history is another way of expressing the significance of Contextual Qualifiers discussed in Section 13, and the unnecessary risk of blind adherence to "*best* practices" rather than "*good* practices." An agent is defined by its containing boundary. A prevalent complex excludes traits into its contour (path or trajectory). An alescent complex admits or excludes traits into its contour by the three usual mechanisms:

Augmentative alescence: a prevailing complex is extended, increased or enhanced.

For example, an organization or business expands its capabilities; Amazon expands from selling books to selling much more than books. In an innovation ecosystem an incubator may extend its functions as a business accelerator also.

. . . .

93   Adapted from Justus Buchler, "Metaphysics of Natural Complexes," *Columbia University Press* (1966).

94   John H. Holland, "Signals and Boundaries: Building Blocks for Complex Adaptive Systems," *MIT Press* (2012), p 54.

Spoliative alescence: there is a loss or attenuation or expiration of a complex that has prevailed.

A business such as IBM divests its PC division. In an innovation ecosystem a centralized technology commercialization office may distribute some of its activities to individual universities and research centers when enough opportunities appear to provide sufficient business to decentralized units.

Coalescent alescence: a complex arising from injunction or intersection or novel configurations of complexes.

One business acquires another through a merger. In an innovation ecosystem an independent seed fund becomes a feeder fund and combines with a venture fund. This can be done by setting boundary entry and exit for the *differentially permeable* boundaries of complexes which are communicating in some way. In nature's rainforests, each organism uses resources passed on from other organisms. Resources can be used multiple times via recirculation.

Conditions may be set up within a bounded sub-system to allow some signals to be accepted and other to be ignored. As people or groups of people we do this all the time without thinking about it, either because we want to be deliberately selective about whom we listen to and how we add to our corpus of knowledge or because of limits to how much information we are able to absorb. Selectivity also helps an agent to adapt to changing circumstances as they accumulate knowledge and experience and can create a shared vocabulary to reduce misunderstanding. Basic biological systems exhibit similar behavior. Thus, a boundary acts as a signal filter.

Because of emergence, effective combinations of building blocks may not be obvious or foreseen; therefore the connection rules must be sufficiently flexible, as the work of Rick Dove shows.

Building blocks and signals exchanged between them are not only used to construct innovation ecosystems but also to analyze them. Note also that building blocks do not have to be physically proximate to exchange signals. A common feature among building blocks that are sub-systems of an innovation ecosystem is those which have a great number of internal connections (as a network) but relatively low signal exchange via external connections. These are sometimes called *niche* communities. Middle-income countries often have valuable research performed by universities and government or private research institutes. Although encouraged to cooperate with the county's innovation system they typically have insufficient connections globally to create economic value from their research because of past isolation and budget constraints on travel for example. Boundary spanners are needed (see Section 12)

Signals

The agents in nature's rainforests are organisms interacting via exchange of resources. In an economy, agents may be buyers and sellers exchanging desired transaction signals. Agents may change rapidly and take immediate action or evolve more slowly. Constant fast back-and-forth interactions produce nonlinear flows in the system. "On a human scale, markets can change radically on the basis of anticipations, a change that takes place even if the anticipation isn't realized. In general, anticipation appears whenever an agent, conscious or otherwise, requires an internal model of its environment." [95]

A rule might be: IF a required signal or set of signals is present THEN send an outgoing signal based on the incoming signals.

"Building blocks are often not at all evident when we first look at some complex adaptive systems. How do we extract building blocks from unfamiliar systems? A search for barriers or filters, namely boundaries, often guides the search for building blocks. A building block is a *generator* if it is immutable over the span of its existence. It may be copied and it may be combined with other generators but it has a fixed set of connections subject to a fixed set of connection rules. If a generator is removed from a structure the structure is changed, typically to a structure with a very different function or interpretation. Removal of the generator is often disastrous, as in the removal of a single instruction from a computer program." [96]

Emergence in this format comes from patterns or properties that appear under the constraints imposed by the rules for combining building blocks.

. . . .

95   John H. Holland, "Signals and Boundaries: Building Blocks for Complex Adaptive Systems," *MIT Press* (2012), p 60.

96   *ibid* p 111.

Emergent properties often occur when co-evolving signals and boundaries generate new levels of organization. Newer signals and boundaries can then emerge from combinations of building blocks at this new level of organization. Some properties can emerge only when the system reaches a high enough level of organization. There are hazards involved in attempting to connect building blocks and match their properties for efficient communication and reduction of social barriers. Disconnects can result (Figure 9).

A connection/signal may be:

1. *Broken or never formed* (a connection which is needed, preferred, and necessary).

2. *In place but not functioning optimally* (although there are cases when it may not need to be functioning optimally as in cost/benefit consideration, see Section 22).

3. *In place but better it was not in place* (too many people or organizations involved causing lack of focus and constraining actions).

Signals pass along links between building blocks and between building blocks and their environment. If there is no link, no signal can pass. Whether a link is strong, weak, or relevant determines the nature of the signal not necessarily their efficiency (strong links may lead to an echo chamber effect, weak links may or may not bring in new thinking, relevant links may or may not be a focus for development and help identify core modules. This description is based on the picture of signals (e.g. information) somehow flowing along links.

There is an alternative picture. Ada and Alan are having a lively conversation about the basics of computing and programming. They are able to exchange ideas because they are speaking the same language (English in this case) and because they both understand the concepts being discussed; there is a match between what Ada is saying and Alan is hearing and *vice versa*. The matching of signals being transmitted and received gives us another way of thinking about signals; signals are both transmitted and received. Frequently this is not the case and disconnects occur because of low levels of trust, misunderstandings, cultural mismatches, and other causes not easy to spot.

In the figure below the left column lists capabilities of a research institute, in this case, one which specializes in developing chemical catalysts. The right column lists the need of the corporate R&D partner. Overlap in the Venn diagram shows features and needs each have in common. In this case, the corporate partner paid the institute to demonstrate proof of concept of a developed product or process up to a prototype stage.

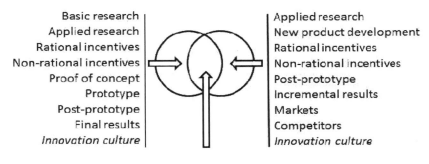

Basic research		Applied research
Applied research		New product development
Rational incentives		Rational incentives
Non-rational incentives		Non-rational incentives
Proof of concept		Post-prototype
Prototype		Incremental results
Post-prototype		Markets
Final results		Competitors
Innovation culture		*Innovation culture*

Applied research
Rational incentives
Non-rational incentives
Post-prototype
Innovation culture

Figure 8. Matching of capabilities.

Many innovation ecosystems, especially in developing and middle-income nations, are intended to support technology commercialization. This is fertile ground for disconnects to arise as in the example below. Disconnects here are more than simply broken links; they may be inefficiently performing links.

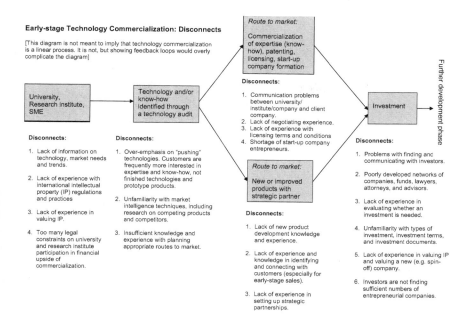

Figure 9. Technology Commercialization Disconnects.

A succinct way to generalize these concepts and illustrate the transmission and receipt of signals is to introduce classifier rules. [97] A signal alphabet {0, 1, #} specifies conditions for accepting signals. A condition is a string such as 1, 0, 1, #, #, 0 as an example. The string can be of any length. This example means that an incoming signal, also a string of these symbols, with a 1 in the first position, 0 in the second position, 1 in the third position, and a zero in the final position will be accepted. The # means a 1, 0, or # will be accepted; what Holland calls a 'don't care' symbol.

So, if the condition is 0, 1, 1, # the following signals will be accepted: 0, 1, 1, #, and 0, 1, 1, 1, and 0, 1, 1, 0 but not 1, 1, 0, 1. There is much more in Holland's book about applications of this method, but intuitively we can translate such symbols into real events.

A few reoccurring examples of difficulties with system links seen in countries as diverse as the UK and Colombia, or the USA and Russia, include: poor relationships between educational organizations and industry (it is

· ·

97   John H. Holland, "Signals and Boundaries: Building Blocks for Complex Adaptive Systems," *MIT Press* (2012), p 64.

commonly believed that developed nations such as the USA have completely solved the problem – but it's not so); help for small and medium sized enterprises (SMEs) during early stage growth which proved, in fact, to be unattractive to SMEs; new business incubators for which there is poor deal-flow; proof of concept, prototype development, and scale-up centers which are underutilized or lack needed services; and technology transfer offices at universities and research centers which may be inadequately staffed or supported – or have unclear missions.

What happens when the problem has not been correctly understood by one party or the other party or different groups define the problem differently or when simply informing one community with knowledge from the other is ineffective? The Rainforest idea is to build trust, but what happens if this is simply not possible? This is where the boundary spanner comes into play.

12

Boundary Spanners: Network Holes and How to Plug Them

· ·

Section Summary: When two separate clusters possess complementary information, there is said to be a structural hole between them. Brokerage is about coordinating people between whom it will be valuable to trust, and where there is an inherent degree of risk. The effectiveness, or otherwise, of brokerage is also highly dependent on context. Bridging structural holes between disconnected networks brings a diversity of potential scientific approaches to a problem and can be a significant predictor of problem solving success. There is strong evidence that linking networks of entrepreneurs generates valuable new ideas. No two knowledge intermediaries are the same; because their work is entirely context specific, this means that, while it is possible to draw general lessons as to how they could choose to act, it is impossible to develop a standard set of rules as to how they should act.

"There's a hole in the bucket, dear Liza, dear Liza. There's a hole in the bucket, dear Liza, a hole...."

— A children's song with obscure origins in 18th century Germany.

Having discussed strong links, weak links, and relevant links in networks. We should now talk about how to connect networks and what is meant by a network 'hole.'

Networks, like the bucket in the song, may suffer from holes. In buckets, holes need to be plugged; in networks, holes are bridged. In social networks they are called 'structural holes' formally defined by Ronald

S. Burt,[98] [99] a leading researcher in networks and structural holes at the University of Chicago, as "when two separate clusters possess non-redundant (that is, complementary) information, there is said to be a structural hole between them." This suggests that a broker or boundary spanner – such as an entrepreneur – who bridges the hole could gain competitive advantage by engaging in information arbitrage. Connecting networks of entrepreneurs with their own strong, weak, and relevant links, by bridging structural holes may provide access to valuable new ideas, alternative opinion and practice, early access to new opinions, and an ability to move ideas between groups where there is an advantage in doing so. Although, over time the value from arbitrage may diminish, especially as more bridges are built.

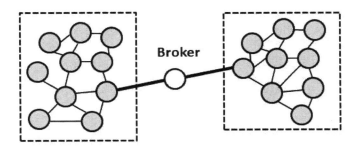

Figure 10. A boundary spanner between building blocks.

Previously we noted evidence from **Innocentive** [100] that as the number of unique scientific interests in the overall submitter population increased, the higher the probability that a scientific or engineering problem was successfully solved through **Innocentive's** crowdsourcing method. Bridging structural holes between disconnected networks brought a diversity of potential scientific approaches to a problem and was a significant predictor of problem solving success. [101] Boundary spanners are usually pictured

98   Ronald S. Burt, "Brokerage and Closure: An Introduction to Social Capital," *Oxford University Press* (2005).

99   "Structural Holes and Good Ideas" http://www.econ.upf.edu/docs/seminars/burt.pdf

100 http://www.innocentive.com

101 "Innocentive and ideas coming from other industries than the seekers" http://www.innocentive.com/blog/2008/07/25/5-questions-with-dr-karim-lakhani/

as bridging network holes; in the building block perspective they bridge building blocks or clusters of building blocks.

However, let's control our enthusiasm because in a moment we will see that there may also be a downside. Brokerage is about coordinating people between whom it will be valuable to trust, but where there is an inherent degree of risk. The effectiveness, or otherwise, of brokerage is also highly dependent on context.

When a network is closed, with many strong links, no behavior goes unnoticed. Problems may be identified early and at low cost so that non-performing people, for example, can be removed from the network. In the early 1990's, while working in an Eastern European country on technology commercialization issues I was surprised that the organization for which I was consulting employed several people who were related to the boss. Nepotism? No, said the boss; it's an incentive for them not to mess up and have it immediately known by their relatives and be the cause of family shame.

In a highly connected world, networking know-how can be a key resource in finding jobs and business opportunities, but a series of studies by Dr. Yuval Kalish of the Leon Recanati Graduate School of Business Administration at Tel Aviv University suggests that, in some cases, bridging networks can do more harm than good. "If you're at the intersection of two previously unconnected niches of a network, you're occupying what I call a 'structural hole,'" says Dr. Kalish. Filling that space can lead to prestige, opportunities and power — or it may have quite the opposite effect. "While it's been reported that people who occupy these structural holes become more successful, some structural holes may be 'social potholes' that can harm you and your business," he warns. For example, someone who cut across formal hierarchical organizational boundaries within a company may be resented. Furthermore, bridging structural holes often means dealing with wicked problems [102] (Section 15).

Finally, networks are useless unless transactions occur among the networked parties. Communication is a transaction – an exchange of knowledge – and is also context dependent. The six degrees of *separation* theory

. . . .

102 Paul Williams, "The Competent Boundary Spanner," *Public Administration*, Vol 8 No 1 (2002), p 104.

that everyone is six or fewer steps away, by way of introduction, from any other person in the world is well known, but not much practical use unless at each stage a request – a signal – gets transmitted. I figure I'm two links from the leader of one the world's most powerful countries, but I very much doubt if any advice I send him would be received, and thus no transaction would occur.

Once when studying two linked group of researchers from a research center and a corporation in two different countries, my colleagues noticed an occasion when communications (transactions) between both groups had been acting effectively, but then stopped. It was a mystery. Why? Answer: 'culture' prevented further transactions. The culture of the country in which the research center was located was that it was not good to transmit bad news. So, when their R&D work ran into problems – completely normal and to be expected – they decided that giving *no* news to their corporate partners was better than giving what was perceived as *bad* news. Of course, from the company's viewpoint, it was essential to know as soon as possible if there were problems so that the two partners could work together to correct them and proceed.

Note that each network, the research center and the corporation may each have high levels of trust within them. Thus, a boundary spanner has to create trust and understanding between these two high internal trust groups. There is a net cost to boundary spanning if the direct or indirect benefits don't exceed the direct or indirect costs. In the past four or five decades universities, and research institutes, around the globe in developed and developing counties have established technology transfer offices (TTOs) to move research to market. There is a common misconception that the only purpose of TTOs at universities is to earn revenues through licenses and cashing out stakes in spin-off companies. Even though total annual research-related income generated by all universities in the USA runs at around $1.5 billion, most of this is generated by a relatively small number of large institutions. The majority of the rest hover around the break-even point. So why bother? TTOs also help bridge the gap between academia and industry, they create trusted networks of researchers in each and bring indirect benefits to the university such as keeping curricula relevant.

When companies begin working with universities and research institutes it is common to start with minor transactions so partners can prove they are worthy of trust and can delivery as promised. A physics and engineering research institute employing some 700 researchers is working hard to build on its good reputation for innovation to increase its income from joint R&D contracts with industry. Several large domestic and foreign firms have negotiated new contracts with the institute, but these are mostly short term, for proof of concept or initial prototype developments. After these are completed the contracting firms said they will continue future work themselves. These kinds of short term contracts go not produce much profit, and costs can exceed income. Carrying out and managing multiple small short-term contracts will normally have higher costs than for a large, long-term, institute/industry R&D project. Furthermore, short-term contracts are likely to produce few additional benefits, such as embarking on entirely new lines of scientific inquiry and improved access to current corporate R&D.

The research institute is caught in a 'positioning trap.' Positioning traps are similar to poverty traps which have been heavily analyzed by economists. The book **Poor Economics** notes: [103] "There will be a poverty trap whenever the scope for *growing income or wealth at a very fast rate* is limited for those who have too little to invest, but expands dramatically for those who can invest a bit more." This is an exact description of the research institute's state – its income growth was limited by not having sufficient funds to invest to be able to offer the ability to move beyond proof of concept or prototype phases which attract longer term, larger, contracts. There is a need to "invest a bit more" to "dramatically" expand income.

Therefore to escape the positioning trap the research institute should try to *position* itself to (1) provide relatively small amounts (compared with expected returns) of internal retained earnings and quickly accessible grant financing to demonstrate to a corporate partner that the institute has the capacity to move beyond proof of concept and early prototype R&D, and (2) reduce transactions costs by increasing trust levels, in fact, action (1) will help to do so.

Did applying these solutions help? Yes, they did. The institute becomes more selective about taking on short-term R&D contracts and is able to obtain large long-term joint corporate R&D contracts yielding substantial income. A combination of retained earnings from other projects, internal budgets, and limited grant support is used to escape the 'positioning trap.'

. . . .

103   Abhijit Banerjees and Esther Duflo, "Poor Economics," *Public Affairs* (2011), p 11.

Early stage development grants are common but we don't always think of them in terms of helping to escape a 'positioning trap.'

The remainder of the children's song describes, in some 20 verses, an increasingly frustrating tale of attempts to plug the bucket's hole. Network brokers balancing cultures, transaction effectiveness and costs, trust, and so forth, may have a similar frustrating experience.

To sum up, "The three benefits of bridging structural holes may be expected: access to alternative opinion and practice, early access to new opinion, and an ability to move ideas between groups where there is an advantage in doing so." [104]

Intermediaries as Knowledge Brokers

Transferring good practice is another level of brokerage. People familiar with activities in two groups are better able than people confined within either group to see how a belief or practice in one group could create value in the other, and perform the necessary 'translation.' A word of caution about organizations that claim to broker those with inventions or 'technologies' and those seeking them. An inspection may show that there are many more offers of technologies than requests for them, indicating ineffective boundary spanning matches. Corporate R&D or new business development divisions don't have time to review multiple lists and websites. Effective brokers are individuals or groups of individuals who have wide professional networks of industry contacts.

Intermediaries as Connectors

Companies benefitting from the support of an innovation ecosystem should ask questions such as "is an intermediary needed, how will the intermediary add value, how much value could be added?" Typically, although there are exceptions, the less developed the region or country, the more intermediaries can add significant value. Organizations and individuals in more developed regions or countries have better connections to better

. . . .

104   Ronald S. Burt, "Brokerage and Closure: An Introduction to Social Capital," *Oxford University Press* (2005).

developed networks than in less developed environments, and thus have less need of help to make connections. An effective intermediary may:

1. Help find technical solutions for users of technologies and innovations.
2. Find users for new technologies.
3. Help in identifying the technology/needs match.
4. Identify where similar or the same technology are already in the marketplace.
5. Identify potential development or marketing partners.
6. Identify competitors and competing products or services.
7. Find and help leverage resources.
8. Package and promote expertise available at universities and research institutes.
9. Help with negotiations and business development.
10. Reduce transaction costs.
11. Help with IP issues in inward and outward licensing.
12. Provide access to finance.

The task of an intermediary will be made easier if there is a 'champion' or 'integrator' within the organizations being matched who will support the project and help overcome internal barriers. An integrator can bring together all the necessary components to work with the intermediary. One such intermediary is **Connect**[105] founded by the University of California-San Diego which helps to create and scale companies through access to the resources needed most by entrepreneurs and growing companies, namely people, capital, and technology.

An intermediary is needed to bridge the gap between early stage product development and later stage product development and placement in markets. An ideal intermediary, in this case, will be a Contract Research Organization (CRO). CROs solve problems or develop products for corporate clients who have decided to 'outsource' selected R&D or don't have the necessary in-house capacity.

. . . .

105 http://www.connect.org

Questions to ask include:

1. Will an intermediary – an organization or an individual - with experience of common situations make the transfer process more efficient?

2. Is an intermediary really needed or not?

3. How will the intermediary add value?

4. How much value could be added?

Attempts to set up innovation intermediaries will usually fail if they are driven 'top down' by those who see an opportunity to earn income by managing the intermediary. It's better for the intermediary to be driven 'bottom up' and created by potential users of the services to be provided.

Because of insufficient participation in international business and R&D networks by technology companies in most middle-income countries or less developed regions of advanced nations, potential customers, strategic partners, and investors remain unaware of the know-how, resources, and new product ideas these companies may provide. Individual companies or groups of companies need to know how to package and promote their aggregate capabilities. The use of intermediaries may be effective, but as already cautioned, frequently technology bid/offer markets are inefficient with too many offers and not enough bids.

13

Contextual Qualifiers: One Size Doesn't Fit All

Section Summary: Contextual qualifiers are those knowledge fragments that allow a user to assess whether a given policy or practice, implemented elsewhere, is truly relevant or applicable to the user's environment. Contextual qualifiers are statements, which refer to knowledge sources, which 'qualify' the knowledge presented as being dependent on certain conditions. Contextual qualifiers can reduce transaction costs of knowledge acquisition by a user. Contextual qualifiers acknowledge that "one size doesn't fit all" and that a tool is needed that helps people to better appreciate the influence of contextual factors when engaging in taking actions. Contextual qualifiers facilitate the presentation and comprehension of context when locating potentially relevant resources. Contextual qualifiers provide guidance for intervening to make corrections to poorly functioning innovation ecosystems. Examples are discussed.

"I see a picture which represents a smiling face. What do I do if I take the smile as a kind one, now as malicious? Don't I often imagine it with a spatial and temporal context of kindness or malice? Thus I might, when looking at the picture, imagine it to be of a smiler smiling down on a child at play, or again at the suffering of an enemy. This is in no way altered by the fact that I can also take the apparently genial situation and interpret it differently by putting it into a wider context."

— Ludwig Wittgenstein, philosopher (1889 – 1951).

Understanding Ludwig Wittgenstein is a tough assignment but in my opinion worth the effort. In his *Philosophical Investigations* (Number 539) he discusses context in the quote above. [106]

How a system behaves is determined by its internal parameters and connectivity and also by influences from its surrounding environment, or in other words its context. Just as these parameters change over time so also may a system's context (remember, in linear systems these parameters by definition are fixed but in non-linear complex systems they may change, see Section 8). Furthermore, a system's environmental context may be a feature of top down causation (see Section 17).

We need to introduce the concept of a 'contextual qualifier.'

1. Contextual qualifiers are those knowledge fragments (also called facets) that allow a user to assess whether a given policy or practice, implemented elsewhere, is truly relevant or applicable to the user's environment.

2. Contextual qualifiers are statements, which refer to knowledge sources (documents, images, videos, etc.) which qualify the knowledge presented as being dependent on certain conditions.

3. Contextual qualifiers acknowledge that "one size doesn't fit all" and that a tool is needed that helps people to better appreciate the influence of contextual factors when engaging in learning and taking actions.

4. Contextual qualifiers facilitate the presentation and comprehension of context when locating potentially relevant resources.

5. Contextual qualifiers provide guidance for intervening to make corrections to poorly functioning innovation ecosystems.

6. Users should be able to contribute contextual qualifiers such as "how to use" or "when to use," or "when not to use" based on their experience.

7. Various products and services include embedded contextual qualifiers where appropriate.

. . . .

106   B R Tilghman, "Wittgenstein, Ethics and Aesthetics: The View from Eternity" *Macmillan* (1991).P M S Hacker, Joachim Schulte (Eds.), "Philosophical Investigations," Revised 4th edition, *Blackwell* (2009).

In my kitchen I have several bowls, some plastic some stainless steel. A contextual qualifier for the plastic one is "the oven is hot and will melt plastic." The result of this qualifier is "do not put in an oven." Many new business incubators have failed because their context generated an insufficient deal flow. Contextual qualifiers are important not only when selecting, designing, and implementing policies – what we might call formulating solutions – but also in diagnosing where the failures and bottlenecks lie – what we might call identifying problems – and asking the right questions as guidance towards appropriate answers (more problem solving in Section 24). Nobel Laureate Ilya Prigogine one of the founders of complexity science wrote: "The evolution of such a [human] system is an interplay between the behavior of its actors and impinging constraints from the environment" [107]

Our model assumes that context matters substantively and that innovative solutions to challenges are unlikely to emerge out of a market economy absent very specific constraining conditions. This also makes intuitive sense. "If the system is not constrained at all, the requisite conditions for qualitative change never happen because the individuals in the system, being unconstrained, just maneuver around difficulties. Constraints, such as the need for seed capital, or capacity restrictions in a factory, limit this ability of individuals to maneuver within the system to the point where qualitative change becomes inevitable." [108] Having too little money to develop a national innovation ecosystem, or parts thereof, is a constraint. When new nations join the European Union they receive substantial pre-accession and accession funds, some of which have been for the ever popular, and justified, innovation capacity development. However, many governments are not prepared or experienced to use these large funds to support innovation; better for such funds to be gradually phased in with evaluated milestones to be reached along the way. In another example of insufficient constraints, several governments have created national venture capital funds in which too much cash has created an inefficient investment

- -

107   James K. Hazy Jeffery Goldstein, "Generative Conditions for Entrepreneurship: A Complexity Science Model," *Adelphi University School of Business Working Paper Series*: SB-WP-2010-05 (November, 2010), p 7.

108   *ibid.*

strategy. Most of these funds have learned that investing smaller rather than larger amounts produces a better chance of success.[109]

These cases reflect our observation that many countries borrow policy solutions for problems of economic development or building innovation that aren't the critical ones for *their* innovation systems in *their* context. A better approach is to first diagnose where the real problems lie before searching for appropriate solutions. It is important to support diagnostic analysis, where contextual qualifiers will be a central concern.

Contextual qualifiers can affect how a knowledge intermediary functions, noting that "… no two knowledge intermediaries are the same; their work is entirely context specific, which means that, while it is possible to draw general lessons as to how they [a user] *could* choose to act (italics added), it is impossible to develop a standard set of rules as to how they *should* act (italics added)." [110] The authors also caution that … "it will not be possible to anticipate how the information will be used [by those seeking solutions] and its likely effects." [111]

Contextual qualifiers can reduce transaction costs, especially the cost of time, of knowledge acquisition by a user. If innovation is to occur it cannot be assumed, as in neo-classical economics, that actors are rational. Innovation deals with complex systems where, by definition, the same input will not always yield the same output. Knowing an initial state or set of conditions does not imply we can then predict a trajectory measured in state space. Trajectories change as variables change; this is the key reason why 'contextual qualifiers' or 'contextual constraints' are necessary.

We should frame concepts in terms of others' experience and how an option is possible, not that it is definitely the best way to go. The way to chart this course is to focus on presenting options with qualifiers and examples, rather than prescriptive "do this." In some instances, possible unintended consequences may be illustrated, but not predicted. For example, overly restrictive technology transfer office policies at a research

. . . .

109   See Victor W. Hwang and Greg Horowitt, "The Rainforest: The Secret to Building the Next Silicon Valley," *Los Altos Hills: Regenwald* (2012), p 229 for a Rainforest view of investment.

110   Harry Jones, *et al* "Knowledge Policy and Power in International Development: A Practical Guide." *The Policy Press* (2012) Chapter Five: Facilitation knowledge interaction, p 123.

111   *ibid* p 135.

institute (which may seem necessary to make sure that all transactions are managed appropriately by the technology transfer office) may have the unwanted effect of encouraging staff to circumvent the system and negotiate their own deals, resulting in lost revenues for the institution – not to mention unknown liabilities.

Context should not always be thought of as a constraint. Some corporate innovation ecosystems are both internal, to share knowledge and create transparency and efficient communication for example, and have an external reach to connect to new sources of innovation. [112]

Some typical contextual qualifier categories

For these or other categories a user can be taken through a series of structured steps in support of problem diagnosis and policy formulation that invites them at several stages to consider contextual qualifiers which fall into these categories.

Culture and politics

1. Support for innovation and entrepreneurship.
2. Existence of rigid organizational hierarchies.
3. Attitudes to what is seen as failure.
4. Existence of social networks.

Science, technology, innovation (STI) capacity

1. Development stage of the country/region.
2. Quality of universities and research institutions.
3. University/research institutes relations with business.
4. Capacity of SMEs and large companies.
5. Technology adoption/adaption, transfer, and commercialization capacity.

112   See Figure 17, Section 22, for the 'tree' analogy.

Regulatory environment

1. Intellectual property regulations and enforcement.

2. Difficulties of doing business and legal/bureaucratic barriers to business creation and growth.

Capital access

1. Availability of public finance for business development.

2. Availability of private finance for business development.

3. Availability of hybrid finance for business development.

Infrastructure/ecosystem

1. Existence of boundary spanning and linking organizations.

2. Existence and capacity of service providers.

Examples of contextual qualifiers

1. In attempting to respond to a demand for financing high risk small business development projects through grants and equity funding, public sector organizations may be prevented from efficiently doing so due to the existence of risk-averse rigid hierarchies within the organization (*Culture and politics #3 above*).

2. Policies for improving relations between universities and the business sector are more likely to succeed if the history of, and lessons learned from, past attempts is understood. For example, a university president may be supportive, but without a buy-in from department heads and faculty the effort may fail (*STI capacity #3*).

3. Where intellectual property (IP) regulations and their level of enforcement are under-developed a decision will have to be made on the level of acceptable risk that IP created under a policy of supporting new technology development may, in fact, have unclear ownership, versus waiting for regulatory improvements. Waiting reduces risk but may lead to lost opportunities and stagnation (*Regulatory environment #1*).

4. A practical problem for many developing countries in negotiating financing agreements to either acquire a technology or license IP to

others is that someone has to take the first step and agree to provide initial funding, which could be matched later by others. Sometimes this funding can be in the form of a grant for early-stage development, but if these grants take too long to be approved, as is often the case, the deal may be lost. This is a frequent situation. Therefore it is useful to have sources of small but quickly available finance available (*Capital access #2*).

5. In addition to factors such as legal/bureaucratic barriers to doing business, firms need experienced and competent services providers, which are present in most developed countries but not always in developing ones, including but not limited to: lawyers, accountants, advisors, fellow entrepreneurs, and mentors, as well as reliable communications, and networks to allow ideas, talent, and capital to come together (*Infrastructure/ecosystem #2*).

6. A contextual qualifier may be a clarification on a *detailed issue*. For example, there is a common confusion between patents solely as property rights (to exclude others) and monopolization (of a market). A patent is certainly an exclusive right, but in most circumstances patented technologies have substitutes, so they're not economic monopolies. Moreover, in many situations patents don't confer rights over finished consumer products or even product components, and therefore they aren't monopolies in any sense of the word. For instance, a patent might cover a particular technology or process used in given component that is incorporated into a finished mobile device. In this instance, the patent isn't a monopoly at all; indeed, it doesn't even guarantee its holder the right to sell a single product.[113]

Time is a contextual qualifier. A study of the history or trajectory of an innovation ecosystem or its building blocks and communications may yield knowledge of what works at one time/history will not in another. An official who was heavily involved in the rapid growth of Korean technology capabilities decades ago told me it could not be repeated now. How many regions have tried to grow their own 'Silicon Valleys' without success? [114]

. . . .

113   Thanks to Prof. Stanley Kowalski, University of New Hampshire Law Center, for this example.

114   Josh Lerner, "Boulevard of Broken Dreams," *The Kauffman Foundation Series on Innovation and Entrepreneurship* (2012).

Robert L. Goldstone at Indiana University came up with another view of contextualization or, in fact, de-contextualization, that is untying knowledge from context; [115] the opposite of the 'contextual qualifiers' or 'contextual constraints' process. Goldstone's argument is that if specific knowledge is too strongly tied a particular context or case then it will be difficult to apply it elsewhere. This implies the requirement to have compartmentalized re-usable knowledge units (see Section 21) for which "… extracting the perceptually grounded principles from their specific scenario will often allow the principle to be better appreciated and transferred." From our discussion of near decomposability of building blocks (Section 10) we know that when we try to decompose building blocks it's not always easy to identify which connections are important and which are less so. Similarly, difficulties arise when we try to remove extraneous details from a knowledge unit to expose the transferrable core.

Contextual qualifiers are important not only when selecting, designing and implementing actions – what we might call 'formulating solutions' – but also in diagnosing where the failures and bottlenecks lie – what we might call 'identifying problems.'

Finally, it should be clear from this section that context is a way to consider the surrounding environment of any system. For example, a business co-evolves with its environment meaning that both change over time because of these interactions. As we noted in Section 8 "because complex systems are open systems, we need to understand the system's complete environment before we can understand the system, and, of course, the environment is complex in itself."

---

115   Robert L. Goldstone, "The Complex Systems See-Change in Education," *Indiana University*, p 5.

14
Networks and Feedback

· ·

Section Summary: An innovation ecosystem can be viewed as a network of nodes or points connected by links rather than a system of connected building blocks. Emergence through re-arrangement of sub-complexes and re-arranging links in a network are different perspectives of the same action. Emergence in networks is due to relationships and interactions between the network's nodes, not within the elements of the network as the nodes have no internal structure. Positive feedback encourages deviation from the existing state of affairs. When order emerges a system it will tend to stabilize itself if it is creating value. Negative feedback reduces deviations from an existing state and acts as a stabilizing force and slows down the processes that caused the new order to emerge as attractor basins. The changes then become institutionalized, until the next set of stimuli create new emergence and a move to a new attractor basin. Positive feedback in far from equilibrium complex systems provided self-reinforcement which can amplify small actions and events and create large changes.

"We are willing to have some inefficient lack of access to information every day, in exchange for getting more people involved in information production over time."

— Yochai Benkler, *The Wealth of Networks: How Social Production Transforms Markets and Freedom.*

Networks are a fundamental aspect of highly innovative ecosystems. This section will not discuss networks in general – there are many other sources for this – but network properties as they are important for innovation ecosystems. Both social and professional networks greatly expand the number of interactions that can happen in a system leading to a higher probability of 'engineered serendipity' or ideas and people coming together that would have been unlikely in the absence of the connections provided by networks. There are numerous paths from one member of the system to any other so that not only bottlenecks in the system become readily avoidable, but people are able to gather much more information about the rest of the system, and environment, in which they work. The network model has yielded a mass of valuable practical results.

It's useful on many occasions to imagine an innovation ecosystem as a network of nodes or points connected by links rather than a system of connected complex building blocks. It is basic to social network analysis that connective structure matters just as for building blocks. For example, we can make the point that emergence through re-arrangement of sub-complexes and re-arranging links in a network are simply different perspectives of the same action. Emergence in networks is due to relationships and interactions between the network's nodes. Networks have structure in that sub-networks may be formed. These sub-networks into which the whole network system may be divided correspond to building blocks with internal structure and traits.

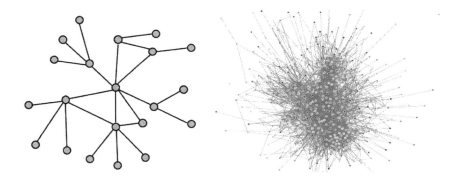

Figure 11. Left: A Simple Personal Network: Nodes and Links.
Right: The author's LinkedIn network.

Both the building block and network models have their limitations as different perspectives. Network models are limited because they imagine connected nodes with the nodes lacking any internal structure. This gives the model an inherent rigidity. [116] Building block models are differently limited because they don't always show the total system network. Both models are dynamic; they will look different at different times.

Networks have nodes (ourselves and our friends in a social network for example) connected by links. In the conventional representation of a network the nodes have no internal structure, unlike agents/building blocks, therefore nodes represent boundary rules for signals passing among nodes. We need to know much more about how clusters of nodes can form building blocks. As so often happens when we view a system from a different perspective, new characteristics appear. For example, how the shape of elements which are connected (a network's topology) such as clusters of nodes or nodes as hubs with many links can influence the system's behavior. Connectivity is an important part of network dynamics not just number of nodes but this does not imply that everything should be connected to everything as demonstrated later (Section 22).

Network decision making scales up better than hierarchical decision making, depending on context and subject to the need to balance local decisions with the good of the whole system (see Section 14 for more on hierarchies).

Network decision making is effective when decisions require, or greatly benefit from, local knowledge – for example in uncertain system states where projections into the future are highly restricted. It's important for participants to keep their local identities and loyalties. Network decision making is not as effective in more predictable system states where goals are top down, and localized participants are required to follow these.

Alescence in Networks

Networks, just like assemblies of building blocks, experience Buchler's three forms of alescence (Section 25):

Augmentative – a prevailing complex is extended, increased or enhanced.

. . . .

116   Karen Jane Tesson, "An Interdisciplinary Study of Network Organization in Biological and Human Social Systems," Ph.D. dissertation, University of Bath, UK (2006), p 32. http://www. jackwhitehead.com/teesonphd/007c6.pdf

Spoliative – there is a loss or attenuation or expiration of a complex that has prevailed.

Coalescent – a complex arising from injunction or intersection of novel configuration of complexes.

These forms produce changes to the network's structure with new nodes and links being formed and old ones disappearing. This is the network perspective of the picture of innovation through rearranging building blocks. "In many cases we can expect the construction of links to be a much slower process than the creation of new nodes. When, as a result of new discoveries, new nodes are introduced in our network of knowledge we can expect connectivity to fall. As links are established with the newly created nodes, the connectivity of the system can start rising again." [117] Emergent new nodes tend to be poorly connected at first but as knowledge diffuses through these nodes and links, and factors such as trust grow, connectivity is increased. A system will go through several transitions some of which may be dead ends.

Connectivity is measured by the density of links per node in a network. As experience in social networks indicate, those individuals with more connections tend to grow more rapidly than those with fewer. This is why in supporting technology commercialization it is critical to build networks of scientists, companies, funders, and so forth in addition to 'programs.' Karen Tesson has argued that "The rigid nature of a node-based network is largely due the manner in which the focus, in conventional network theory, is on the nodes themselves. Nodes in a nodal network are *discrete* entities; they have finite boundaries that distinguish them from their surroundings. These are nodes that have been *abstracted* from their normal contexts." Tesson suggests that abstraction from context is also seen in the point-to-point, transactional, nature of links.

"Nodal networks focus on the *relationships* between the nodes in the network, but not at all on the relationship between the network and its context. There is no inherent way of representing *context* in a nodal network

117   Cristiano Antonelli (Ed) "Handbook on the Economic Complexity of Technological Change," *Edward Elgar* (2011), p 152.

model." [118] However, with Buchler's concept of complex systems having traits, whether viewed from the perspective of building blocks or networks, it is possible to represent the model within a context.

We must look at networks that change as its agents adapt. Changes in the exterior boundaries of the agent changes the agent's possibilities for interaction with other agents; changes in its interior boundaries change its interior signal processing." [119] (See Section 17).

Some of these characteristics, for example exchanging signals among component parts, produce a picture familiar to us as a network, but one which is continually changing – at typically unpredictable rates (we lose touch with friends and work colleagues and gain new ones, strong links become weaker ones and *vice versa*).

Feedback

Why is feedback important in Rainforest systems?

In Section 5 the main characteristics of a complex adaptive system are listed. Characteristics 7 and 8 are:

7. It has *feedback* loops. If new emergent order is creating value it will stabilize itself, finding variable and parameters that best increase its overall sustainability in an ecosystem. Stability results by slowing the non-linear process that led to the amplification of emergence in the first place. Because complex systems exist in far-from-equilibrium states, small actions and events, fluctuations in the system, can be amplified through positive feedback and a cycle of self-reinforcement. This process creates a dynamic which increases the likelihood that other similar events will emerge. Positive feedback encourages deviation from the existing state of affairs and adaptation, but also helps to keep small adaptations localized. Negative feedback reduces deviations from an existing state and acts as a stabilizing force.

· ·

118 Karen Jane Tesson, "An Interdisciplinary Study of Network Organization in Biological and Human Social Systems," Ph.D. dissertation, University of Bath, UK (2006), p 32. http://www.actionresearch.net/living/tesson.shtml

119 John H. Holland, "Signals and Boundaries: Building Blocks for Complex Adaptive Systems," *MIT Press* (2012), p 50. Network theory.

8. Its behavior is *non-linear.* Non-linear change occurs when a response is neither directly nor inversely proportional to its cause; thus, small changes or disturbances may cause large changes in the system's behavior.

Just to be clear, 'feedback loops' includes 'feed-forward loops.' Feedback loops may be short term and cost effective or longer term with uncertain costs. In new product development (Section 10) when feedback takes time to evolve, significant costs will occur if R&D or product development conducted to date ends up being wasted. For example, it is not uncommon in universities and research institutes, especially in developing countries where researchers may be inadequately connected to market intelligence, that development proceeds without sufficient knowledge of competing products. Wasted time and money is the usual result, together with disappointment and frustration among the developers.

The term positive does not mean 'good.' The term negative does not mean 'bad.' Positive feedback encourages deviation from the existing state of affairs and adaptation and thus produces emergence/alescence. When order emerges a system will tend to stabilize itself if it is creating value. An example of positive feedback is when an innovation ecosystem's members have many new and diverse ideas for developing or expanding businesses in their region. These ideas result from assessments (such as the Rainforest Scorecard), brainstorming, and focus groups. Great, but are there sufficient human and other resources to pursue all opportunities even after some stability has emerged from initial apparent randomness? This question is taken up in Section 19.

Negative feedback reduces deviations from an existing state and acts as a stabilizing force. It keeps minor changes and adjustments (which may be needed) from becoming too large by re-stabilizing the system post-changes. In the above example, negative feedback from a reality assessment of all the possibilities unleashed produces a decision to first work on those possibilities which are close to the ecosystem's existing experience and skills.

Negative feedback slows down the processes that caused the new order to emerge as attractor basins. The changes then because institutionalized, until the next set of stimuli create new emergence and a move to a new attractor basin.

Self-reinforcing feedback occurs in networks with their culture and sub-systems rather than individuals making decisions.

Positive feedback in far from equilibrium complex systems provided self-reinforcement which can amplify small actions and events and create large changes.

Feedback can come from top-down causation.

Systems which seek steady state equilibrium can achieve it through negative feedback loops which absorb deviations.

When talking about feedback loops it should be recognized that these behave differently if they are present in (1) time sequential systems such as the stages of new product development, or (2) in systems such as innovation ecosystems comprised of building blocks which function as a group at any one time, even though they may change over time (see the concept of 'core' building blocks in Section 11). In (1) feedback may cause the need to return to an earlier stage in the new product development sequence resulting in delays and additional expense.

Complexity science shows that when systems are in a dis-equilibrium state, small actions and events, 'perturbations' in the system, can be amplified through a positive feedback cycle of self-reinforcement. This effect has been observed, for example, in studies of leadership in groups of people.

In his book **Streetlights and Shadows; Searching for the Keys to Adaptive Decision Making**, Gary Klein discusses the limits of feedback and the often expressed claim that "To get people to learn, give them feedback on the consequences of their actions." [120] There are two kinds of feedback which need to be distinguished. "[F]eedback isn't sufficient.... Researchers have found that outcome feedback – knowledge of results – doesn't improve our performance as much as process feedback, which helps us understand how to correct flaws."

Feedback from customers or potential customers provides essential guidance in the development of new products or services. It can reduce risk of creating products or services for which there are no markets. It can either

. . . .

120   Gary Klein, "Streetlights and Shadows: Searching for the Keys to Adaptive Decision Making," *MIT Press* (2009), p 165.

encourage bold moves or more modest incremental innovation. This is not outcome feedback; knowing there is no market for a fully developed product or service is too late. This is Klein's process feedback allowing us to correct flaws during the development process and through formal and informal development networks.

Furthermore "To learn that a certain set of actions will lead to good outcomes, we have to figure out the cause and effect relationships [121] between the actions we took and the later events." See Sections 17 and 25 for more on cause and effect and why causality may not be valid in Rainforests.

As Henry Doss notes, "It seems inevitable that in most - all? - organizations, *rewarding* is deeply linked to *recognizing*. This emphasis on recognition, in turn, creates a value set that causes individuals to seek recognition. Work is evaluated in terms of how much recognition any particular action might realize, not in what value that action might have for the organization." [122]

He goes on to note that incentive structures — "the great demon of unintended consequences" can create feedback loops that might cause someone else to be recognized, or to cause a negative recognition in the event of failure. "Which, of course, ensures the long-term failure of any organization." Systems of recognition, rewards, and evaluation must be focused on something other than the individual. These might be contributions of work to the overall objective (outcome) or the achievement of the objective more quickly (process). The opposite also applied in cases where feedback must be constraining.

Hwang and Horowitt talk about rational and extra-rational incentives in Rainforests. [123] In an innovation ecosystem we might refer to rational and less-rational incentives. When a university or research institute licenses a technology, most distribute a portion of license income, typically one-third, to the researchers concerned as a rational incentive. Perhaps a less rational, but important, incentives are the professional recognition they

121 *ibid* p 166.

122 Henry Doss Forbes blog, http://www.forbes.com/sites/henrydoss/2015/09/16/five-character-traits-of-innovation-leaders/

123 Victor W. Hwang and Greg Horowitt, "The Rainforest: The Secret to Building the Next Silicon Valley," *Los Altos Hills: Regenwald* (2012), p 122ff.

receive. For some researchers rather than extra income, a rational incentive, which may seem non-rational to a non-scientist, is the acquisition of a new instrument vital to their work.

15

Wicked Problems are Everywhere

Section Summary: A wicked problem is a social or cultural problem that is the opposite of a 'tame problem.' Tame problems are susceptible to logical analysis. Wicked problems are not. Every wicked problem can be considered a symptom of another problem. There is no identifiable root cause and it is not possible to be sure of the appropriate level at which to intervene; parts cannot always be easily separated from the whole. In linear systems cause and effect is determinable and typically modeled using Logical Framework Analysis methods, which deal with inputs and outputs and the tasks which produce the latter from the former – a defined cause and effect relationship. The behaviors of complex systems don't fit into such analysis. It is necessary to inspect the system's cause-and-effect assumptions and focus on applying assessments such as the Balanced Scorecard methodology within regions of quasi-stability (attractors, or farms in Rainforest language) where linear cause-and-effect relationships are more likely to hold. Strategic planning in building innovation ecosystems is considered.

Wicked: Adjective (slang) meaning very good, excellent; "cool"; "awesome" from 13th Century Middle English wikked, wikke, an alteration of wicke, adjectival use of Old English wicca ("wizard, sorcerer"). "Going beyond reasonable or predictable limits." Or, the Merriam-Webster dictionary's [nicely understated] "very bad or unpleasant."

Nepalese citizens viewed the impact of climate change on their country in a 2009 survey of local views as "A problem with many layers of nested and intractable predicaments,… complex inter-linkages between elements… small perturbations can quickly transform into catastrophic events…"

Wicked problems

Innovation ecosystems, as well as climate systems, have their share of nested and intractable predicaments where inter-linkages are hidden like the layers of an onion. New business creation is linked with leadership; leadership linked with culture; resources are linked with frameworks and policies, and so forth.

In economic development, especially in developing countries, poverty is linked with education, nutrition with poverty, the economy with nutrition, and so on as described by Ben Ramalingam.[124] Partly as a result of Ramalingam's book the global aid community is starting to understand that countries and regions are complex adaptive systems, and in turn are made up of sub-complexes, rather than linear modules.

Here we introduce an additional wrinkle on complexity, namely 'wicked problems.' A wicked problem is a social or cultural problem that is the opposite of a 'tame problem' as set out below. Tame problems are susceptible to logical analysis. Wicked problems are not. A wicked problem is an extreme case of a complex problem. In the 1970's Russell Ackoff, well known for his work in organizational theory, coined the delightful name 'messes' for these problems

· ·

124   Ben Ramalingam, "Aid at the Edge of Chaos," *Oxford University Press* (2013).

Characteristic	Tame problems	Wicked problems
Problem formulation	The problem can be clearly written down. The problem can be stated as a gap between what is and what ought to be. There is easy agreement about the problem definition.	The problem is difficult to define. Many possible explanations may exist. Individuals perceive the issue differently. Depending on the explanation, the solution takes on a different form.
Testability	Potential solutions can be tested as either correct or false.	There is no single set of criteria for whether solutions are right or wrong; they can only be more or less acceptable.
Finality	Problems have a clear solution and end point.	There is always room for more improvement and potential consequences may continue indefinitely.
Level of analysis	It is possible to bound the problem and identify its root cause and subsequent effects; the problem's parts can be easily separated from the whole.	Every problem can be considered a symptom of another problem. There is no identifiable root cause and it is not possible to be sure of the appropriate level at which to intervene; parts cannot always be easily separated from the whole.
Replicability	The problem may repeat itself many times because it is linear; applying formulaic responses will produce predictable results.	Every problem is essentially unique; formulae are of limited value because the problem is non-linear.
Reproducibility	Solutions can be tested and excluded until the correct solution is found.	Each problem is a one-shot operation. Once a solution is attempted, you cannot undo what you have already done.

Table 5. Comparison of Tame and Wicked Problems

As we noted before, it's not just understanding complexity which is important but *solving problems* in complex systems. This is what we are called upon to do. It's of little use understanding the complex nature of innovation ecosystems unless we can understand and resolve issues with which we are confronted, such as how to improve the flow of innovation, how to predict disruptions, how to optimize leadership, and many others.

Inspecting the right side column in the table above [125] shows that many, possibly most, challenges in innovation ecosystems are indeed 'wicked.' So what should we do? Throw up our hands and admit defeat, or try to make these wicked problems if not tame then at least a little less wicked?

One way to try and 'tame' a wicked problem is to use a standard engineering approach and approximate the complex, non-linear, wicked problem as a linear one, or several linear ones to get at least some rough solution. However, experience shows that wicked problems are too intractable for this procedure to work in the real world with any confidence. Even if the method did work, it's unlikely to scale. Furthermore, it may be thought that 'complicated' systems rather than complex ones are somehow better. But complicated systems can be easily copied and we may not always want this if we need to be competitive. Linear predicable systems, by definition, will show scant emergence and will not be innovative. This is an example of the wrong model being used (see Section 8).

Should traditional planning models be used in complex adaptive systems?

In linear systems causes and their effects are determinable and typically modeled using Logical Framework Analysis, or 'logframe' methods, which deal with inputs and outputs and the tasks which produce the latter from the former – that is, a defined cause and effect relationship. Logframes are ubiquitous in the global aid community using methodology created in the 1960s by the U.S. Agency for International Development (USAID). Logical Framework design is not an evaluation in itself; it provides a plan of the project against which project progress can be assessed by evaluators. It was also intended to make evaluation less threatening. Furthermore, where there are clear and logical relationships between inputs and outputs this can lead to efficient task delegation.

Donor agencies typically require the use of logframes to try and assess the likelihood that a project will perform as predicted. However, the behaviors

. . . .

125   Adapted from: Ben Ramalingam, Miguel Laric and John Primrose, "From best practice to best fit; Understanding and navigating wicked problems in international development," *UK Department for International Development (DFID)* (September 2014). http://www.odi.org/publications/8571-complexity-wiked-problems-tools-ramalingam-dfid

of complex systems don't fit into logframes [126] which assume a linear sequence of events and also assume that planned outputs will be obtained if all activities are carried out according to the plan – unlikely if wicked problems are present.

Some international development agencies have recognized the need for changes because "…'traditional,' well-established and strongly embedded approaches to implementation rely on the policy problem involving stable hierarchies, well-understood causality and agreed policy goals" [127] which is, again, not necessarily the case among wicked problem environments. Furthermore, "tools which are perfectly suitable for some problems have serious side-effects when applied to complex problems. Where incentives for staff are aligned around assumptions that problems are simple, this can lead to them being pushed towards aspects of the problem that suit these assumptions – focusing on the 'low-hanging fruit' and working with high risk aversion. These are both likely to lead, in the long run, to irrelevant programming in the face of complexity."

The world is not linear and effects may have multiple causes (Section 17). A non-linear world drives the conversation about the need for non-deductive reasoning (Section 24). Global development organizations are beginning to pay more attention to complexity *"Many development partner tools and business processes deal with static, simple or linear problems. There is considerable demand for new methods and principles that can help development partners better navigate the complex, dynamic realities they face on a day-to-day basis."* [128] Searching for new methods recognizes that attempting to reduce complex systems to merely complicated ones with causal chains, by increasing centralized control, and by drastically limiting goals and objectives, will not help solve wicked problems.

. . . .

126   The Logical Framework Approach is sometimes confused with Logical Framework (or Logframe). The Logical Framework Approach is a project design methodology, whereas the Logical Frame is a document. https://en.wikipedia.org/wiki/Logical_framework_approach

127   "A guide for planning and strategy complexity development in the face of Complexity," *ODI Background Note* (March 2013).

128   Ben Ramalingam, Miguel Laric and John Primrose, "From best practice to best fit: Understanding and navigating wicked problems in international development, *UK Department for International Development (DfID)* p iv. http://www.odi.org/sites/odi.org.uk/files/odi-assets/publications-opinion-files/9159.pdf

To illustrate what we are talking about a rather simplified logframe might look something like this (it's typically a 4×4 matrix):

Goal	Improve creation of spin-off companies from universities.
Purpose/Outcome	An effective improved company creation system is operating.
Output	New spin-off companies developed. New incentives created. Increased number of role models and mentors. New methods in place.
Activities	Analyze problems with current methods to create spin-off companies. Provide more early stage, start-up, funding. Find more brokers available to help match R&D needs to sources. Provide more incentives to researchers. Identify role models and mentors. Create an entrepreneurship culture. Inventory physical and people assets. Provide training on IP and finance.

Table 6. Simplified logframe.

This table suggests we can produce a certain set of outputs from a certain set of inputs to achieve the required outcome. These concepts can help us think through a project in an orderly logical fashion assuming there are definite cause and effect relationships between any level and the level immediately above it; in wicked problems this is not the case. Finally, an emphasis on cause and effect suggests a rational expectations hypothesis, which does not take into consideration extra-rational motives which influence behavior.

The question of cause and effect relationships between different levels in complex systems is taken up in Section 16.

Logic models fail to account for the complex connection between programs and communities.[129] In an innovation ecosystem there may be no obvious causal chain of events. Impacts and outcomes may not be direct and immediately measurable. "However, practically speaking, logframes often reflect a blueprint or 'control-oriented' project planning approach whereas many Theories of Change proponents advocate for a more

. . . .

129   Philip L. Lee, "What's Wrong with Logic Models," *Local Community Services Association: Occasional Paper* No. 1, p 5.

process-orientated approach. To overcome this issue, logframes could be based on tightly defined inputs and outputs that reflect what is initially realistically implementable. These need to have the option of being revised regularly." [130] [131] The question of frequent plan revision will be considered in detail in Section 25.

The United Nations Industrial Development Organization (UNIDO) has recommended ways in which logframes may be a more adaptive planning tool. [132] Expected deliverables are categorized into simple, complicated, and complex domains.

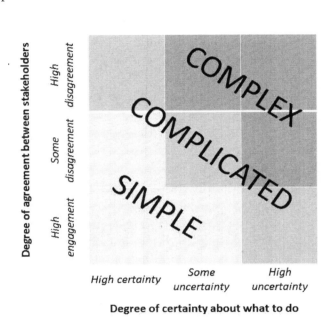

Figure 12. Simple, complicated, and complex domains.[133]

130   "Theories of Change," *UK Overseas Development Institute* (2015), p 6.

131   For more on pros and cons of logframes see "The logframe and the beautiful game: Project logic v football logic," Politically Agile Programming. Paper 1, 2014 http://www.gpgovernance.net/wp-content/uploads/2014/01/Politically-Agile-Programming-paper-1.pdf

132   This summary is taken from a more detailed explanation in Richard Hummelbrunner and Harry Jones "A guide for planning and strategy complexity development in the face of Complexity," *ODI Background Note* (March 2013).

133   Source: *ibid* p 10.

Simple: There is agreement on goals and ways to achieve them. The system is fully decomposable and therefore what has worked elsewhere may be reused.

Complicated: Where indicators and assumptions should be identified carefully to enable monitoring and evaluation for relevance and context.

Complex: High levels of uncertainty and disagreement.

If many outputs are expected to be complex, then it will be necessary to take account of initial conditions and emergence. Indicators should capture emerging phenomena. In Section 5, property #10 noted that the state of a complex system depends on its *trajectory or history*. Complex adaptive systems are sensitive to *initial conditions*, and self-organizing networks are development path-dependent.

What this means is looking carefully, and possibly suspiciously, at the usual Assumptions & Risks column of a logframe. If outputs are expected to be complex it is necessary to decide whether the assumptions which connect the various levels in a logframe are reasonable or not, and whether what is expected to be achieved at one stage can be expected to be transferred to the next.

Let's look again at the rather simplified logframe from the bottom up and try to identify where there may be clear causal connections and where wicked problems may lurk.

For example, should "Provide more early stage, start-up, funding" cause more spin-off companies to be created, or will "training" as is often assumed? Will "New incentives" be created? Is there a clear bottom up causal hierarchy (see Section 16 for details)? Almost certainly not. These questions, and others, fall into the "Complex: High levels of uncertainty and disagreement" category where *initial conditions trajectory or history* (path-dependency) are critical. Consequently, interdependent relations and communications among elements need to be assessed.

Earlier, we saw that innovation ecosystems are made up of sub-systems. Some of these are farms in the Rainforest language (linear, causal, systems – hosting complicated problems), and others are Rainforests (non-linear, non-causal, systems – hosting wicked problems). We need to know which are which in order to decide what approaches to use to address needs and solve problems. Section 25 provides a tool for this assessment.

In the Balanced Scorecard methodology developed initially by Kaplan and Norton[134] a cause-and-effect hypothesis is the basis for Balanced Scorecard metrics applied across its four stages in a chain of cause and effect relationships. If strategic planning, like the Balanced Scorecard, is to be applied in complex systems it will be similarly necessary to (i) inspect the system's cause-and-effect assumptions to see if they model the real world, (ii) assess our level of trust in these assumptions, and (iii) focus on applying the traditional strategic planning methodology within regions of quasi-stability (attractors – or farms in Rainforest language) where linear cause and effect relationships are more likely to hold. Especially important for strategic planning is to recognize that emergence produces new causal relationships.

These ideas are discussed and described in detail in Section 25.

We expressed this similarly in Section 4:

> A notion of causality based on regularities can only be meaningfully defined for systems with linear interactions among their variables. This implies that we cannot understand causation in complex systems by a process of analysis of variables because complex systems have emergent properties, and a change in one variable will probably affect all the other variables. This further implies that a notion of causation can only be meaningful for regions in which the behavior of a nonlinear system is topologically equivalent to that of a linear system. However, it may be possible to track cause and effect by studying cases which take different paths to the same results. This approach puts emphasis on cases and trajectories rather than variables. Knowledge of how complex adaptive systems behave enables some leading indicators to be developed. Another way of expressing this is that because complex systems are adaptable and can self-repair it is sometimes possible to assume linearity – until the next disruption arrives.

This situation when a variable is regulated to keep nearly constant is called 'dynamic homeostasis.' An example is regulation of human body

....

134   "The Balanced Scorecard" https://balancedscorecard.org/BSC-Knowledge-Management

temperature, or a thermostat regulating room temperature by means of negative feedback. See Section 14 for more on feedback, and Section 8 for attractors.

The ubiquity of wicked problems, non-linearity, and the properties of complex systems generally, also raises similar questions about conventional strategic planning methods – described in detail in Section 25.

16
Hierarchy and Necessity

. . . .

Section Summary: Many innovation ecosystems exhibit a hierarchical structure. The description of properties at a particular level offers necessary but not sufficient conditions to derive the description of properties at a higher level. Additional contingent contextual conditions are required. Examples of hierarchical innovation ecosystems are discussed. Considerations for innovation management which are higher level contingent contextual conditions include: competitive advantage, business alignment, knowing the customers who will benefit from your innovation, and identifying resources, processes, risks, partners, and suppliers. Adherence to the 'status quo' may sound completely antithetical to the concept of innovation, but an idea that requires too much change in an organization, or too much disruption to the marketplace, may never see the light of day. There is a need to balance farms and Rainforests.

"The hierarchical concept allows us to define components of an ecosystem and their links between different scales of ecological organization. The systematic hierarchical approach offers a means for establishing the context of species viability, biodiversity and determining management objectives."

— Mark Twain National Forest Resources Management Plan,
  USDA, 2005.

When discussing the powerful effect on emergence (alescence) by rearranging basic building blocks of an innovation ecosystem we assumed a certain basic simplicity of the building blocks. Herbert Simon (Section10) suggested that complex systems form hierarchies which are more robust by virtue of being simple. Furthermore, hierarchies can be self-reinforcing.

The meaning of hierarchy

A hierarchy is a successive set of subsystems. The term 'hierarchy' does not imply that one level is more important than another as it tends to in common usage of the word. Hierarchies are about structure not dominance. Our interest in hierarchy is that many innovation ecosystems exhibit a hierarchical structure; novel features which are irreducible to lower level features emerge at higher hierarchical levels. If a system is reducible then a description of features of a system at a particular level of description offers *both necessary and sufficient* conditions to rigorously derive the description of features at a higher level. [135]

Hierarchical systems have been studied in physics, chemistry, and biology especially, but much less so for complex adaptive innovation systems. The hierarchical picture leads naturally to an analysis of upward and downward causation (Section 12).

An admission here from your author: when I first starting looking into hierarchies it was not clear to me if the hierarchy picture would be of any value in modeling innovation ecosystems. Shortly after, I was asked to provide advice on how to resolve problems encountered in an ecosystem designed to support technology transfer from universities (described in Section 16). By looking at what hierarchies were in place it was simple to see the reason for the problem. It's a question of "knowing what to look for" which we will pick up again in Section 25.

Emergence, or alescence, in its augmentative, spoliative, or coalescence form, may be explained in terms of the results of a relationship between a lower and a higher level as it appears at the higher level. Let's see how this works and how it relates two important themes of this book: emergence of innovation and context. The explanation involves something called by Bishop *et al* [136] *contextual property emergence* and the concept, much

135 Harald Atmanspacher, Robert C. Bishop, "Stability Conditions in Contextual Emergence," (2007) https://www.researchgate.net/publication/253295067 explain that there may be a case where the description of features of a system at a lower level of description offers *sufficient but not necessary* conditions to derive the description of features at a higher level. To put it another way, lower-level description offers multiple realizations of a particular feature at a higher level, which is referred to as 'supervenience.'

136 Robert C. Bishop, Harald Atmanspacher, "Contextual Emergence in the Description of Properties," *Foundations of Physics* 36 (12), (2006). http://citeseerx.ist.psu.edu/viewdoc/download?doi=10.1.1.586.4804&rep=rep1&type=pdf

beloved by mathematicians and philosophers, of necessary and sufficient conditions. For example, air is a necessary condition for human life. It is not a sufficient condition; food is also needed to support life.

Following the proofs of Bishop *et al* we make the statement:

The description of properties at a particular level of description offers *necessary but not sufficient* conditions to derive the description of properties at a higher level in a hierarchy.

Additional *contingent contextual conditions* are required for the transition from the lower to the higher level of description in order to provide such sufficient conditions. So even if we have a detailed analysis of lower level properties in a hierarchy, emergent (alescence) properties of the system which may occur at the higher level cannot be predicted without taking into account contextual conditions such as contextual qualifiers (Section 13) to create what is sometimes called the contextual topology.

A potentially intriguing case is when the description of features of a system at a particular level of description offers *neither necessary nor sufficient* conditions to derive the description of features at a higher level. Consequently, there are no relevant conditions connecting the two levels whatsoever. Atmanspacher and Bishop refer to this condition as 'radical emergence.' It's not clear how such radical emergence is exhibited in innovation ecosystems – possibly in disruptive situations – and more study is needed. Investigation of hierarchies is an effective problem identification and problem solving tool, as shown in the case below, but cannot be used in radical emergence cases.

The preceding discussion may sound painfully arcane so let's look into practical applications. An innovation ecosystem may have a lower level of hierarchy made up of traits say, training programs, mentors, an innovation culture (remember, a trait does not have to be an organization), an early stage investment fund, research centers, a variety of entrepreneurial businesses, and policies to support economic development. There will be more traits present but let's say a choice has been made that these are the most significant or influential. As always, there is the possibility of making the error of leaving out a trait of importance. These traits may not be sufficient to create a higher level policy for the innovation ecosystem without bringing in *contingent contextual* issues.

Hierarchies need to be identified. An illustrative case comes from a small country which, as part of an economic development strategy, sets about improving commercialization of research from the nation's universities. To get started, many of the activities described in the above paragraph are set up as programs with a focus on training for university Technology Transfer Office (TTOs) staff in the basics of technology commercialization. Training programs (a common feature, but not necessarily effective) and mentoring (often neglected, but frequently more effective) are established for TTO staff. This is a necessary initiative but not a sufficient one. Missing at a higher level of hierarchy was a necessary policy and practical commitment to support TTOs. Only short term contracts are given to TTO staff, there are no incentives and no reward structure in place, and TTO staff feel that the university has no confidence in their abilities or dedication. Missing at the lower level are mentors with hands-on industry experience. The effort falters. This story illustrates the importance of inputs from lower levels being a part of a system's design. Tacit knowledge resided at lower levels where employees often have knowledge and information that upper level management does not. Furthermore, when decisions are made at lower levels those making the decisions are likely to want to implement them by applying their tacit knowledge.

In the example above there are two additional questions (i) at what level does optimum knowledge and know-how reside, and (ii) what are ways in which knowledge can be applied to make good, if not the best, non-deductive decisions (see Section 24 for details of non-deductive decision making). In fact, in this case those at the lower level have more knowledge and are better placed to make decisions about supportive policies than higher level policy makers. A frequent impediment is that those at lower levels may have knowledge but lack capacity to capitalize on their knowledge or know-how.

"Complexity science highlights how there is often untapped potential for change in lower-level decision-making units, and for groups of actors not linked by formal hierarchies to 'self-organise' and work coherently towards a common goal. Lower levels can sometimes address complex problems more effectively for three main reasons. First, they often have a strong understanding of the local dynamics, with long-built and largely tacit knowledge of the drivers of behavior and how issues relate to these."

[137] Another common university technology commercialization example, which can be generalized to hierarchies in most organizations and endeavors other than commercialization, is the hierarchy of approvals. Within the university setting at the faculty and research staff level there may be enthusiasm for commercialization. At an upper level the university dean or president may strongly approve. However, at the middle level if a department head does not value such activities it is likely nothing will happen.

A word of caution: hierarchies are a property of complex systems and we should be careful not to use hierarchical descriptions to over simplify the actual complexity of the system being analyzed. Reducing complexity in one place may increase complexity elsewhere – like poking a balloon.

Hierarchy and new product development

When evaluating the financial feasibility of a project a common first step is to carry out a high level, top-down, go/no-go decision process. At this stage it is assumed other factors which may adversely affect the project's feasibility, such as ownership and protection of intellectual property, an available team development team, suitable market conditions, and others have been assessed as not to be project killers. The StageGate™ procedure typically used in new product development is illustrated in the Figures 13 and 14 below. It consists of a series of development stages and continue or stop decision gates.

For example, when applied to commercializing a technology through licensing, the top down approach may be a sufficient way to give an estimate of potential value but not necessarily market price. It also does not usually determine the customer value proposition. When the StageGate™ procedure is not sufficient, an alternative way to evaluating the financial feasibility of a project is to use a more detailed bottom-up process which evaluates financial statements and projections, product development, marketing and sales costs, and revenue projections based on discussions with potential customers. This process is needed when a business is already functioning. In many cases, a decision will be made to discontinue the

137 Harry Jones, "Taking Responsibility for Complexity," *Overseas Development Institute (ODI) Report Notes,* Working Paper 330 (June 2011).

development of a new product. Adherence to the 'status quo' may sound completely antithetical to the concept of innovation. But an idea that requires too much change in an organization, or too much disruption to the marketplace, may never see the light of day. Once again we see the need to balance farms and Rainforests.

Bishop's result that the description of properties at a particular level of description offers *necessary but not sufficient* conditions to derive the description of properties at a higher level will sometimes mean, in the financial modeling case, that more detailed upper level conditions found by using StageGate™ methods need to be considered.

Tech Stage Gate™ Process

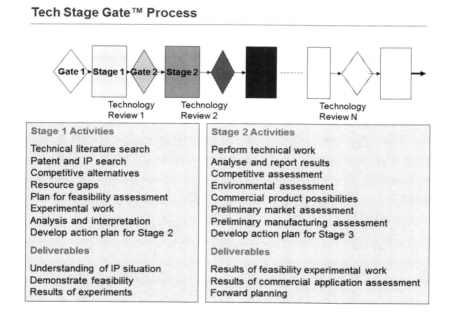

Figure 13. StageGate™ activities.

Even though the StageGate™ may appear to be highly linear, decisions to proceed, stop, or modify, which must be made at each gate may be based on non-deductive reasoning (Section 24). Different phases of development, different segments of the chain, may begin at differing times and run in parallel. The process may also have several tracks. Illustrated are commercial new product development track and a research track.

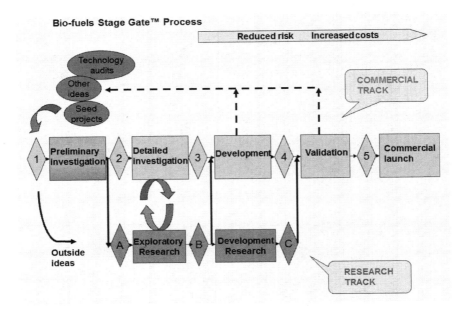

Figure 14. StageGate™ parallel tracks.

The hierarchical nature of parallel tracks allows possible application of Bishop's result suggesting that upper level conditions found by using StageGate™ need to be considered. If we expect effective emergence at the upper level what additional *contingent contextual conditions* will be required?

Considerations for innovation management [138] which are higher level *contingent contextual conditions* are:

1. Competitive advantage: Your innovation should provide a unique competitive position for the enterprise in the marketplace.

2. Business alignment: The differentiating factors of your innovation should be conceptualized around the key strategic focus of the enterprise and its goals.

. . . .

138 "How to build a framework to conceptualize your ideas into successful innovations," *Innovation Management.*
http://www.innovationmanagement.se/2012/01/23/how-to-build-a-framework-to-conceptualize-your-ideas-into-successful-innovations/

3. Customers: Knowing the customers who will benefit from your innovation is paramount.

4. Execution: Identifying resources, processes, risks, partners, suppliers, and the ecosystem in the market for succeeding with the innovation are all important.

5. Business value: Assessing the value (monetary, market size, etc.) of the innovation and how the idea will bring that value into the organization is a critical underlying factor in selecting which idea to pursue.

Hierarchy and transaction costs

In their book [139] Hwang and Horowitt make the point that transaction cost can be reduced by increases in levels of trust and teamwork between transacting parties in the context of a firm as an organizational structure, first introduced by Nobel Laureate Ronald Coase. [140] Trust in innovation ecosystems is, in part, determined by communication between building blocks. Reducing transaction costs makes additional resources available for reinvestment in new opportunities. Shocks to a complex innovation ecosystem (Section 18) can alter the structure of the system and, in turn, factors which determined transactions costs. For example, a network may be disrupted when links are severed by shocks resulting in damaged or lost trusted contacts.

Transaction cost economics are also related to other characteristics of complex adaptive systems, including hierarchy. Transaction cost economics "tells us that focusing on the microelements of an organizational structure need not be very enlightening because all that will be observed will be component complexity – it is necessary to choose an appropriate level of organization, such as the firm, before an understanding can emerge... Complexity science gives us a much clearer idea why the costs associated with different organizational arrangements to produce different kinds of

139 Victor W. Hwang and Greg Horowitt, "The Rainforest: The Secret to Building the Next Silicon Valley," *Los Altos Hills: Regenwald* (2012), pp 162-165.

140 Coase, R., "The Nature of the Firm," *Economica N.S.*, 4, (1937) pp 386-405.

products vary so much." [141] In other words, the ability to see patterns in behavior and transactions matter as much as the observation and analysis of the individual elements of each. This, again, is Bishop's result that the description of properties at a particular level of hierarchy offers *necessary but not sufficient* conditions to derive the description of properties at a higher level.

Obviously, identifying where knowledge actually resides in a hierarchy is of little use unless, for example, entrepreneurs or intrapreneurs at these levels are listened to. "Rather than develop policies abstractly intended to correct 'market failures' policymakers should engage local entrepreneurs in person to develop and implement practically focused policies intended to encourage dynamism, increase diversity, and stimulate 'metabolic' activity such as idea exploration, product development, and increased rates of deal flow." [142] From the public perspective, this point cannot be overemphasized. The above discussions illustrate the importance of inputs from lower levels being a part of a system's design. To emphasize what was noted earlier: tacit knowledge resides at lower levels where employees often have knowledge and information that management does not. Furthermore, when decisions are made at lower levels those making the decisions are likely to want to implement them.

. . . .

141 John Foster "Is There a Role For Transaction Cost Economics If We View Firms as Complex Adaptive Systems?" page 12. http://www.thefreelibrary.com/IS+THERE+A+ROLE+FOR+TRANSACTION+COST+ECONOMICS+IF+WE+VIEW+FIRMS+AS...-a066881360

142 Philip E. Auerswald, "Enabling Entrepreneurial Ecosystems: Insights from Ecology to Inform Effective Entrepreneurship Policy," *Ewing Marion Kauffman Foundation* (October 2015).

17

Cause, Effect, and Trying to Predict

....

Section Summary: Chance, probability, cause and effect are so embedded in our daily lives that we may give scant thought to the mechanisms of causality – what cause produces what effect, either immediately or at a later time. If, in building innovation ecosystems, we propose interventions that adjust the ecosystem's sub-systems and especially their connections we need to know what the effect of these actions are likely to be. Top-down causation (also called downward causation) is a causal relationship between higher hierarchical levels of a system to lower-level parts of that system: for example, mental events acting to cause physical events. Applications of these ideas to engineering innovation ecosystems and analyzing malfunctioning ones are discussed. However, any discussion of causality in complex adaptive systems is bound to be slippery.

As cousin Zeb spreads his money on the table, ready to play poker with Cuthbert J. Twillie (played in the movie by W.C. Fields) he excitedly asks, "Is this a game of chance?"

"Not the way I play it, no," comes Twillie's reply.

— *My Little Chickadee* (1940) movie starring W.C. Fields and Mae West.

What genetic factors caused a particular disease? Is poverty a cause of crime, did forgetting to change the oil in my car cause the engine to seize, was the lack of funding for patenting inventions in my university the cause of low technology commercialization compared to peer institutions, what was the cause of the sudden rise in the value of my company stock? Was a remark I made without thinking sufficiently about its consequences the cause of the breakdown of a friendship?

Chance, probability, and cause and effect, are so embedded in our daily lives that we may give scant thought to the mechanisms of *causality*, that is, what cause might be the first step to an effect, either immediately or at a later time. Most of us are inclined to believe that all effects have causes even though they may not be clear to us. The 18th century philosopher ago David Hume noted that causation and correlation are notions fundamental to human cognition, conveniences so fundamental that they are unlikely to ever be eradicated, [143] although Hume himself did not believe in causal powers that brought about causal regularities. Probability is not discussed in this book; sufficient to note that Judea Pearl in his book **Causality** [144] points out that "people prefer to encode knowledge in causal rather than probabilistic structures." He goes on to note, as many other authors have, that most of us are not good at estimating probabilities – although collectively, we may be exceptional; a reinforcement for encouraging collective power in innovation. In Section 25 we will be considering how to plan under conditions of uncertainty where attempting to assign probabilities will not be helpful or indeed possible.

Causality would seem to imply that we can create simple models such as event A causes B and in turn action B may be the cause of an effect C. For example, the diagram below depicts a causal model relating price and demand, for which algebraic equations can be written. Q is the quantity of household demand for a product, P is the unit price, I is household income, W is the wage rate for producing the product, and U_1, U_2 are unmodeled error factors affecting quantity and price.

. . . .

143   For more on causality in philosophy see: https://en.wikipedia.org/wiki/Correlation_does_not_imply_causation

http://blog.oup.com/2013/11/correlation-is-not-causation/

"Causal Processes." Stanford Encyclopedia of Philosophy. http://plato.stanford.edu/entries/causation-process/

144   Judea Pearl, "Causality, Models: Reasoning, and Inference," *Cambridge University Press* (2000,) p25.

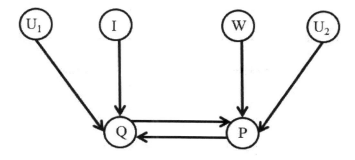

Figure 15. Causal relationships.[145]

But wait a moment. Previously we discussed how innovation ecosystems are non-linear complex adaptive systems where the same inputs don't always produce the same outputs, where the behavior of a system is not the sum of its individual parts, where there are disruptions and emergence, and where effects occur in far-from-equilibrium states. Surely then, complex adaptive systems make a mockery of simple causation? So, what should we do to get a hold on cause and effect in complex adaptive innovation ecosystems? If we cannot, then have we lost our way completely?

It is to these questions we shall now turn our attention. Much of what is discussed next is taken from the thought-provoking work of David Byrne and Emma Uprichard. [146]

Deterministic equations cannot be written for complex systems as they can for the linear system diagramed above. Other means are needed. A valuable concept is the 'causal narrative' – descriptions or cases, which may contain both text and numbers, that help to explain why some event happened in a complex system and how the state of the system came about. Such narratives are reconstructions of events similar to case examples and studies familiar from learning methods, although here we are typically talking about short narratives and maybe reusable knowledge facets as introduced in Section 21.

. . . .

145 *ibid.*

146 David Byrne and Emma Uprichard, "Useful Complex Causality," *The Oxford Handbook of Philosophy of Social Science* (2012).

In practice, preparation of a roadmap for an innovation ecosystem demands an understanding of causality. A roadmap is a trajectory over time which might show what actions or projects are recommended and when they should begin and when they should be completed. In this situation causality means causality by comparison – comparison with the trajectories of systems which have similarities, or in the language of complexity, those which are 'near neighbors.' Knowledge of what happened to produce an existing state can enable choices to be made of which actions – causes – can produce future expected results – effects. Fritz Ringer, professor emeritus of history at the University of Pittsburgh, described this as "the kind of causal analysis that will explain why the course of historical development ultimately led to the explanandum [147] in question, rather than to some other outcome."

W.C. Fields was correct; it's not a game of chance.

We know from our everyday lives that there are causal relations and we don't take the time, or have the knowledge, to investigate if the systems are linear or not or what their state space looks like. We tend to think of cause and effect as *If/Then* relationships. However, for the mass of nonlinear systems around us and in which we are embedded cause and effect relations change from *If/Then* to *If/Maybe* or to *If/It's Probable That.*

So, what's the explanation?

If, in building innovation ecosystems, we propose interventions that adjust the ecosystem's sub-systems and especially their connections, we need to know what the effects of these actions are likely to be. For example, in many cases, improving communications and shared goals among universities, incubators and accelerators, resulted in improved efficiency and 'fitness' of the innovation landscape (see Section 22 for more on the concept of fitness).

. . . .

147 "Explanandum" is not a familiar word to many of us, but quite a handy one. An explanandum is a phenomenon that needs to be explained, and its explanans is the explanation of that phenomenon.

Intervening in ecosystems

Donella Meadows, who wrote about world events from a systems point of view, created a list of places to intervene in a system. [148] These are, in *increasing* order of effectiveness:

12. Constants, parameters, numbers (such as subsidies, taxes, standards).

11. The sizes of buffers and other stabilizing stocks, relative to their flows.

10. The structure of material stocks and flows (such as transport networks, population age structures).

9. The lengths of delays, relative to the rate of system change.

8. The strength of negative feedback loops, relative to the impacts they are trying to correct against.

7. The gain around driving positive feedback loops.

6. The structure of information flows (who does and does not have access to information).

5. The rules of the system (such as incentives, punishments, constraints).

4. The power to add, change, evolve, or self-organize system structure

3. The goals of the system.

2. The mindset or paradigm out of which the system – its goals, structure, rules, delays, parameters – arises.

1. The power to transcend paradigms.

Most of these points are already covered in this book or will be.

When may causation be meaningful?

Causation is an example of many cases in this book where it's possible to keep digging further and further down into a topic, but we must stop somewhere. So the difficulty can be succinctly summarized thus: "A

148 http://donellameadows.org/archives/leverage-points-places-to-intervene-in-a-system/

regularity notion of causality can only be meaningfully defined for systems with linear interactions among their variables. For the vastly more important class of nonlinear systems, no such notion is likely to exist. …A linear system may be independent of context and of the other state variables. Not so in nonlinear systems…In sum, a notion of causation based on regularities can only be meaningful for areas of the state space in which the behavior of a nonlinear system is topologically equivalent to that of a linear system." [149] State space was introduced in Section 8. In the social sciences, for instance, it is common to assume linear interactions among variables in investigating causal relationships.

As discussed in Section 15, popular tools such as Logical Framework ('Logframe') analysis and the Balanced Scorecard which, because of their assumptions of linear cause and effect relations, may only be reliably used in areas of Rainforest state space which exhibit linear behavior ('farms' in Rainforest language).

Philosophers have been debating cause and effect for millennia. Aristotle identified four basic causes and stated that "we do not have knowledge of a thing until we have grasped its why, that is to say, its cause." David Hume's readers think about whether we are justified in using inductive reasoning to understand events. Ludwig Wittgenstein, with his usual ability to both enlighten and confuse, dropped in the idea that "outside logic everything is accidental."

Still another factor is: "Outcomes are determined not by single causes but by multiple causes, and these causes may, and usually do, interact in a non-additive fashion. In other words, the combined effect is not necessarily the sum of separate effects. It may be greater or less because factors can reinforce or cancel out each other in nonlinear ways. It should be noted that interactions are not confined to the second order. We can have higher-order interactions and interactions among interactions." [150]

A cause can be thought of as a change in a state variable. Because state variables in complex systems are not simple relations between variables and parameters, cause and effect will not be a simple relationship; this

....

149   Andreas Wagner, "Causality in Complex Systems," Biology and Philosophy 14, *Netherlands: Kluwer Academic Publishers* (1999), p 83.

150   "Complexity Theory and the Social Sciences" *Routledge* (1998), p 20.

is how the world works. In addition to a single event as a cause, multiple events contained within changes to entire systems may count as causes. For example, it has been found that most commercial aircraft crashes are due to several factors none of which alone would have caused the accident. There is frequently a time lag in causality, however small, before the effect of a certain input may be seen, such as a bathtub filling and overflowing, or frequently a long delay between developing prototypes, financing further R&D, setting up production systems, and final sales of products or systems in the market.

The notion of making predictions in complex systems is related to maybe the most important feature of complex systems – that of emergence/alescence. There's an inevitable trade off; emergence produces innovation but also reduces predictability. The steam engine and the internet were aslescent events and thus unpredictable.

Upward and Downward Causation in Complex Systems

"In philosophy, top-down causation (also called downward causation) is a causal relationship from higher levels of a system to lower-level parts of that system: for example, mental events acting to cause physical events." Some theories state that downward causation in biological systems always involves the environment but not by "direct causal effects from higher to lower levels of system organization." [151] This idea seems to be consistent with the proof in the previous Section 16, namely:

> The description of properties at a particular level of description offers *necessary but not sufficient* conditions to derive the description of properties at a higher level.

The higher level, although being materially related to the lower one cannot be simply deduced from the lower one for non-linear regions of state space. Using the language of philosophy, direct causation occurs when emergent higher level property causes the 'instantiation' of a lower level property.

Another effect is that signals from the environmental context tell the lower levels of an organization when there are incoming external (exogenous)

. . . .

151   Wikipedia, Downward Causation.

shocks to the system (Section 18) and re-organization of building blocks is needed. Thus, higher levels of organization can be the cause of effects at lower levels, e.g. emergence. These ideas are completely consistent with the statement that context is a trait of an innovation ecosystem (Section 10). Remember that traits are not necessarily *contained* in a complex building block.

Another result from Herbert Simon's investigations into the architecture of complexity (Section 10) proposed that complex systems are hierarchical with complex sub-systems within sub-complexes, which is also the basis of Buchler's description of complex systems. Simon added the evolutionary concept that non-hierarchical structures would be replaced with hierarchical structures over time because non-hierarchical structures are less robust and less able to respond efficiently to perturbations (Section 18).[152] In discussing Building Blocks (Section 10), and in the description of the characteristics of complex adaptive systems, it was emphasized that although innovation ecosystems can be both broken down into building blocks this did not imply that such systems are *reductionist* – that is, capable of ultimately being divided into simple non-interacting parts. A reminder: if this were so the resulting linear elements would not enable emergence and hence innovation. Explaining causation takes us back to non-reductionism. This led to the practical result of seeking *nearly decomposable* real systems.

---

152   Andrew Haldane, Prasanna Gai, and Sujit Kapadia, "Complexity, Concentration and Contagion," *Journal of Monetary Economics*, 58(5) (2011) p 2. "The modern financial system seems to have bucked this evolutionary trend. In recent years, it has become much more complex, concentrated and interconnected. In [Herbert] Simon's words, the financial system has become less modular, less hierarchical and thus less decomposable. In consequence, it became markedly more susceptible to systemic collapse. This sowed the seeds of the global financial crisis of 2007/8."

18

Sowing the Seeds of Resilience: Shocks to the System

· ·

Section Summary: For an innovation ecosystem to thrive it should be able to recover from shocks. Even if the organization is on a high 'fitness landscape' peak, a shock can dislodge it. It is known that multiple weak links can stabilize a network, stop perturbations spreading too far within a network, and allow fast recovery from shocks, leading to the emergence in complex systems of defenses against failure. In innovation ecosystems such defenses might be culture, knowledge, trust, diversity and openness, and various forms of physical and intellectual resources and capacity. Ashby's Law states if you are being attacked, having many defensive options is an effective strategy to manage the threat. Conversely, tightly controlled systems designed to operate efficiently under prevailing conditions, with too many strong links and too few weak ones, reduce communications and become unresponsive to external shocks leading to instability or even collapse. A feature of complex systems that small changes may give rise to disproportionally large consequence.

"All of the interesting systems (e.g. transportation, healthcare, power generation) are inherently and unavoidably hazardous by their own nature. The frequency of hazard exposure can sometimes be changed but the processes involved in the system are themselves intrinsically and irreducibly hazardous. It is the presence of these hazards that drives the creation of defenses against hazards that characterize these systems."

— How Complex Systems Fail: Being a Short Treatise on the Nature of Failure; How Failure is Evaluated; How Failure is Attributed to Proximate Cause; and the Resulting New Understanding of Patient Safety. Richard I. Cook, 2000.

We have seen that relating cause to effect in complex systems is inherently difficult. Therefore, if the future cannot be predicted let's try to be resilient when it arrives.

Innovation Ecosystem Resilience

For an innovation ecosystem to thrive it should be able to recover from shocks to the system (also referred to as 'perturbations,' a less melodramatic word than 'shocks'). Even if the organization is on a high 'fitness landscape' peak (Section 24), a shock can dislodge it.

In thinking about a complex innovation ecosystem as a network, it is known that multiple weak links can stabilize a network, stop the perturbation spreading too far within the network, and allow fast recovery from shocks. The government of an Asian country decided to privatize most government research facilities. Reasons for this bold action included the belief that resulting outcomes should include an improved reputation for efficiency and reliability of R&D problem solving for clients, access to partners for joint development R&D, access to short and long term project finance or subcontracting, and integration with the domestic innovation eco-system. Even with advanced warning, the decree was a sizeable perturbation to the government research institute system. Another example is when new technologies dislodge successful companies.

Dr. Richard Cook is a physician at the University of Chicago's Cognitive Technologies Laboratory[153] who has analyzed and written extensively about the failure of complex systems. Let's look into Dr. Cook's research from **How Complex Systems Fail**, cited on the Cognitive Technologies Laboratory website, to see what this tells us about how we should build innovation ecosystems which will withstand all the ills that complex adaptive systems are heir to.

First, we have to accept that complex systems are intrinsically hazardous systems and, as noted in the quote above, "It is the presence of these hazards that drives the creation of defenses against hazard that characterize these systems" – that is the emergence in complex systems of defenses against failure. In innovation ecosystems such defenses might be a robust

. . . .

153 http://www.ctlab.org/

innovation culture, knowledge, trust, diversity and openness, and various forms of physical and intellectual resources and capacity.

This brings to mind Ashby's Law, also known as the Law of Requisite Variety or the First Law of Cybernetics, which states that the variety in a network control system must be equal to, or larger than, the variety of the *perturbations* in the system in order to achieve control. In other words, if you are being attacked having many options is an effective strategy to manage the threat. Conversely, tightly controlled, not so agile, systems designed to operate efficiently under prevailing conditions, with too many strong links and too few weak ones, reduce communications and become unresponsive to external shocks, leading to instability or even collapse. It's worth remembering that it is also a feature of complex systems that small changes may give rise to disproportionally favorable or unfavorable large consequences.

This simply means that a flexible system is better able to deal with change than one which is apparently optimized (see Section 22) or has mostly strong links (Section 9). Furthermore, hierarchical systems tend to be more robust than non-hierarchical ones. In its original setting of control theory, Ashby's Law concerns controllers trying to keep a system stable. The more options the controller has, the better able the controller is to deal with fluctuations in the system. Variety of input can only be dealt with by variety of action. The processes of deciding what actions to take and how to implement and motivate them are introduced in Sections 24 and 25.

Perturbations or shocks disturb systems, whether in the network or building blocks perspectives. A system is stable if it shows a tendency to return to its original parameter values after a perturbation. The speed at which a network relaxes after a perturbation is an important measure (see discussion of RRA RAI in Section 19). Shocks may be harmful or helpful depending on context. Possibilities include:[154]

- Perturbations trigger innovations – change happens when people or organizations reach a threshold of opportunity or dissatisfaction.

- Ideas proliferate – after starting out in a single direction the process proliferates into multiple, divergent progressions.

....

154 Adapted from "Innovation Models," Tanaka Business School, Imperial College, London (2006).

- Setbacks frequently arise, plans are overoptimistic, commitments escalate, mistakes accumulate, and vicious cycles can develop.

- Restructuring of the innovating unit often occurs through external intervention, personnel changes, or other unexpected events.

- Top management plays a key role in sponsoring, criticizing, and shaping innovation.

- Criteria for success shift over time, differ between groups, and make innovation a political process.

These possibilities are consistent with the discussion of hierarchies in the previous Section.

In fact, perturbations are necessary for ecosystem networks to survive. We may think of this as an innovative ecosystem needing a constant flow of energy throughout its networks (see Section 20). Networks with many weak links allow perturbations to be dissipated and the system remains intact. Incidentally, some investigations indicate that the speed at which innovations move through networks increases when there are a "greater number of errors, experimentation, or unobserved payoff shocks in the system" (also called noise or variability, see Section 20).

Cook also suggests that "Human practitioners are the adaptable element of complex systems" in optimizing the system's productive capacity and reducing vulnerability to failure. We know that a feature of complex systems is adaptability. Adaptation may be catalyzed by early detection of changes in system performance and the provision of new paths to recover from perturbations and shocks; as we have seen, the presence of weak links helps here. Adaptation allows systems to be more resilient (the ability to bounce back) from internal confusion or external disturbances, subject to the always present constraints of finite time and resources.

We will end with another finding from Cook's investigations into accidents varying from aircraft crashes to errors in hospital patient care, namely "Hindsight biases post-accident assessments of human performance." This means that when the outcome of some event, or more likely a series of events, leading to an accident is known, an after-the-event analysis is frequently inaccurate or misleading. For ecosystems, this might be a serious disruption due to external shocks. Knowledge of the outcome reduces our ability to re-create stories from the viewpoint of those involved. For example, we might say of some event "surely they should have known that such and such a policy would lead to problems."

We have promoted the learning benefits of extracting re-usable knowledge components from descriptive cases, i.e. stories. So how could hindsight bias, in constructing an *ex post facto* narrative, affect the learning value of these re-usable knowledge facets? I'm not sure. It's worth thinking about, especially as stories are an important method of communication.

We can all think of many system examples of hazards and resilience ranging from the disintegration of communism in Europe to companies which were ill prepared for technological change, such as Kodak's slow response to digital photography. Cities and regions – clearly complex systems – have experienced the consequences of Ashby's Law where a major local employer or even an entire industry has declined, reduced employment due to improved production technologies, or moved elsewhere. An essential resource may be removed, a key person may leave, or a supportive regulation of law may change.

A perturbation changes, damages, or removes a building block in an innovation ecosystem complex through spoliative alescence. Spoliative alescence was defined in Section 11 and appears several times in this book and its definition repeated here:

Spoliative – there is a loss or attenuation or expiration of a complex that has prevailed in an existing complex system. Spoliative alescense suggests it's something to be avoided. This is not necessarily so; the result may be the emergence of new capabilities.

The resulting challenge is how can the results of the perturbation be repaired? How can the system adapt? Rearranging remaining building blocks is usually the place to begin because we know this can produce beneficial alescence/emergence.

19
Indicators and Fallibility

. . . .

Section Summary: There may be difficulties in understanding the degree of fallibility of an indicator, and cognitive traps which are characteristics of complex ecosystems which support innovation. Attempting to avoid such troubles by retreating into more ordered domains will only reduce access to new ideas and thus reduce innovative activity. Rainforest Scorecard indicators and leading indicators for disruptions in innovation ecosystems and resilience of innovation ecosystems are discussed. The Rate of Resource Appropriation (RAA) is a measure of the extent that people in the ecosystem organize to acquire improved resources when the environment presents improved access to necessary resources. That is, can we organize to acquire resources? The Rate of Accessible Information (RAI) is an opportunity tension which presumes a context in which a problem or opportunity implies the availability of additional resources. That is, can we organize to use resources?

"TITANIC SENDING OUT SIGNALS OF DISTRESS. WE HAVE STRUCK AN ICE BERG"

— From a telegram sent by the S.S. Olympic's Marconi radio operator.

On April 14, 1912, a decision was made based on an observation which proved to be fatally flawed. For ships sailing the North Atlantic routes at night in conditions where icebergs could be expected it was common practice to detect the presence of an iceberg from the white foam produced by waves splashing against the base of its dark bulk so that a decision could be made to steer the ship port or starboard to avoid a collision. Under the prevailing conditions of an ocean smooth as glass, the lookouts on the Titanic saw no such indicator and the rest is history. A more mundane example of an indicator is when we look for the presence of dark clouds in the sky to see if it's going to rain and whether to make the decision to take an umbrella when we venture out. As we know from experience it may not rain; indicators for rain or for the presence of icebergs are unreliable or 'fallible.'

What are indicators and why may they be fallible?

Leading indicators signal future events. An amber traffic light indicates the coming of the red light – we can depend on it. For a business, leading indicators may include falling sales for a product line, competitors introducing new technologies, or currency exchange rate shifts, among many others. The opposite of a leading indicator is a lagging indicator which follows an event. The unemployment rate is a commonly used lagging indicator for an economy in trouble.

Much more work is needed to develop leading indicators for innovation ecosystems, a difficult task because of what we have already said about causes and their effects. However, let us see how leading indicators can be developed for:

- Resilience of innovation ecosystems
- Imminent disruptions in innovation ecosystems

Indicators describe the observable states of a system. Ideally, indicators should be clearly defined, reproducible, understandable, and unambiguous. Because indicators may be fallible, these features are not always present.

We constantly, and unconsciously, make decisions (Section 24) based on multiple fallible indicators. Indicators are the critical step between identifying a problem and determining a possible practical solution in the appropriate problem context. Not recognizing this frequently leads to 'jump to' solutions; ones which may have worked elsewhere or ones whose unintended consequences have not been carefully thought through. This may happen because our personal networks are not sufficiently open to new thinking, typically due to the presence of too many strong links and insufficient weak or relevant links (Section 9).

As Kenneth R. Hammond points out in his fascinating book **Beyond Rationality: The Search for Wisdom in a Troubled Time**, "Because indicators vary considerably in their fallibility, from complete fallibility to perfect infallibility, whether the fallibility is due to random or deliberate factors, it is essential that we be able to measure their degree of fallibility so that we can discriminate among them. These measures simply indicate, in one form or another, how often an observable indicator is associated with an observable fact, condition, or event."[155]

Indicators related to technology commercialization outcomes for example will always have different levels of fallibility. The Association of University Technology Managers (AUTM) annual survey of US and Canadian universities and teaching hospitals focuses on a relatively small indicator set. I list these here so you can assess them for fallibility. Also note that one indicator may, in turn, depend on other indicators. Relations between indicators, measures, and metrics is a conversation for another time.

- Number of staff employed in technology transfer offices
- Research expenditure
- Legal expenditure and reimbursement
- Patent related activity
- Start-up activity
- Licenses and options
- License income

For many developing countries, or indeed developed ones, these indicators are not sufficient for capturing contract research, skills development, indirect benefits, or other outcome-related metrics. These metrics focus

155   Kenneth R. Hammond, "Beyond Rationality: The Search for Wisdom in a Troubled Time," *Oxford University Press* (2007), p 33.

mostly on outputs (numbers) rather than outcomes (impact). An excellent set of more comprehensive measurements has been proposed.[156]

In his collected essays, Isaac Levi has described seeking to identify potential answers to questions as a strategy to expand our personal body of knowledge ('knowledge corpus' or as we might say in this book 'knowledge complex'). However, Prof Levy notes that all knowledge expansion bears the risk of importing error, for example making predictions can lead to error. Refusing to expand our body of knowledge of course incurs no such risk whatsoever.[157] But, as has been previously stressed, alescense is the admittance of new traits into a complex; no risk would mean no admittance of new traits and would consequently mean no alescence and no innovation.

These ideas also re-appeared in **Research Technology Management**, a journal for R&D managers.[158] Searching to identify ideas for radical innovation, companies may frame their searches within the frame of existing markets or well understood applications. But, limiting peripheral vision in this way may not recognize discontinuous innovation shifts occurring. The article notes however, as did Levy, that reframing an existing cognitive frame presents a significant risk which not all of us may be willing to take. For example, a business may be reluctant to move from let's say using the Balanced Scorecard to embracing ways to create strategies in complex environments (Section 25).

- - - - - - - - - -

156 "Report to the CCST (Australia): Metrics for Research Commercialisation"

http://www.ausicom.com/filelib/PDF/ResearchLibrary/DEST%20Metrics%20CCST%20Group%202005.pdf

This report contains a detailed discussion of metrics with many examples. After examining current practice the report concluded that current metrics for commercialization of publicly funded research need to be extended to reflect a broader understanding of the commercial and economic benefits of research commercialization. Current metrics emphasize the commercialization of intellectual property through patents, licenses, and spin-out company formation. These data capture only a small portion of the commercially significant interactions that take place between the publicly funded research sector and private enterprise. The report proposes how metrics can be expanded.

157 Isaac Levi, "Decisions and Revisions: Philosophical essays on knowledge and value," *Cambridge University Press* (1984), p 118.

158 John Nicholas, Ann Ledwith & John Bessant, "Reframing the Search Space for Radical Innovation," *Research Technology Management* (March-April, 2013), p 27.

Difficulties in identifying the right problem, understanding the degree of an indicator's fallibility, and cognitive traps, are all characteristics of those complex ecosystems which support innovation. These are the ecosystems in which we will increasingly live and work. Attempting to avoid such troubles by retreating into more ordered domains will only reduce our access to new ideas and thus reduce innovative activity.

References to philosophers such as Levy, whose writings are somewhat dense with the language of symbolic logic, may seem disconnected from practical problems of innovation ecosystems. I have tried to show that it *is* valuable to expand our knowledge of these domains and that doing so increases our ability to make better practical decisions.

We can expect problem solving for, among others, innovation, technology commercialization, and new product development in Rainforests to throw up challenges, and that the fallibility of multiple fallible indicators is increased in complex spaces such as Rainforests. I will try and show how these challenges become less intimidating and how new and energizing good practices can be developed, once the *characteristics* of such complex spaces are understood.

The idea proposed here is that indicators, and especially leading indicators, can be developed for innovation ecosystems by interpreting measurements and narratives from the deployment of tools described in this book. Some tentative hypotheses to think about how we might test them are:

H1. The fallibility of multiple fallible indicators is reduced in spaces where the characteristics are a balance of strong and weak links, with a sufficient number of weak links for stability and enabling access to divergent opinions and experiences.

H2. The fallibility of multiple fallible indicators is reduced in spaces where the characteristics are high trust levels and low transaction costs.

H3. The fallibility of multiple fallible indicators is reduced in spaces where the characteristics are efficient boundary spanning organizations.

Note what connects H2 and H3 is not just transaction costs but transaction value.

H4. The fallibility of multiple fallible indicators is reduced in spaces where the characteristics are ordered domains focused on efficiency (such as 'farms'), where the whole is the sum of the parts, and where optimizing the parts optimizes the whole.

H5. The fallibility of multiple fallible indicators is increased in complex spaces (such as Rainforests) where the characteristics are such that small actions may significantly change the nature of the system. As a result, to optimize the whole system sub-optimal behavior of each of the components needs to be allowed (Section 22).

Rainforest Scorecard Indicators

Any pairing can be used, but suppose there are strong links between say the **Rainforest Scorecard** categories of Role Models and Culture to take one example (Rainforest Scorecard categories are Leadership; Frameworks, Infrastructure, and Policies; Resources; Activities and Engagements; Role Models; and Culture. Actually, a *direction* of influence or 'relevance' is also implied here (Section 9). Suppose there is one person who is a Role Model in the organization who has been responsible for creating much of the organization's present culture which is supporting innovation. This person is attracted elsewhere and leaves the organization (a perturbation), and thus the link is broken; the organization becomes unstable and no longer thrives as well as previously.

This suggests that having a high score on the Scorecard for Role Models is not only not sufficient, but might be detrimental. We need the Scorecard's long-form sub-questions to determine if, for example, there are only a few strong Role Models, or if there are multiple Role Models which are not too strongly linked to, in this case, Culture. In this latter case, losing any one Role Model should be easily absorbed. However, if there are only a few strong Role Models this is a warning indicator. The situation is the same as we already discussed in relation to strong leaders several times in this book. If an organization is not worried about external shocks then having a high score may be all they need to know. We also know that too many strong links in an organization can produce an echo chamber effect of not listening to outsiders.

Other Rainforest Scorecard Examples

The below is about scores from Scorecard *sub-questions* only (numbering from published version). We will have to add narrative results from Scorecard sub-questions to further develop indicators.

2.1.3 Knowledge leaders. Who are the key thought leaders in research and development?

What is their level of support for a knowledge-based innovation organization? How prominent are they in supporting new and breakthrough thinking that encourages innovation?

High scores may indicate that emergence of new ideas and procedures are likely to be encouraged (*Leading Indicator for Innovation Ecosystem Growth*).

Low scores may indicate that emergence will be constrained and the organization will remain too stable and unresponsive (*Leading Indicator for Innovation Ecosystem Growth and Resiliency*).

Leaders with mostly strong links and few weak links may not be responsive to internal or external shocks to the system (*Leading Indicator for Innovation Ecosystem Resilience*).

Note: Leadership which is strongly linked to other Scorecard categories can produce the echo chamber effect and stifle new thinking resulting in trending away from innovation. Having fewer strong and more weak links should correct this situation.

2.2.4 Trust. To what degree are leaders trusted by their constituencies? How do they foster this trust? What is leadership's commitment to ethical behavior?

High scores may indicate that leaders trust and are trusted, leading to increased transaction efficiency and a lowering of transaction costs (*Leading Indicator for Innovation Ecosystem Efficiency*).

Low scores may indicate a lack of trust leading to decreased transaction efficiency and higher transaction costs (*Leading Indicator for Innovation Ecosystem Efficiency*).

2.2.5 Diversity, Networks, and Openness. *What is the degree of diversity among organizational leadership? Experience? Culture? Gender? How is diversity among leadership promoted? To what degree do leaders' networks span different boundaries? Social boundaries across different levels of social class? Professional boundaries across different disciplines and professionals? Cultural boundaries across different organizations and cultures? To what degree do leaders possess a keystone ability? How open and accessible are leaders, in general?*

High scores may indicate that leaders are effective boundary spanners (*Leading Indicator for Innovation Ecosystem Growth*).

Low scores may indicate low boundary spanning ability (*Leading Indicator for Innovation Ecosystem Growth*).

Note: In social networks when two separate systems possess non-redundant, complementary, information, there is said to be a structural hole between them. This suggests that a broker or boundary spanner – such as an entrepreneur – who bridges the hole could gain competitive advantage by engaging in information arbitrage. Connecting networks of entrepreneurs with their own strong and weak links by bridging structural holes may provide access to valuable new ideas, alternative opinion and practice, early access to new opinion, and an ability to move ideas between groups where there is an advantage in doing so (Section 12).

Leading Indicator for Rapid Change in an Innovation Ecosystem

Research into complexity models of entrepreneurial innovation has identified two critical parameters which determine entrepreneurial innovation success.[159] These parameters can become metrics for measurement if a way to measure their values can be found – which may not be easy.

The ***Rate of Resource Appropriation (RRA)*** is a measure of the extent that people in the ecosystem organize to acquire improved resources when the

159   James K. Hazy Jeffery Goldstein, "Generative Conditions for Entrepreneurship: A Complexity Science Model," *Adelphi University School of Business Working Paper Series*: SB-WP-2010-05 (November, 2010).

environment presents improved access to necessary resources. That is, the potential to acquire additional resources generates a need for coordination that may not have previously been in place.

In other words, can we organize to *acquire* resources? As RRA increases beyond a certain threshold a bifurcation (a splitting of something into two parts), also known as a tipping point, may occur.

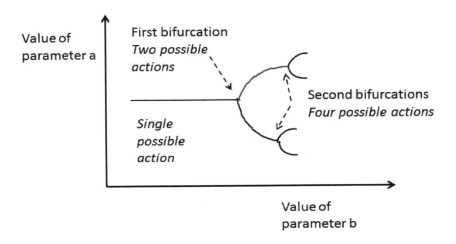

Figure 16. Bifurcations.

Bifurcations occur in complex adaptive systems such as Rainforests when controlling parameters (Section 8) reach a certain level. A bifurcation re-shapes state space as in figure 6. A bifurcation may be helpful of harmful or it may open up new alternatives to business-as-usual, because the system has moved to a new attractor, for example acting in greater collective unison rather than acting alone. A bifurcation may also cause a disruption in business processes that are painful or costly to repair. An example of a bifurcation from metallurgy is the buckling of a rod. If a straight rod is compressed by a small force its length shrinks but it remains straight. If the load is increased beyond a critical value, the rod starts to buckle. Another example is the sudden climate shift which changed a verdant region of North Africa into desert some 5000 years ago. To generalize, we can say that bifurcations are points in the slow evolution of a system at which qualitative changes or even sudden jumps of behavior occur.

In these cases the bifurcation is usually explained by the changes in a few parameters. Evidence from climate change suggests that these parameters can frequently be combined into a single control parameter for which there exists a critical control value. Exceeding this critical value leads to a qualitative change in a crucial system feature after prescribed times. Complex (Rainforest) ecosystems are functions of both parameters and sub-functions – because a complex system is made up of sub-complexes which in turn are made up of other sub-complexes and so on as we have seen.

The *Rate of Accessible Information (RAI)* is described as an adaptive or opportunity *tension* since it presumes a context in which a problem or opportunity implies the availability of additional resources. However, there is a gap between actual and potential performance because the availability of resources also depends upon the generation of innovative modes in which people and technology are organized.

To illustrate, when individuals or groups act *alone*, the environment might have a particular level of resource availability. At the same time however, there might be another, greater level of resource availability that is only exploitable if individuals act in *collective unison*, but this requires organizing.

That is, can we organize to *use resources*?

"RAI is a crucial parameter. Even in the case when there is a high level of RRA, entrepreneurial innovation may not ensue if the relevant informational differences to address the problem are too widely dispersed, or if they are not accessible to be parsed and processed in a cogent fashion. Only those groups with a capacity to gather and use the relevant information about opportunities can organize to exploit them." [160]

Measurement of the *change* of RRA and RIA over time is more important than measuring absolute values (assuming this is possible). A rapid change in RRA for example could be an *indicator* that a bifurcation is immanent. If a system has already passed a bifurcation point it may be too late for a correction. The transition cannot be reversed.

. . . .

160   James K. Hazy Jeffery Goldstein, "Generative Conditions for Entrepreneurship: A Complexity Science Model," *Adelphi University School of Business Working Paper Series*: SB-WP-2010-05 (November, 2010) p 11.

Rainforest Scorecard Measurement

The Rainforest Scorecard could measure RRA by analyzing Short and Long Form responses to existing questions. And/or by adding a question such as "How much do different units or individuals cooperate to find and access new resources?"

The Scorecard could measure RAI by analyzing Short and Long Form responses to existing questions, and/or by adding a question such as "Are cooperating groups in your organization able to organize to make effective use of relevant information?"

Another Scorecard question might be "Is useful information about how to best approach an opportunity held by individuals who are in a position to influence decisions about organizing a response to the opportunity?"

It is also known, again from climate change as one example, that a system which is close to a bifurcation transition tends to recover more slowly than normal from perturbations. We need a system to exhibit a fast recovery from perturbations and return to its original locally stable state to maintain resilience.

The Scorecard could assess this situation by asking a question such as "Has a slower recovery than usual been noticed when the system being assessed has been subjected to internal or external disturbances."

In all of these cases, the dynamics of the system are shown to slow down before the transition. "The values taken by RRA reflect the recognition that when the environment presents improved access to necessary resources including better sales or profits, these resources only become fully exploitable to the extent that people in the system organize to acquire them. In effect, the potential to acquire additional resources generates a need for coordination that was not previously forthcoming."[161] A slow recovery following a perturbation such as a bifurcation is a sign of a system having too few weak links to acquire additional resources.

....

161   James K. Hazy Jeffery Goldstein, "Generative Conditions for Entrepreneurship: A Complexity Science Model," *Adelphi University School of Business Working Paper Series*: SB-WP-2010-05 (November, 2010) p 11.

20

Noise and Housekeeping

Section Summary: Noise is a series of perturbations changing a network's state. For an innovation ecosystem, good noise keeps the system, and its people, alert by being connected to the larger environment and responsive to needed change. Not-so-good-noise is a perturbation which may disrupt a key link and cause a serious malfunction not by virtue of the magnitude of the perturbation but its type. For an innovation ecosystem no noise means isolation from its external environment. A completely static, isolated, network which is not connected to the environment will become dysfunctional. An apparently minor event could trigger a breakdown in trust between two critical organizations which in turn may create a damaging disruption. Another way of understanding the role of noise is that some form of energy is needed to prevent self-organizing complex innovation ecosystems from dropping into a dysfunctional, static, equilibrium state. 'Housekeeping heat' is the energy preventing non-equilibrium steady states from shifting to equilibrium where little innovation will occur. This process requires energy, which is input as perturbations or noise.

"Every body has their taste in noises as well as other matters; and sounds are quite innoxious, or most distressing, by their sort rather than their quantity."

— Persuasion, Jane Austen, 1817.

Jane Austen was describing the feelings of one of her characters on entering the town of Bath, England, "driving through the long course of streets …. amidst the dash of other carriages, the heavy rumble of carts and drays, the bawling of newsmen, muffin-men and milkmen, and the ceaseless clink of pattens [*the model of the required casting made in wood or metal is used to produce the mould cavity in sand*] .... these were noises which belonged to the winter pleasures; her spirits rose under their influence."

From Section 5 describing What is a Complex Adaptive System?

"The concept of equilibrium is fundamental to the physics of Isaac Newton, neoclassical economics, and much of social organization theory. In physics, equilibrium refers to a body or physical system at rest or in steady, un-accelerated, motion. The ball bearing on the rim of a bowl is a classic example of equilibrium; when released it quickly settles at the bottom of the bowl and that is that. In economics, equilibrium is a point of rest from which there is no external cause creating a tendency for any individual, firm, or market to change. Organizations or social systems are said to be in equilibrium when all influences on the system are canceled or balanced by others, resulting in an unchanging state of affairs. Nonlinearity, by contrast, is exhibited by systems that are far from equilibrium. If I try to balance a pencil by its point on my finger I must continually make small adjustments to keep the pencil balanced. The pencil is in unstable equilibrium (also called dynamic equilibrium)."

In Section 23 discussing diffusion, investigations will be cited indicating that the speed at which innovations move through networks increases when there are a "greater number of errors, experimentation, or unobserved payoff shocks in the system" – also called noise or variability. How does a network see noise? Noise is experienced as a series of perturbations changing the network's state. Picture kicking a network (the network view of an innovation ecosystem) and watching the resulting impact rippling through it. In Section 19 it was noted that the time to 'regain its composure,' so to speak, is a useful indicator.

Instinctively we think of noise as something to be eliminated but as you may have already realized this is not necessarily so. Some people find listening to music to be an aid to learning (we don't have space here to get into why music, and not just the kind we dislike, may be referred to as noise). As I write this book I feel comforted by sounds of the city coming through my open window; I find it difficult to work and learn in a completely silent environment. Likewise, for an innovation ecosystem, no noise means isolation from its external environment. A completely static, isolated, network which is not connected to the environment will become dysfunctional. We can probably all cite examples.

For an innovation ecosystem, good noise keeps the system, and the people and organizations comprising the system, alert by being connected to the larger environment and responsive to needed change. Not-so-good-noise is, for example, a perturbation which may disrupt a key link and cause a serious malfunction, not by virtue of the magnitude of the perturbation but its type. Some apparently minor event could trigger a breakdown in trust between two critical organizations, or between individuals within an organization, which in turn create a damaging disruption.

Another way of understanding the role of noise is that some form of energy is needed to prevent self-organizing complex innovation ecosystems, which as we know are in non-equilibrium states, from dropping into the dysfunctional, static, equilibrium state mentioned earlier. A non-equilibrium state is called a *steady state* system. Such states were discussed in Section 8.

To sum up: noise can be a friend or an enemy to innovation ecosystems depending on whether it keeps the system alert or damages critical parts of the network. Two centuries ago Jane Austin was right; it is the sort of noise that matters. Buchler did not use the term but put it this way: "In the ongoing history of a people or of an individual, the prevalence or continuing order seems to require numerous alescent stresses, from minor conflicts and ostensible discontinuities to crises and portents." [162]

Housekeeping heat (introduced In Section 8) is defined as the energy preventing non-equilibrium steady states from shifting to equilibrium. Self-organizing systems are subject to damage from perturbations. This process requires energy, which is input as perturbations or noise. System restructuring provides a continuous repair function, as it adapts to the system's environment. This noise is housekeeping heat. The term originates from thermodynamics when transitions occur between different non-equilibrium steady states. The total heat dissipated in such transitions into consists of two contributions, a housekeeping heat and an excess heat. The housekeeping heat is the one permanently dissipated while maintaining a non-equilibrium steady state at fixed external parameters. The excess heat is the one associated with a transition between different steady states. For transitions between equilibrium states, the housekeeping heat vanishes and the total heat reduces to the excess heat.

162   Justus Buchler, "Metaphysics of Natural Complexes," *Columbia University Press* (1966), p 58.

There are many examples of organizations which have set up web-based networks which begin with enthusiasm but fade away or Facebook pages which are abandoned for lack of housekeeping heat, some stimuli to keep the top spinning. Excessive external 'heat'– people working under pressure – can produce surprising achievements although to work that way constantly would be intolerable.

Writing about checks and balances in republics Niccolo Machiavelli (1469-1527) the Italian Renaissance politician and writer who is often called the founder of modern political science realized that, "Paradoxically, then, stability can be achieved only by permitting a degree of internal dissension and channeling these passions to constructive ends."[163]

There is no single definition of what constitutes housekeeping heat. It may have some common features between applications but will be different for each case. Assessing needs for the kind of support which housekeeping heat provides to a system (unit of analysis) can be investigated using questionnaires and client interviews. It is the perceptions of individuals and groups – human factors – that matter. This step will not only measure important variables, such as those in the Rainforest Scorecard, when future measurements are carried out, but also provide a baseline measurement from which changes over time will become apparent. Monitoring progress enables corrections to be made. Factors include: Capacity, Sustainability, Emergence, Decision Making, Strategies, Networks, Culture, Optimization and Non-optimization, Communication and Trust, among others. Necessary interventions and their cost may then be planned and executed.

. . . .

163   Miles J Unger, "Machiavelli: A Biography," *Simon & Shuster* (2011), p 267.

21

Reusing Knowledge: Create Early, Use Often

· ·

Section Summary: One type of innovation ecosystems building block is knowledge. Motivations for knowledge reuse in radical innovation situations are identified including: work processes that optimize exposure to diverse knowledge sources, use of extensive personal knowledge bases with both weak and strong links, culture within the project which encourages reuse, availability of flexible ways to assess the credibility of potentially reusable knowledge, ability to scan for fit, and ability to quickly determine malleability of reusable knowledge. There is unnecessary and frequent reinvention in creating technology commercialization systems, and innovation ecosystems, especially in developing and middle-income countries, resulting in unnecessarily high transaction costs and less than optimum efficiency. Reusable knowledge tools, analogous to more general reusable knowledge or learning objects, can reduce reinvention of known processes, lower transaction costs, and increase efficiency. This is important because more and more countries need, are attempting to build, ecosystems around technological innovation.

"Mankind are so much the same, in all times and places, that history informs us of nothing new or strange in this particular. Its chief use is only to discover the constant and universal principles of human nature."

— David Hume (1711–76), An Enquiry Concerning Human Understanding.

We have described innovation ecosystems as being made up of building blocks. One such is knowledge. We have also discussed how building blocks can be re-arranged and re-used, subject to contextual qualifiers. In

Section 13, Goldstone's argument was presented that if specific knowledge is too strongly tied a particular context or case then it will be difficult to apply it elsewhere. From our discussion of near decomposability of building blocks (Section 10) we know that when we try to decompose building blocks it's not always easy to identify which connections are important and which are less so. Similar difficulties arise when we try to remove extraneous details from a knowledge unit to expose the transferrable core.

Studies from NASA's Jet Propulsion Lab at Caltech[164] on the process of knowledge reuse in radical innovation situations found that users were motivated to reuse others' ideas if:

1. There exists a culture within the project which encourages malleable knowledge reuse.

2. Work processes optimize exposure to diverse knowledge sources.

3. There are efficient ways to locate, assess for credibility, determine malleability of reusable knowledge, and an ability to scan for fit.

4. They are confronted with an insurmountable problem with their current knowledge and resources.

5. They re-conceptualized the problem and approach to require an ambitious new perspective.

6. They believed that they can find useful existing ideas elsewhere.

7. They use extensive personal knowledge bases with both weak and strong ties

Are not these common challenges of developing supportive innovation ecosystems?

Aristotle (384-322 BC) in his **Nicomachean Ethics**, Book III, in writing about a person's voluntary and involuntary acts, distinguishes between (i) who is acting, (ii) what is the act, (iii) the circumstances of the act, (iv) the instrument or tool, (v) the aim of the action, and (vi) the manner of doing the act; for example quickly or slowly. The issues of actions will re-surface in Section 25 when the process of making a decision and acting on it will be analyzed.

Aristotle might have expressed the above 6 stages as (i) person seeking a solution to a problem, (ii) applying the solution, (iii) context, (iv) tools, (v) re-conceptualizing the problem, (vi) short-term or long-term impacts.

A handful of years ago a colleague of mine from the World Bank and I were having coffee in Washington DC with a visitor from South Africa. She was listing the skills and tools that she believed South Africa needed to improve technology transfer and commercialization, especially from universities. At that time I had never worked anywhere in Africa, but I was surprised by the realization that some 90% of the items in our visitor's list of wants and needs were identical to those of the countries in Eastern and Central Europe where I had more experience. Since then this commonality of needs has been verified by working in many other countries from Colombia to Kazakhstan.

In this section I argue that there is unnecessary and frequent reinvention in creating technology commercialization systems, and innovation ecosystems, especially in developing and middle-income countries, resulting in unnecessarily high transaction costs and less than optimum efficiency. Reusable knowledge tools, analogous to more general reusable knowledge or learning objects, can reduce reinvention of known processes, lower transaction costs, and increase efficiency. This is important because more and more developing countries are attempting to build ecosystems around technological innovation. To be clear, when I use the terms 'learning object' I mean a digital resource that can be reused to facilitate learning. In the application discussed here it's helpful to think of a learning object for what it *does* (an agent) rather than what it *is* (its properties).

Wait a moment. Am I going against what I was preaching in Section 13 about context and cutting and pasting solutions without paying attention to *context*? Solving the right problem is all about *context*. A problem comes with its own context trait. Apparently similar problems in different contexts may have very different solutions. Likewise, solutions have their own contexts. In Section 24 problem solving and decision making in Rainforest ecosystems will be discussed in some detail. Meanwhile, let's see if anything has changed.

The Lego™ block analogy is used frequently whenever knowledge is being collected and assembled from disparate resources. Mary Adams and Michael Oleksak in their 2010 book on intellectual capital[165] speak about using Lego™ blocks to build models of a 'knowledge factory' such as Google search or a medical device company. Alphabet blocks appeared as early as 1693 when philosopher John Locke pointed out that "dice and play-things, with the letters on them to teach children the alphabet by playing" would make learning to read a more enjoyable experience.

Wouldn't it be great if we could build supportive innovation ecosystems, by plugging Lego™ blocks of learning into each other? There is an appealing simplicity. Shortly, we will use some examples to see how far we might go, discuss the limitations of the Lego™ block analogy, and suggest that a reluctance to apply reusable knowledge tools to problems arises from a misunderstanding of the role of context. Actually, the Lego™ block idea has been discussed extensively by educators and found to be an imperfect analogy. The difficulty is that the analogy's assumption suggests any learning object should be combinable with any other learning object; this is not always the case as we shall see – because of our old acquaintance: *context*.

It's not that you cannot reuse these learning objects (we will call them 'tools' from now on) because contexts are never the same, it's that context must be fully understood. For example, the tool to decide whether to license a technology or create a spin-off company which will be introduced in Section 24 is largely context independent. By contrast, a tool for use in developing network intermediaries and how to plug network holes is highly context dependent. This is mostly because "... no two knowledge intermediaries are the same; their work is entirely context specific, which means that, while it is possible to draw general lessons as to how they [a user] *could* choose to act, it is impossible to develop a standard set of rules as to how they *should* act." [166] The authors also caution that (p. 135) ... "it

. . . .

165   Mary Adams and Michael Oleksak in their book "Intangible Capital: Putting knowledge to work in the 21ˢᵗ century organization" *Praeger* (2010), speak about using Lego™ blocks to build models of a knowledge factory such as Google search or a medical device company p 61 (see the video "You can grow like Google" http://www.youtube.com/watch?v=brBwWqiSg8g) 2009.

166   Harry Jones, *et al* "Knowledge Policy and Power in International Development: A Practical Guide." *The Policy Press* (2012) Chapter Five: Facilitation knowledge interaction, p 123.

will not be possible to anticipate how the information will be used [by those seeking solutions] and its likely effects." I have not been able to come up with any tool which is entirely context free.

A Harvard Business Review article discusses how incumbent consulting firms are being eroded by technology and other forces. The authors note that "...only a limited number of consulting jobs can be productized but that will change as consultants develop new intellectual property. New IP leads to new toolkits and frameworks, which in turn lead to further automation and technology products."[167] In this new business model, consultants may not always re-invent solutions; a move away from work where value depends primarily on "...consultants' judgment rather than repeatable processes." The authors call this "value-adding process business" in which "processes are usually repeatable and controllable."

. . . .

167 Clayton Christensen, Dina Wang, and Derek van Bever, "Consulting on the Cusp of Innovation" *HBR* (October 2013), pp. 106 – 114.

22
Should Everything be Optimized?

∙∙

Section Summary: To optimize an innovation ecosystem it is not necessary or sometimes even desirable, to optimize the operation of all its building blocks. Optimize means obtaining the best that can be achieved in the prevailing circumstances – within an existing context and constraints. Making cost/benefit decisions helps to decide what to optimize. Optimization is about a corporation wanting to optimize the generation of new products; a community wants to optimize new job creation; a university wants to optimize the creation of spin-off businesses, and so forth. Finding and visualizing fitness landscapes for innovation ecosystems is a measure of how well the ecosystem is functioning. What is meant by fitness will depend on the objectives of the system. Fitness could be measured as the number of sustainable new companies created over a certain period of time. Fitness could be a measure of a less tangible property such as an improved innovation culture or quality of life.

"The best is the enemy of good."

— Voltaire (1694 – 1778), Dictionnaire Philosophique.

It's natural for us to seek, if not perfection, at least to try and optimize impacts and outcomes. We may seek to optimize our individual happiness, live in communities which function efficiently, or optimize opportunities for our families. So, while wanting to optimize everything or all elements of our existence is a laudable sentiment it is in fact not always necessary, or desirable, thus saving effort and expense. This applies to the collection of building blocks which support effective innovation ecosystems.

So let's not strive for perfection but be happy with fit-for-purpose. Furthermore, optimized systems also have the disadvantage of tending to be fragile and unstable (see Section 18). Striving for exactitude may result in damping emergence.

In the classical, complicated systems view, an optimized system has all its sub-systems optimized. This is because a complicated system is the sum of its parts and changing one element has no unpredictable, effect on any of the other elements. The non-classical, complexity view differs; an optimized system may have sub-systems operating sub-optimally. "Just as it makes no sense to try and define an optimal rainforest, so it is with complex adaptive systems in general. For individual agents, the mechanisms of change aim at improvement rather than optimization." [168] This is why we should talk about 'effective practices' or 'good practices' rather than 'best practices.' The latter term suggests that there is a best practice which should be always followed. What practices are best will depend on the particular overall environment or circumstances.

When should optimization not be attempted?

'Optimize' is used rather than 'maximize.' By optimize we mean obtaining the best that can be achieved in the prevailing circumstances – within an existing context and constraints. Maximizing means obtaining the highest theorletical limit. In this section we will discuss making innovation ecosystem fitness as good as possible within a whole system, even though individual components may not be operating in the best way they can. Furthermore, what is being optimized under prevailing conditions may no longer be optimal if conditions change over time, which in complex systems they most assuredly will. Innovation ecosystem fitness is a measure of how well the ecosystem is functioning. What is meant by fitness will depend on the objectives of the system. For example, if an objective is to create new businesses, and thus economic development for a region (unit of analysis), then fitness could be measured as the number of sustainable new companies created over a certain period of time. Similarly, fitness could be a measure of jobs created or sustained, perhaps to absorb recent university graduates or those made redundant by declining industries.

· ·

168   John H. Holland, "Signals and Boundaries: Building Blocks for Complex Adaptive Systems," *MIT Press* (2012), p 57.

Fitness could be a measure of a less tangible property such as an improved innovation culture or quality of life.

In 2008 Neil F. Johnson wrote a mathematical paper together with Damien Challet with the intriguing title (well, maybe not for everyone) of **Optimal Combinations of Imperfect Objects.**[169] Their research shows how to make the best use of imperfect objects, such as defective analog and digital components, and how perfect, or near-perfect, devices can be constructed by taking combinations of such imperfect ones. Johnson, in his book **Simply Complexity** (mentioned in Section 9) tells the story of how sailors used to deduce the correct time at sea, before accurate clocks were invented, by taking a collection of imperfect timekeeping clocks on board and averaging their displayed times.

Optimizing the environment for electronics manufacturing is a set of complex problems where optimization should be carried out within a framework not in isolation. Again, subsystems do not need to be optimize in order to optimize the whole.

In a research paper [170] with colleagues, Johnson describes populations which might, for example, be competing for business. In a population with modest resources, low levels of interconnectivity increase the disparity between successful and unsuccessful agents. By contrast in a higher-resource population with low inter-connectivity, high-performing collective states can spontaneously arise in which nearly all agents are reasonably successful. At high levels of inter-connectivity, the overall population becomes fairer (i.e. smaller spread in success-rates) but less efficient (i.e. smaller mean success-rate) irrespective of the global resource level. These results were based on a fairly simple mathematical model and applying these findings to real world systems should be interpreted with caution.

Intellectual property regulations, intelligence about markets and their access, research and development, early-stage business funding, new product development experience, transaction costs, culture, trust, incubators, science parks, competence in the English language, are all, like

. . . .

169   Neil F. Johnson, "Optimal Combinations of Imperfect Objects," *cond-mat.stat-mech*, 14 May 2002.

170   S. Gourley, S.C. Choe, P.M. Hui, and N.F. Johnson, "Dynamical Interplay Between Local Connectivity and Global Competition in a Networked Population" http://arxiv.org/pdf/cond-mat/0401527.pdf

the sailor's clocks or the defective analog and digital components, imperfect objects. If the cost of perfecting each component, including transaction costs, becomes not worth the effort then stop, use for now; it's good enough,[171] improve later. If no advance towards improving an ecosystem component can be made at the present time, consider making the best of what you have, use for now, improve later.

This attitude follows the 'minimum viable product' (MVP) concept, namely a non-optimum product with just enough features to show to customers in order to receive process feedback (Section 14) at that stage of incomplete development. The MVP should reduce wasted engineering effort and get the product in the hands of early visionary customers. Rather than asking customers about their need for certain features – they will probably say "we want them all"– the MVP is about finding the smallest or simplest problem that the customer will pay to solve. There is not space here to go into more detail which may be found in many articles and books on the topic, most notably by Steve Blank. David Snowden in his work on complexity [172] believes we are all engaged in a constant process of sense-making; trying to find the best available explanation for something based on previous experience rather than the perfect logical solution. Snowden also contrasts classic efficiency-seeking organizational management with organic approaches that can optimize the effectiveness of a system even though its individual component agents may be operating sub-optimally.

Another way is to look at optimization as a cost/benefit decision. The **Rainforest Scorecard** shows strengths and weaknesses as a spider diagram. Optimization is about a corporation wanting to optimize the generation of new products; a community wants to optimize new job creation; a university wants to optimize the creation of spin-off businesses; and so forth. Each has a 'vision of success.' Remember, by optimize we mean obtaining the best that can be achieved in the prevailing circumstances – within an existing context and constraints. One such constraint will be limited human and financial resources.

. . . .

171   In early 1990s IP regulations in former Communist countries were not at all clear. Start-up companies with mostly IP assets had to decide of the existing regulations were good enough to balance future risk.

172   C. F. Kurtz D. J. Snowden "The new dynamics of strategy: Sense-making in a complex and complicated world." *IBM Systems Journal*, Vol 42, No 3 (2003).

That is, there is some factor to be optimized which depends, in our model, on the six Rainforest Scorecard variables of Leadership; Resources; Role Models; Culture; Resources; and Networks, Infrastructure, Policies, as shown in the Rainforest Radar. Do we always want to optimize these variables to produce success? I'm suggesting not.

The issue of optimizing complex non-linear systems is very difficult but extremely important – especially in manufacturing where optimization can make a difference between profit or loss. In fact, optimizing linear systems under constraints has been investigated for decades. In complex systems the usual way is to apply computer modeling and heuristics.

We need to distinguish between optimizing a complex system and optimizing this same system but *subject to constraints.* In the first case pushing all Rainforest Scorecard scores outward on the radar plot makes intuitive sense. When constraints are introduced the picture is different.

For example, a community wants to optimize new job creation. One constraint to achieving this objective is limited financial resources. A prudent community will not want to increase the Resources score (push the score outwards on the Radar plot), as an example, if the cost of developing Resources such as business attraction strategies (tax breaks, building a new technical college, building infrastructure, and so forth) exceeds revenues plus cost savings from having new employers in the region (taxes, reduced welfare spending, lower unemployment, and so forth). Further Resources should not be allocated in this case; money and time can be better spent increasing one of the other **Rainforest Scorecard** variables to improve the fitness of the whole system.

Optimization will always be subject to some constraint, for example, finite available cash. Another constraint could be could be the ratio: (reputation, or reputation risk)/(income or return on investment potential), a calculus used by some development banks. It can also be argued that without constraints invention and innovation are reduced. The requisite conditions for qualitative change never happen because the individuals in the system, being unconstrained, just maneuver around difficulties (Section 13).

It is assumed in the above example that increasing the Resources category score means spending more money or doing something that has a cost. This is a simplification which I don't think affects the explanation.

The conclusion is: in the highly unlikely event there are no constraints a 'balanced' radar plot is worth aiming for; when there are constraints present aiming for balance may not be a good practice.

Another case of where it does not make sense to necessarily optimize is illustrated in Figure 17. On the left, each of n nodes is linked to every other one; optimum connectivity. On the right, connecting nodes in a hierarchy produce fewer links. For very large numbers of nodes in extensive networks the number of links in a fully connected network become n^2 (Metcalfe's Law) and for hierarchies, it remains n. The importance of communications within innovation ecosystems has been emphasized so the trick is to achieve the right balance between over connecting people, for example, resulting in inefficient and slow decision making or gridlock, but not allowing too much authority to reside in a hierarchical few.

Fully connected nodes   **Nodes connected in a hierarchy**

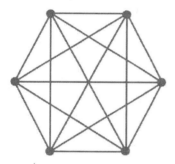 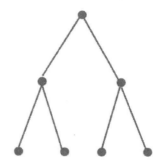

Number of links = n(n-1)/2   Number of links = 6
= 6x5/2 = 15

Figure 17. Connecting nodes.

Eric D. Beinhocker[173] notes that managers are often urged to flatten organizations and to de-layer hierarchies for improved efficiency. Amazon's CEO Jeff Bezos was reported as telling his management team to spend less

---

173   Eric D. Beinhocker "The Origin of Wealth: Evolution, Complexity, and the Radical Remaking of Economics," *Harvard Business School Press*, (2006), pp 154 - 159

time communicating "… small teams should get on with achieving things rather than constantly checking with one another."[174]

Beinhocker continues "… but counterintuitively hierarchy can serve to increase adaptability by reducing interdependencies and enabling an organization to reach a larger size before gridlock sets in." It should be noted that this argument is based on numbers of connections, not their relevancy or efficiency (Section 9). Not everyone needs to be copied by default on every e-mail, however the relevancy and efficiency of connections cannot be ignored. Returning to the **Rainforest Scorecard**, imagine that success depends on only two variables, say Resources and Culture. We could construct a 3 dimensional graph with the horizontal axes representing Resources and Culture. The vertical axis represents success or fitness measured according to some criteria. The result would look like a series of mountains and valleys (Figure 18).

Finally on this topic, another result from Herbert Simon's investigations into the architecture of complexity (Section 10) is that non-hierarchical structures would be replaced with hierarchical structures over time because non-hierarchical structures are less robust and less able to respond efficiently to perturbations.

Innovation ecosystem fitness

Seeking success means tweaking Resources and Culture to find the highest mountain peak. These are the optimum values; trying to maximize them will lead to a lower level, further down the mountain slope. The same holds for six variables, it's just hard to draw a picture. There will be 'minimum viable levels' of optimization for each category. In other words, in order to achieve an objective focused on 'economic growth' each category must be at least some minimum value.

---

174 Messiness celebrates the benefits that messiness has in our lives and why it should be embraced. Tim Harford, "Messy: How to be creative and resilient in a tidy-minded world," *Little, Brown* (2016), p 154.

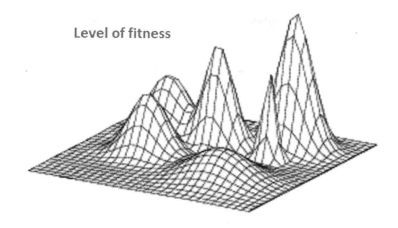

Level of fitness

Figure 18. Representation of a fitness landscape.

The same procedure can be carried out for any number of variables using computer simulations. Searching for optima across such a landscape is the generalized 'NK-model' which is described in detail later in this section.

The generalized NK-model[175] of fitness landscapes differentiates modularity from decomposability. Modular and decomposable systems are both composed of subsystems but in the former these subsystems are connected via interface standards (Section 10) while in the latter, subsystems are completely isolated. A decomposable system is in fact not one system, but a set of several smaller systems. This definition is important to remember because the term modularity is often used loosely to mean any kind of sub-division.

The *optimal level of modularity* in a system is that which minimizes the search time, in a computer simulation, required to globally optimize a system of building blocks within building blocks. Computer simulations find that this result is dependent on interface standards between building blocks not being changed. Studies show that this means optimization

. . . .

175   This introduction to the NK model is taken from Koen Frenken and Stefan Mendritzki, "Optimal modularity: A demonstration of the evolutionary advantage of modular architectures,", Working Paper 11.03, *Eindhoven Centre for Innovation Studies (ECIS), School of Innovation Sciences*, Eindhoven University of Technology (August 2010).

requires *hierarchical* [176] problem-solving, where interface standards are defined first, followed by building block properties within the constraints of the interface standards.

"Modular architectures offer evolutionary advantages because, in most instances, the effect of a change in a given module is confined to that module. Due to this localization of the effects of changes, the probability of a successful change is greatly enhanced. Each module can be improved *more or less* independently of other modules. For example, modular technologies allow for innovation in each module without the risk of creating malfunctions in other modules. Similarly, modular organisational designs allow different departments to change their operating routines without creating problematic side effects in other departments."[177]

We are not usually in a position to set up simulations of innovation ecosystem or experiment too much with them. How then can we apply these findings? Before answering, we need to consider what are standard interfaces? Let's look at an example from manufacturing.

As mentioned earlier (Section 10) Rick Dove in his book on agile enterprises,[178] introduced the concept of 'Response Ability' He notes that "The agile enterprise can respond to opportunities and threats with the immediacy and grace of a cat prowling its territory" and goes on to explain that 'response-able' components can be designed into enterprise ecosystems.

. . . .

176 Andrew Haldane, Prasanna Gai, and Sujit Kapadia, "Complexity, Concentration and Contagion." *Journal of Monetary Economics*, 58(5) (2011) p 453. "Simon reached the powerful conclusion that even complex systems tended to exhibit a basic simplicity. Systems could be arranged in a natural hierarchy, comprising nested sub-structures. Non-hierarchical structures would tend to be deselected over time because of their inefficiency or lack of robustness relative to simpler, hierarchical structures. Whether the complex system was biological, physical, or social, it would be a case of survival of the simplest….The modern financial system seems to have bucked this evolutionary trend. In recent years, it has become much more complex, concentrated and interconnected. In Simon's words, the financial system has become less modular, less hierarchical and thus less decomposable. In consequence, it became markedly more susceptible to systemic collapse. This sowed the seeds of the global financial crisis of 2007/8.

177 Koen Frenken and Stefan Mendritzki, "Optimal modularity: A demonstration of the evolutionary advantage of modular architectures,", Working Paper 11.03, *Eindhoven Centre for Innovation Studies (ECIS), School of Innovation Sciences*, Eindhoven University of Technology (August 2010), p 4.

178 R. Dove, "Response Ability: The Language, Structure, and Culture of the Agile Enterprise," *John Wiley and Sons, Inc.* (2001).

These ideas are closely related to those of re-usable components within a framework. See Section 21 for more on these issues.

While much of the focus of agility has been in manufacturing and software development, let's see if any of the response-able components concepts illuminate how innovation ecosystems may become agile – an ability to adapt rapidly to system environment changes – and what this has to do with standard interfaces. After all, we have already introduced the idea of self-organization in a complex adaptive system, which implies agility. How can analyzing agile manufacturing systems help us in building agile innovation ecosystems able to self-organize and respond effectively to external shocks (Section 18)?

The gardener's dilemma

A colleague posed this question:

1. We know that if everyone is an entrepreneur, a society will not function.

2. We know that if everyone is a producer, a society will wither.

3. Thus, is it possible to determine the exact proportion of innovators versus producers to maximize the productivity of an ecosystem?

This question is, I think, also about the possibility of adjusting all the various elements, variables, and parameters so that the ecosystem optimizes its outcomes, measured perhaps by key performance indicators (KPIs). These elements may be universities, technology commercialization systems, public sector financing funds, or culture for example. In their paper[179] researchers David G. Post and David R. Johnson present a possible method of finding optimal configurations of elements in complex adaptive systems. The authors pose the Gardener's Dilemma: how can a gardener find the best or at least a good configuration of a collection of plants whose overall 'fitness' (for example total yield) is dependent upon the behavior of all the other plants? You may begin to see how the garden

. . . .

179   David G. Post and David R. Johnson, "Chaos prevailing on every continent: Towards a new theory of decentralized decision-making in complex systems." http://www.temple.edu/lawschool/dpost/chaos/chaos.htm

is an analogy for an innovation ecosystem. We shall see shortly if this analogy is helpful.

In this imaginary garden there are plants of different species. The behavior of the plants is dependent upon the behavior of many others within the garden's ecosystem. The gardener would like to obtain the most luxuriant overall growth. The gardener must decide for each individual plant: should it be pruned or not? How can the best combination of pruned and un-pruned plants be created that will produce the greatest yield for the whole garden?

As always, we need to make some assumptions to try to make the problem tractable which for this garden are:

1. The relationship between an individual plant's pruned or unpruned state and its growth is different for each plant. For some plants growth will be increased by pruning, for others pruning will reduce their growth.

2. Each individual plant's growth can be affected by the growth of other plants, for example as one plant grows it might block sunlight reaching another plant that needs it. These are sometimes called these *spillover effects* although I prefer to call them *interactions*.

Even with such simplifying assumptions, it turns out that this problem, and many similar ones, are 'computationally intractable' or in other words incapable of true solutions by any known analytical methods, although a gardener may perhaps solve the problems *intuitively*. A little thought may convince us why this is the case for our garden. Suppose there are only three plants each of which may be pruned (we will call this state 0) or unpruned (we will call this state 1). We can use the tree diagram below to help figure that 8 possible configurations exist, namely 2 x 2 x 2 = 2^3.

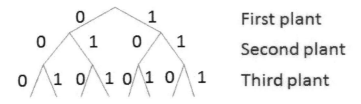

Figure 19. Plant configurations.

A little further arithmetic will show for 4 plants there are 16 possible configurations, namely 2 x 2 x 2 x 2 = 2^4 and so on. To generalize this pattern we can say that in any system with N elements, each of which can take one of S possible states, there are S^N different system configurations. This S^N can rapidly become a very large number. For 10 plants the number of configurations to be tried is already 1,024. Hard work for the gardener!

Is this gardening knowledge of any *practical* use for those of us developing optimal innovation ecosystems? If this ecosystem analogy is computationally intractable, why am I wasting your time discussing it? Stay with me for just another moment and I will demonstrate its practical use – but first a few more research results.

Patching

When a problem cannot be solved by mathematical analysis, computer modeling may help. Even greatly oversimplified models can be used as long as their simplifying assumptions are not forgotten when applying the results to the real world. Stuart Kauffman and his colleagues developed a family of computer models and problem-solving algorithms for complex interconnected systems known as 'NK models' to study various forms of the Gardener's Dilemma in, for example, evolutionary biology and cyberspace law. We don't have space for details (which are in Johnson and Post's publication) but essentially the method consists of modeling interactions between ecosystem elements. The elements in the garden ecosystem are sub-divided into any number of non-overlapping but interacting self-optimizing parts called 'patches,' like a patchwork quilt.

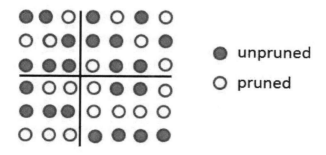

Figure 20. Patches.

To quote Post and Johnson "The result is a fairly remarkable one: It is by no means obvious that the highest aggregate fitness of the system will be achieved if it is broken into quilt patches, each of which tries to maximize its own fitness regardless of the effects on surrounding patches. Yet this is true. *It can be a very good idea, if a problem is complex and full of conflicting constraints, to break it into patches, and let each patch try to optimize, such that all patches co-evolve with one another.*"

The 'adaptive walk' is a trial-and-error algorithm for finding the fitness optima in this kind of system. The overall, aggregate, system fitness is calculated for the initial configuration. Then, a randomly-selected element is 'flipped' from state 0 to 1 or 1 to 0 and overall system fitness recalculated. Remember that this flip will affect the fitness contribution of all elements to which the flipped element is linked. If system fitness following the flip is higher than before the flip then this state is preserved. If the system fitness following the flip is lower than before then the flip is reversed to its original state. This adaptive walk procedure is the repeated until a final optimum fitness state is found.

If the system's elements have no interactions the adaptive walk algorithm is efficient at finding the highest point on the fitness landscape. No interactions mean a fully reductionist system which, as we have seen, is not a good model for innovation ecosystems. In such systems, on average, it will take no more than N/2 flips to find the optimal configuration.

In systems with substantial interactions between elements the adaptive walk algorithm does not work so well and can become stuck in local sub-optimal fitness peaks and not get to the complete system's 'top of the mountain.' In this picture imagine you are climbing among a mountainous landscape and your mission is to reach the top of the highest mountain and you reach one peak only to see another which is higher. Your only option is to descend before tackling the next peak. This is what the adaptive walk algorithm must do. Why patching can be effective is not completely clear; it seems to oppose the finding that it is not necessary to optimize individual systems element to optimize the whole. Post and Johnson suggest it may be that it reduces the tendency of the adaptive walk to become stuck on these suboptimal local fitness peaks, rather like a conversation or argument which becomes stuck in a counterproductive theme.

In Section 25 these ideas of patching and flipping will be applied to creating strategies under uncertain and unpredictable innovation ecosystem environments. It will be seen that the patching concept which may at first seem rather theoretical has a critical role to play. One example can explain the benefits of decentralized decision making. Post and Johnson discuss the case of (US) 'Federalism'[180] but we will apply similar arguments to innovation ecosystems. Decentralized decision making means decision making authority is distributed throughout a larger group of people, typically within a large organization, rather than centralized decision making being the norm.

This is because knowledge of local conditions can be more effectively transferred and incorporated into actions of higher level decision makers. Interactions within these sub-system patches through communication or the movement of individuals help to transfer decision making knowledge. This all sounds similar to hierarchies (Section 16) and in Section 25 we will combine both pictures.

Higher intensity of interactions between patches may make decentralized decision making less effective because, as we saw when explaining the theory, the adaptive walk algorithm does not work so well and can become stuck in local sub-optimal fitness peaks and not reach optimum system fitness. However, overall patching is considered to be effective as it "allows local configurations to change in ways that may be sub-optimal in the short term from the standpoint of the system as a whole, driving the system *down* from suboptimal foothills in fitness space; but these moves alter the environment of other local units, generating reactions and adjustments by these adversely affected 'neighbors' and creating a pull and tug among conflicting rule sets that ultimately allows the overall matrix to achieve a better solution over the course of a large number of moves." [181] Again, in Section 26 we will see how this image becomes reality. The same cost/benefit considerations which apply to the desirability of optimizing sub-systems are applicable to patch optimization. This is a practical constraint.

. . . .

180   Federalism is a form of government which combines a division of powers between a general
      government and regional governments in a single political system.

181   David G. Post and David R. Johnson, "Chaos prevailing on every continent: Towards a new
      theory of decentralized decision-making in complex systems," http://www.temple.edu/
      lawschool/dpost/chaos/chaos.htm

A typical innovation ecosystem has N physical elements (building blocks – traits) in states (S) such as universities and research institutes with their technology transfer offices (TTOs), new business incubators and accelerators, some form of central support organization to assist TTOs with issues such as market intelligence and so forth, financing programs such as early-stage R&D grants and seed and venture funds, economic development organizations, a science and technology park, contract research organizations, and sometimes miscellaneous organizations which were formed for different times but are still functioning. In addition, we have seen that innovation ecosystems contain traits such as culture, role models, and leadership. All these can certainly exist in many states so N will be much larger than 2 as in our innovation ecosystem garden.

Applying what we have just learned, it is an effective practice to divide these ecosystems into patches which might have similar features, for example, possible patch groupings in a typical innovation ecosystem could be:

Universities and research institutes technology transfer offices (TTOs) Central, regional, support organization to assist TTOs	Early-stage R&D grants, seed and venture funds New business incubators and accelerators
Contract research organizations Science and technology parks	Economic development organizations Miscellaneous organizations which were formed for different time
Culture Role models Mentors	Networks Feedback Hierarchies

Table 7. Some possible patches.

Having the elements trying to maximize their fitness within their patches improves trust and communications between them, and as a result increases transaction efficiently. Furthermore, this should break down the rigid hierarchical structure from which some ecosystems suffer. Although, hierarchies are not all bad as discussed earlier where a hierarchy was both the cause of a problem but also its solution. Other practical applications of the Gardener's Dilemma can be found, such as explaining the familiar S-shaped curves of technology growth and stabilization, supply chain management, and generally allowing sub-systems to make timely independent decisions which will optimize objectives under constraints imposed by the whole system.

The reader may want to try some patching and flipping algorithm 'thought experiments'[182] ('what if' scenarios) on existing or planned innovation ecosystems. As Philip E. Auerswald[183] points out "Entrepreneurs and members of entrepreneurial communities are not potted plants" and care needs to be taken in segmenting communities or strategies especially where participants may have multiple roles and memberships in groups. Patching may also benefit from the property of a complex adaptive system for small changes to have large impacts.

Let's look at a simple case of patching which many of us may be familiar with but have not thought of it as an example of patching. In a project to design and implement an innovation ecosystem one of the first stages (I'm simplifying a bit here) was to have a group decision making session where people were assigned to a series of separate tables to assure a mix of affiliations and work experience at each table. This method will be familiar to many of us who have attended training programs and workshops. After discussion of assigned themes – usually within a tight time limit – a representative of each table presents conclusions from their table's group; an example of distributed decision making.

Later in the meeting session in order to address a set of combined and new themes arising from extensive discussion among the whole group, the groups of tables were labeled with a set of revised themes. In this case, the themes were: creating an innovation culture; funding for start-up companies; developing role models; retaining talent in the region; and promoting the region as a magnet for innovative companies. Now, instead of being assigned to tables participants were asked to 'vote with their feet,' that is joining a table where they have the most knowledge or interest in contributing. New patching and sets of discussions at each table produce a set of refined results thus improving overall landscape fitness. Thus, patching is

182 The possibility should be investigated of carrying out small interventions or changes to test ideas where these will not damage the ecosystem – sometimes called 'fail-safe' experiments.

183 Philip E. Auerswald, "Enabling Entrepreneurial Ecosystems: Insights from Ecology to Inform Effective Entrepreneurship Policy," *Ewing Marion Kauffman Foundation* (October 2015), p 1.

similar to a sorting algorithm where for example these initial results from tables are first sorted into an initial set of patches or groupings. This will usually produce a reasonable but not optimum set, and a second sort is carried out. Repeating this procedure 3 or 4 times will typically produce working optimal final patches or groupings.

Finally, it appears that distributed decision making systems are robust in absorbing shocks to the system (Section 18) probably because if one sub-system is damaged the others will continue functioning; the same effect as in networks with multiple hub and spoke structures. There are many examples of distributed partnerships and distributed manufacturing in the aerospace, automotive, and information technology industries.

23

Thinking about Diffusion

Section Summary: Innovations often spread through social networks as we respond to what our 'friends' are doing. However, in looking at how diffusion of information occurs there is a difficulty; did my behavior influence yours or do you and I behave similarly because we have common characteristics or interests? Although the probability of influence is significantly higher for those that interact frequently, most contagion occurs along weak links, which are more abundant. Research has discovered that diffusion is fast whenever the payoff gain from the innovation is sufficiently high. For example, a technology may be adopted more quickly if the benefit payoffs are substantial. The speed of innovation diffusion increases when there are a greater number of errors, experimentation, or unobserved payoff shocks in the system. Experimenting with different ways in which the building block components of the ecosystem communicate and work with each other, bringing people together in new settings, and encourage unstructured events, can all positively change the relationship-space culture in an innovation ecosystem.

"Patience is the art of concealing your impatience."

— Guy Kawasaki, marketing specialist, author, and Silicon Valley venture capitalist.

It affects nearly all of us, whether we are drumming our fingers in front of the microwave oven telling it to hurry up, wanting ever faster internet connections, or finding our attention spans are getting shorter – we have a need for speed.

In Section 10 we discussed agile innovation ecosystems and suggested that there is a need for rapid diffusion, spread, or flow, of information (knowledge, learning, innovations) if such networks are to be responsive. It is to this feature we shall turn our attention with two *caveats*.

First, the results presented here are from several different contexts and there is no certainty that they will be directly relevant to innovation ecosystems. However, they should at least catalyze our thinking. Second, all these results are based on modeling information flow along links between nodes connected in networks. There are ongoing investigations among researchers as to just how the structure, or topology, of a network of nodes and links influences information flow. Past research has also investigated the type of network structure, such as clustering, which enables rapid diffusion and social learning, and what features can block social learning. Investigations carried out at Oxford University and MIT derived results that are independent of a network's structure and size. We will get to their results in a moment. Further study is needed on how matching of signals between innovation system building blocks affects diffusion and learning which was introduced in Section 11. An alternate, and less researched, model is that of fluid flow through pipes as an analogy for knowledge flow. It should be noted that it is not easy to measure flow directly but rather by the effects of interactions caused by the flow; that is, have I have acquired some new knowledge that somehow flowed to me?

In other recent work, a team of researchers at Facebook and the University of Michigan have also been looking into information diffusion among over 200 million Facebook users.[184] Let's look at some of the conclusions from these investigations about factors influencing information flow. Some appear to be common sense, others possibly less so. Both groups note that innovations often spread through social networks as we respond to what our 'friends' are doing. However, in looking at how diffusion of information occurs there is a difficulty; did my behavior influence yours or do you and I behave similarly because we have common characteristics or interests (i.e. similar peer behavior)?

It would seem to make sense that if I only interact infrequently with others, meaning that my links are weak and there is not much similarity between myself and these weakly linked individuals, then not much

----

184 Eytan Bakshy, Cameron Marlow, Itamar Rosenn, Lada Adamic, "Role of Social Networks in Information Diffusion." International World Wide Web Conference Committee (2012). http://www.scribd.com/doc/78445521/Role-of-Social-Networks-in-Information-Diffusion

volume of information is likely to flow through these weak links. On the other hand, information flow should be strong between me and those people with whom I frequently interact; my strong links or strongly clustered ones. Strong links, weak links, and relevant links, and their role in stabilizing networks were discussed in Section 9. The Facebook studies have surfaced results demonstrating the function of strong and weak links in the diffusion of information.

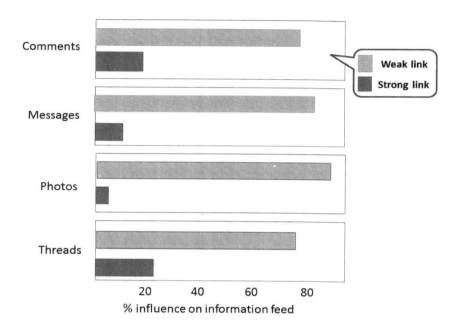

Figure 21. Social Networks and Links Information Diffusion.

To quote the Facebook study report: "Weak ties are collectively more influential ties. Although the probability of influence is significantly higher for those that interact frequently, most contagion occurs along weak ties, which are more abundant." Used in this context, 'contagion' means the spread of information or ideas from person to person.[185] These results extend the classic studies of weak links by Mark Granovetter described in Section 9.

185 Influences may be correlative or *contextual* (depends on exogenous characteristics of a group). W. Brian Arthur, "Complexity and the Economy," *Oxford University Press* (2015), p 100.

The MIT/Oxford studies[186] discovered that diffusion is fast whenever the payoff gain from the innovation is sufficiently high; greater payoffs produce a greater speed of diffusion. For example, a technology may be adopted more quickly if the benefit payoffs are substantial. This seems intuitive.

Less obvious is another finding that the speed of innovation diffusion increases when there are a "greater number of errors, experimentation, or unobserved payoff shocks in the system" (also called noise or variability). This may explain the remarkable results which are sometimes achieved in some circumstances by people working under unexpected crisis conditions. It also suggests that 'amplifying actions' such as experiments and collective action should be encouraged to produce novelty and new emergent order.[187] These amplifying actions result from the fact that in complex systems small changes can be amplified through positive feedback producing much more significant changes to other parts of the system because of the system's nonlinearity. The result may be novel as a move to a new attractor occurs (Figure 6). Allowing, or encouraging, such amplifying actions in innovation ecosystems can be beneficial. Experimenting with different ways in which the building block components of the ecosystem communicate and work with each other, bringing people together in new settings, encouraging unstructured events, can all positively change the relationship-space culture in an innovation ecosystem. Finally, we know it is the connections between the individual innovation ecosystem components which are critical; non-existent or non-functioning links can destroy communication and knowledge flow without adequate redundancy built in.

How seriously should we take all these findings? How do they relate to the Rainforest model and complex adaptive innovation ecosystems? I wonder if a paradox is emerging. Might designing lean and agile ecosystems, in fact, discourage adequate experimentation and learning from mistakes, thus defeating their very purpose? We need "time for reflection, meaning that the necessary focus on meeting immediate targets does not undercut what should be a long-term commitment to patient analysis and creative

....

186   Gabriel E. Kreindlera, H. Peyton Young, "Rapid innovation diffusion in social networks" (2014). http://www.econ2.jhu.edu/people/young/KreindlerYoung.pdf

187   Lichtenstein, B.B. & Plowman, D.A., "The leadership of emergence: A complex systems leadership theory of emergence at successive organizational levels," *The Leadership Quarterly*, vol. 20, no. 4 (2009), pp. 617-630.

thinking."[188] Could rapid diffusion in innovation ecosystem networks be increased if we curb our impatience?

What might this mean for the popular hackathon?[189] "Arguably the biggest disadvantage of hackathons is also their draw. They're often willfully divorced from reality. ... Throw a bunch of diverse teams together in a novel setting. Provide them with more playful materials than they'd normally encounter. Then put them to work on a worthy challenge where, at least at first, no ideas are rejected. This can have some real upsides; exposing people to different perspectives is a surefire way to get them to look at problems in a new light. New spaces and unusual materials can stimulate creativity." The authors go on to give their opinion that solving a problem in a vacuum, however, is a waste of time and money and continue "When hackathon participants don't have the right contextual knowledge and technical expertise, they tend to come up with ideas that are neither feasible nor inventive. Worse yet, these flaws tend to go unrecognized in the limited time that the events take place." This sentiment, not shared by all hackathon researchers, resonates with what is in this book about the importance of context. In the short time allotted to most hackathons it's typically not possible to reveal all contextual issues. Furthermore, because of time constraints, wicked non-linear problems (Section 15) will have to be reduced to complicated linear ones to allow any kind of solution, which is likely divorced from reality.

. . . .

188 "Learning and Results in World Bank Operations: How the Bank Learns," (2014), p 60. http://documents.worldbank.org/curated/en/589531468338471638/text/894210WP0learn0Box385279B00PUBLIC01.txt

189 "Why Hackathons are bad for Innovation," *Fast Company* (December 9, 2015). Anjali Sastry, a senior lecturer at MIT Sloan School of Management, and Kara Penn, co-founder and principal consultant at Mission Spark, are the authors of "Fail Better: Design Smart Mistakes and Succeed Sooner," *Harvard Business Review (2014)*.

24

Practical Reasoning: Decision Making and Solving the Right Problem

Section Summary: Making decisions in complex innovation ecosystems. Stating that there is a problem means being unable to get from a present system state to a desired one by carrying out some actions. If an action can be taken which transforms the present state to the desired one, then the problem has been solved. Relating decision making to action, or to a series of actions, based on these decisions, goes far beyond explaining how a system state came to be, but produces interventions to change the present system state to a future desired state through reasoned actions. Steps to addressing a problem are: identifying the right problem, which might not be obvious, and its context unclear; making a decision about what might be an effective solution in the present context; and taking actions to apply the solution. Non-deductive reasoning is close to the real world where decision makers have biases and subconscious feelings, and may be driven by extra-rational motives.

"Yes, I have a turn both for observation and for deduction. The theories which I have expressed there, and which appear to you to be so chimerical are really extremely practical – so practical that I depend upon them for my bread and cheese."

— Sir Arthur Conan Doyle, *Sherlock Holmes. The Sign of Four, Chapter 2: The Science of Deduction. 1890.*

In this section we attempt is to use what we have learned so far and apply this knowledge to solving problems and making decisions in complex innovation ecosystems. This cannot be a section on problem solving in general. There are many excellent books and journals on this topic as well as methodologies such as TRIZ. [190] The following is restricted to issues of problem solving in Rainforest system state spaces, where wicked problems roam, and where causal relationships may be murky.

Problems and actions

To begin let's define what we mean by a problem in the context of this book. A problem exists if we are unable to get from a present system state to the desired one by carrying out some action or actions. Identifying a problem is often intuitive (more on intuition later in this Section). If an action or actions can be taken which transforms the present state to the desired one, then the problem has been solved. Whenever an action takes place it means that a decision has been made to carry out that action. Problem solving always involves decision making and actions (see Section 25 for more on actions).

Relating decision making to action, or a series of actions, based on these decisions goes far beyond explaining how a system state came to be, but produces interventions to change the present system state to a future desired state through reasoned actions.

In Rainforest ecosystems decision making and decision making authority is likely to be *decentralized* and should be carried out at the most effective *level* in a hierarchy, as discussed in Section 16. This usually means trying to make decisions at the level where there are the most knowledgeable or experienced people, or where most are affected. Such an approach also provides better feedback to decision makers at other levels in the hierarchy as a basis for proposed interventions. In the case cited in Section 16, critical knowledge resided at a lower level but this will not always be the case.

An ODI report was quoted earlier (Section 16) "Complexity science highlights how there is often untapped potential for change in lower-level decision-making units, and for groups of actors not linked by formal hierarchies to 'self-organise' and work coherently towards a common goal."

190 "What is TRIZ?" TRIZ Journal, https://triz-journal.com/triz-what-is-triz/ TRIZ is a problem solving method based on logic and data, *not* intuition.

How does problem solving in less structured Rainforest ecosystems differ from problem solving in more structured environments? What Rainforest elements impact on problem solving? Is identifying problems and possible solutions easier or harder in the Rainforest? In selecting a possible solution to a problem we may first use multiple indicators to select one or more possible solutions. Solutions requires the new thinking discussed in this Section.

If we are to have any hope of solving at least some parts of wicked problems (Section 15) where logic cannot necessarily be applied and where there are no clear causal relations between where we are and where we want to be it will be necessary to search for non-deductive ways of reasoning and decision making. Furthermore, we will have to make decisions in spaces where indicators may be fallible (Section 19). In an innovation ecosystem, a problem might be identified such as a low level of entrepreneurship in a community compared to similar communities. This problem will be solved if the level of entrepreneurship can be raised to what is regarded as the desired higher level (however measured).

Some researchers have noted that decision making by a person or groups of people is a form of self-organization, a property of Rainforests. That is:

1. Self-organization is the process of evaluating the probabilities of system states in the search for the most stable states.

2. Decision making is the process of evaluating the probabilities of decision prospects in the search for the most preferable prospect.[191]

Decision making is also importantly related to the presence of hierarchies. Recognizing the presence of hierarchies and upward/downward causation is an extra check on decision making. For example, if a decision concerns elements at the lower level we will need to check if there are supportive upper level features. Likewise, upper level decisions can affect lower levels via downward causation (see Section 16 for details).

In many cases, we also wish to know how well solutions will scale up for widespread applications. There is a paradox in how we approach scaling of innovation. In theory, we test an innovation in order to determine whether

....

191   V.I. Yukalov , D. Sornette, "Self-organization in complex systems as decision making,"
       Advances in Complex Systems, Vol. 17, 1450016 (2014), p 4.

it works and has potential for scaling up, but in practice the decision to move toward scaling up must often be made on the basis of inadequate information, producing fallible indicators, or indicators of unknown reliability, and also before all contextual conditions are in place. The difficulty faced by R&D managers in deciding what investments to make in R&D without feedback on the results of decisions made at an earlier time is a similar situation.

In seeking a solution to a defined problem such as enhancing economic development a common approach is to ask "how did others solve this problem?" Have others had the same or a similar experience? What approaches have others tried to solve the problem or address the need? What does this problem look like in other regions, countries, or environments and what have others done in similar situations? Some describe this as seeking 'near neighbor solutions.' However, solutions which were effective elsewhere may have been, and almost certainly were, applied in different contexts.

In the formative days of building ecosystems to support research commercialization in newly independence Eastern Europe a common problem was identified as not enough developments are progressing beyond the proof of concept or prototype stage resulting in products and services not reaching markets. A frequently proposed solution was that more funds should be made available for product development as this had been effective in Western Europe. But Western European countries had, for example, efficient support ecosystems necessary for these funds to be effective, including developed intellectual property legislation and knowledge of potential markets for commercialized products and services. The *context* was different. More funding for product development was necessary but, because of differences in context, by no means a sufficient to solve the problem. Missing contextual elements included experienced mentors, boundary spanners (Section 5), access to markets and market partners, knowledge of how value can be added to products, and competitive market intelligence.

Sometimes we might think that a proposition or hypothesis is context independent. We learned as children that if we add together all the angles of any triangle the result is always 180 degrees. What the teacher might not have mentioned is that this is only true for a triangle drawn on a flat surface. If we draw one on the outside of a balloon the angles will add up to slightly more than 180 degrees. The truth, or not, of the statement depends on its context (Section 13).

So let's analyze steps we take to do a better job addressing the kind of problems which many innovation ecosystems are engineered to support.

Problem Solving

To solve a problem we have to (1) identify the right problem, which might not be obvious, and its context may be unclear, (2) make a decision about what might be an effective solution in some context, and (3) take actions to apply the solution. A fourth step is to measure and evaluate results, which we will cover in Section 25. Step (2) may involve selecting from a menu of solutions applied elsewhere, as we mentioned earlier, and will *always* require us to make decisions under uncertainties and appeal to multiple fallible indicators (Section 19).

An example of identifying the right problem is when a start-up company supported by an innovation ecosystem was asked to state their biggest problem. The answer was the need for working capital. Upon further investigation by an experienced mentor, the actual problem was the lack of market access for the company's products, a problem that would not be solved by additional working capital. Take the case of wanting to decide whether to license a university-developed technology or use it as the basis for a spin-off company. Many questions need to be asked in order to make a decision; the most important ones are:

Questions to ask	Consider licensing the technology	Consider building a Spin-off company
What is the estimated market size?	Too small to sustain a spin-off company.	Large markets.
What is the competition?	Competition with established companies with strong market shares.	Market niche with few competitors.
What are the development risks?	Large risk or unknown risk. Long path to development, possible regulatory or other hurdles.	Manageable risk. Development path well understood.
How much investment capital is needed?	Unsure if it can be obtained.	Investment committed or high probability of its being available. Founders have social ties to venture capitalists. Government or seed investment received, but will additional larger amounts of investment be available for growing the company?
Is there an experienced management team and CEO?	Little or no experience with building and growing a business.	Experienced team in place.
Has market intelligence been conducted or potential customers contacted about your product or service?	Technology supports incremental changes to existing technologies.	Substantial number of commitments to buy products.
What are future income projections?	Royalty payments are reliable and can be estimated.	Potential of future profits from holding equity in the spin-off company are estimated to be greater than expected royalty payments from a license.
Are experienced external advisors and mentors available?	Few mentors or advisors.	Experienced external advisors and mentors.

Table 8. License versus spin-off decision guide.

- Spin-off companies may create value more quickly and in greater amounts than licenses if the shares in the spin-off increase in value sufficiently.
- License royalties may produce a more reliable and consistent return on investment.

- Creating spin-off companies requires much more work than licensing but may have a larger financial 'upside' in the long term.

Context is embedded in columns 2 and 3.

Asking Questions

Another way to understand context is the Toyota '5 Whys' strategy from the 1970's. Simply ask "Why?" 5 times until the root cause of the problem becomes apparent – a favorite technique of children. There is nothing special about 5, but this is typically a sufficient number of times.

A region is unhappy that new business incubators designed to create technology-driven high growth firms are not doing so. Desired outcome: more high growth firms produced by existing incubators.

1. Why are existing incubators not creating the expected number of high growth technology-driven firms? *Because firms started in incubators are remaining in the incubator.*

2. Why are these firms not achieving self-sustaining business operation so they can leave the incubator? *Because they do not have access to capital needed to support growth.*

3. Why don't they have access to capital needed to support growth? *Because they cannot show potential investors that there are large markets for the firms' products.*

4. Why can the firms not show an investor that that there are large markets for their products? *Because they cannot demonstrate user needs or ability to access markets.*

5. Why can these incubator firms not demonstrate user needs or ability to access markets? *Because the incubator does not provide the needed services, such as mentoring by experienced entrepreneurs, market intelligence training, market surveys, or access to potential marketing partner companies.*

Notice that reacting to what was thought to be the root cause of the problem might produce the wrong solution (a 'jump to' solution). For example, a proposed incorrect solution might be raising incubator rents to encourage firms to leave. Unfortunately in engineering innovation ecosystems 'jump to' solutions are common, for example when there is political pressure from officials to find a quick resolution and demonstrable successes during their term in office. What has worked elsewhere is cut and pasted into a non-compatible (by the measures described in this book) environment.

At the start of this Section, it was noted that identifying a problem is often intuitive. Much has been researched and written about intuition and decision making – and about intuitive versus analytical thinking. There is only space here for a few highlights from these studies relevant to building and sustaining innovation ecosystems.

Problem Solving Heuristics.

The application of heuristics (rules of thumb) is an approach to problem solving, learning, or discovery, which may be a combination of experience from solving similar problems, intuition, or just educated guesses. Heuristics are a way of getting started on solving problems; they are not expected to guarantee an optimal or exact solution, but maybe one that is good enough, or a way to get past brain blocks in initial reasoning.

In order to initiate some program, for example strategic planning, we noted earlier the term "let's pick the low hanging fruit first" is often heard. While this choice makes sense to gain quick wins there is a downside of encouraging a risk-averse approach that needs to be recognized and evaluated. Making this choice may require assuming that a problem which is actually a complex one is not complex, leading to invalid strategic planning methods being used. Ignoring complexities and uncertainties in a situation can produce an impression of clear cause and effect and validity of *ex-ante* assumptions where none exists.

One example of a heuristic is constructing a model (Section 8) as a heuristic device. A model is always a simplified version of what it is a model of and may help to understand what is being modeled. Stories, metaphors, etc., can also be termed heuristic in the sense of being models of reality. Another example is to break down a problem into its constituent parts. Even if these parts are be connected and not operating independently, as in an innovation ecosystem, a clue to solving the real problem may emerge. For instance, if we are trying to find the reason for poor communications within an innovation ecosystem's multiple building blocks the communications between pairs could be checked as a first step.

Looking for a similar problem and comparing it with the present one, assuming you have a solution and working backwards, and applying trial and error, or making an educated guess, are all examples of applying heuristics. There is nothing wrong in applying intuition and educated guesses to get a grip on a problem as Pólya notes "Without considerations which are only plausible and provisional, we could never find the solution which is certain and final." [192] Pólya also cautions "Heuristic reasoning is good in itself. What is bad is to mix up heuristic reasoning with rigorous proof. What is worse is to sell heuristic reasoning for rigorous proof." [193]

Making Judgments

Intuition based judgments are typically rapid, as described by Nobel Economics Prize winner Daniel Kahneman in collaboration with Amos Tversky.[194] They give the example of a familiar intuitive judgment, namely, making a left turn against oncoming traffic when driving (or a right turn if you are reading this book in a country which drives on the left). The driver does not use analysis to calculate the speed of oncoming vehicles and the number of seconds it will take to complete the turn. It is an intuitive judgment – hopefully based on experience. The Titanic crew (Section 19) made an intuitive judgment to turn away from the iceberg instead of ramming it head on which, due to the liner's construction, might have prevented it from sinking

Kenneth Hammond notes that in making judgments based on analysis we often have to apply knowledge that is not yet, in Hammond's terminology, 'fully coherent' where 'coherent' means capable of analysis using methods of mathematics or logic. Hammond defines 'cognitive continuum' as a continuum between intuition and analysis with intuition and analysis as its endpoints. The continuum picture differs from that of Kahneman and Tversky who divide thinking into 'System 1' a fast, intuitive, approach and 'System 2' a slower more analytical, reasoned, approach.

192   G. Pólya, "How to Solve It," *Princeton University Press* (1973,) p 158.

193   *ibid* p 113.

194   Daniel Kahneman, "Thinking, Fast and Slow," *Farrar, Straus and Giroux* (2011).

On the subject of intuition, he writes *"Flexibility* refers to the ease with which cognition moves from intuition to analysis (and back) on the cognitive continuum; *robustness* refers to the capacity to match the properties of the cognitive process to the properties of the task to which judgment applies. That is, when a person begins a task by applying analytical cognition but fails to make successful judgments and thus begins to apply intuitive judgments, she or he is exhibiting flexibility; if she or he has chosen correctly, that is, has applied intuition to an intuition appropriate task, or analysis to an analysis appropriate task, she or he will have demonstrated robustness. Thus, oscillation on the cognitive continuum that occurs in such a way as to match cognitive properties to task properties…" [195] At the risk of stating the obvious, we must always be aware of the fallibility of indicators in making intuitive judgments.

"The interpersonal dimension of learning reflects the way in which the human brain evolved. Kahneman distinguishes two ways of thinking: one mode is fast, automatic, and largely unconscious … and the other mode is slow, rule-based, and largely conscious (typical of the brain needed to function in a bureaucratic society). Fast thinking relies on habits and intuitions. It involves making associations between personal experiences and those gained by observing others. Slow thinking uses reasoning, combining beliefs to reach new conclusions. People use both types of thinking – both are needed, and neither is superior. It may be that in project-based organizations where time for learning is limited and project deadlines are always pending, the staff's learning style may be more inclined to fast thinking, which may reduce the demand for training and learning events geared to developing slow-thinking skills, particularly on the part of the oldest and most experienced staff. There may be a case for paying more attention to ways of enhancing fast brain skills through tweaking the networks and the social interactions that influence learning…" [196]

"[Policy makers] explicitly or unconsciously outline a limited number of policy alternatives which are familiar from past experience. When comparing these alternatives, policymakers tend to rely on previous records or their own experience rather than general theories because the former are

195   Kenneth R. Hammond, "Beyond Rationality: The Search for Wisdom in a Troubled Time," *Oxford University Press*, (2007), p 293.

196   See also: "Learning and Results in World Bank Operations: How the Bank Learns," (2014), pp 9, 39. https://ieg.worldbankgroup.org/Data/reports/chapters/learning_results_eval.pdf

often more available and less demanding in data collection and analysis." [197] This process inhibits introducing new thinking into engineering innovation ecosystems.

Notice also that direct cause and effect is assumed by using the word 'because.' Discussion of causality in Section 17 and 'attractors' in Section 8, and the detailed applications in Section 25 indicates that such direct causality may only apply in a 'farm' space within a dynamically stable attractor supported by housekeeping heat. Wicked problems are intractable, interconnected, problems with unclear cause and effect connections, See Section 15 for details of how wicked problems are defined.

So, what can we do if we must make decisions, fast or slow, regarding wicked problems but cannot use deduction? In this Section, I will suggest that not being able to use deduction does not mean we cannot use reason and deliberation. We *can* measure factors or variables as the basis for decision making because complex adaptive systems have basins of stability, attractors, or niches (Section 8) which are steady state systems maintained by the feeding in of external energy. For corporations and innovation ecosystems this equilibrium is a kind of order. Empirical research has shown that in large complex systems such as communities and corporations, these attractors maintain conditions required for emergent self-organization, adaptive capability – and measurement.

Buridan's donkey, named after the 14th century French philosopher Jean Buridan, had a problem in trying to make a rational decision using deduction. This hungry donkey standing midway between two equally nourishing looking piles of hay is unable to make a rational decision to choose one pile over the other and consequently dies of hunger. The donkey was 'deliberating' that is trying to move from a problem (being hungry) to a solution (selecting a pile of hay) – and also carrying out an *action* (eating hay). It's also possible that the unfortunate donkey was trying to optimize his choice rather than accepting that either pile of hay would assuage his hunger. Either choice was good enough; there was no need to optimize.

---

197   Kevin C. Desouza, Yuan Lin "Towards Evidence-Driven Policy Design: Complex Adaptive Systems and Computational Modeling," *The Innovation Journal: The Public Sector Innovation Journal*, Volume 16 (1), (2011) article 7.

David Milligan, writing about practical reasoning explained that a good deliberative reasoner is "not someone who simply obeys the rules of logic" [198] but someone who is also a sound judge and can make intelligent decisions and can defend his or her decisions about how to act by pointing to reasons which support actions. "The deductivist [a person using deduction] tries to reduce the elements of sound judgment and correct evaluation either to the application of logic or to a kind of subjective response." Milligan does not talk about complex systems, linearity or nonlinearity as such (he was writing in 1980), although everything he discusses applies to complexity. Rather than downgrading the importance of logic, the author is trying to show that "reason is far wider and has a far more important role in action than might appear from the deductivist account." [199]

Deduction is not the only way to reach a conclusion or as Milligan puts it "deductive certainty is far rarer in reasoning than works of logic seem to indicate," [200] a view shared by Hammond. Milligan's work launches us into the necessary search for non-deductive ways of reasoning and decision making where there are an abundance of wicked problems and Rainforests (Section 15) – which is almost everywhere – and where deduction cannot be relied upon.

In fact, non-deductive reasoning is a reflection of the difference between complexity thinking and classical economics utility theory which assumes that decision makers are rational and able to precisely estimate all necessary probabilities. Complexity thinking is closer to the real world where decision makers have biases and subconscious feelings and may be driven by extra-rational motives such as an urge to discover or to make the world a slightly better place.

Another feature to take into account is that decision making will always be 'bounded,' meaning we cannot know all the factors which possibly should be taken into account when making a decision, and thus we cannot

. . . .

198   Deduction is a process of reasoning in which a conclusion follows necessarily from the premises presented so that the conclusion cannot be false if the premises are true. Induction is any form of reasoning in which the conclusion, though supported by the premises, does not follow from them necessarily. Abduction starts with an observation then seeks to find the simplest and most likely explanation. In abductive reasoning, the premises do not guarantee the conclusion.

199   David Milligan, "Reasoning and the Explanations of Actions," *Harvester Press* (1980,) p 75.

200   *ibid*, p74.

reach an optimal solution. This concept was first proposed by the economist Herbert Simon, who we met in Section 10, as an alternative basis for the mathematical modeling of decision making; we have to be satisfied with a less than optimal solution (Section 22). The decision-maker is thus sometimes referred to as a 'satisficer' – someone who is satisfied with a good enough solution. We should point out that being satisfied with boundedness and sub-optimality does not imply accepting an insufficient depth of knowledge of those factors we *do* know about. Note there are also costs involved in finding possible solutions to problems and therefore we must know when to stop digging and evaluate the ones we have found.

Let's see how this works in practice by returning to the previous example about commercializing university research through creating a new business (a spin-off company) around the technology. What characteristics of the university's innovation environment might support greater spin-off company activity? To make things simple, consider the case of trying to reason and choose one of just two options out of many possibilities:

- **Resources**: make available more financial and supportive resources for spin-off company creation.

- **Culture**: develop a culture of innovation throughout the university and its broader stakeholder community.

After deliberation, which incidentally might include the patching methodology of Section 22, two reasons emerge as reasons in favor of Culture which we will call reason P and reason Q. Two reasons against Culture also emerge which we will call reason R and reason S. It turns out that P and Q outweigh R and S, therefore Culture development is the better option, although neither P nor Q is necessarily a *conclusive* reason for Culture. Of course, the reasons P, Q, R, and S are all open to challenge. In linear systems the argument from P and Q to the selection of Culture will be deductive.

In non-linear complex systems (Rainforests) where wicked problems are the norm, and deduction cannot be used, forming an acceptable good reason involves deliberation involving evaluations, sometimes called reason statements, which can be defended, or indeed changed if they fail to hold up against a challenge. This reasoning will typically involve drawing non-deductive conclusions from observations. Note that the reasons P and Q and R, and S, are not imperatives – "you must do P and Q" but rather "reasons in favor of doing P and Q." This method of reasoning can be extended to situations where there are many more than two options as in the example just given. In practice, in complex systems there may be a very large number of possible solutions to problems.

So far nothing has been said about probability and we cannot leave a discussion about decision making without some comments on this subject. We can think of the application of probability as intermediate between deterministic models environments where predictability is high although not complete, and environments where uncertainty prevails. "In deterministic models, a good decision is judged by the outcome alone. However, in probabilistic models, the decision maker is concerned not only with the outcome value but also with the amount of risk each decision carries." [201] Assessing probability is assessing uncertainty. Therein is the difficulty; how to put a number on probabilities? We will take these issues no further in this book. There are many sources for the interested reader who wants to understand more about probability and decision making.

Finally, the problem solving methods we are discussing here are all of the *deliberate – decide – evaluate – act* variety. In the problem of increasing spin-off company creation, with only two options, it was reasoned that culture development is the better option. The next step is to take whatever actions will be effective in improving the culture, recognizing that there may be a considerable time lag before results begin to appear. In some cases 'act' may mean a plan for carrying out an action plan rather than an actual action. A different example is when the problem is solving a puzzle or completing a crossword. After the puzzle is no longer puzzling or the crossword has been filled in the result is apparent and no further action is needed. In Section 25 next, much more about actions, motivations, and strategies are discussed and we will break down the *deliberate – decide – evaluate – act* sequence to help apply it to build innovation ecosystems.

As Milligan notes "reasons can be good and sufficient to justify a conclusion without being deductive… in the context of deliberations reasons which are not deductive are the most important." Or as Sherlock Holmes put it, don't rely entirely on deduction to make a living.

....

201   M. T. Taghavifard, K. Khalili Damghani, R. Tavakkoli Moghaddam, "Decision Making Under Uncertain and Risky Situations," *Society of Actuaries* (2009), p 2.

25

Strategies for Building Innovation Ecosystems: The Workbook

. . . .

Section Summary: The purpose of this book's capstone Section is to apply all we have learned about complex adaptive systems and Rainforest thinking to build innovation ecosystems, or improve and repairing existing systems. How does strategic planning change when the environment is a mix of the certain and the uncertain, of the predictable, the unpredictable, of the continuous and the discontinuous; that is, in complex adaptive systems? Strategic planning is not possible except in regions of linearity ('farms' in Rainforest language or 'attractors' in complex adaptive systems language). Outside of these, planning must be incremental. Therefore strategies, not strategic planning, matter in Rainforests.

Assessing the level of uncertainty, the level of agreement, and the distribution of knowledge, capacities, and decision making are all considered. Many traditional, hierarchical, sequential, strategic planning methods that were developed for factory production environments, which are complicated rather than complex, cannot be applied for strategy planning and implementation in Rainforest-like environments.

What are the goals and objectives for the ecosystem? What short term and long term outcomes are sought? It may only be possible to lay out the best expected outcomes, but recognize these will be modified during the planning process in complex systems. A typical sequence of development stages and actions in designing and building an innovation ecosystem is presented.

"People in any organization are always attached to the obsolete – the things that should have worked but did not, the things that once were productive and no longer are."

— Peter F. Drucker, management thinker.

The purpose of this book's capstone Section is to apply all we have learned about complex adaptive systems and Rainforest thinking and focus on *how to build innovation ecosystems,* or improving and repairing existing systems. Demonstrated will be applications of Building Blocks; Boundaries, Limits, and Connections; Contextual Qualifiers; Strong Links, Weak Links, and Relevant Links; Knowledge Reuse; Emergence; Hierarchies; Feedback; Housekeeping Heat; Resilience; Indicators; and more.

Before reading this Section it will be helpful to review Rick Dove's 'response-able' systems and their relevancy to innovation ecosystems (Section 10).

A 2010 IBM survey [202] of corporate CEOs identified certain organizations from every industry sector, and around the world, which have historically delivered solid business results even in economic downturns. These 'Standout' organizations stated that "they were much more prepared for complexity" and their "CEOs anticipate even greater complexity ahead." Standouts were reported to have "turned increased complexity into financial advantage" during 2005 through 2010. Of significance to this Section is that "Standout CEOs expressed little fear of re-examining their own creations or proven strategic approaches." In fact, "74 percent of them took an iterative approach to strategy, compared to 64 percent of other CEOs." Furthermore "Standouts rely more on continuously re-conceiving their strategy versus an approach based on formal, annual planning."

Those building innovation ecosystems can similarly learn to both embrace complexity and, like the CEOs of Standout organizations in the survey, take an iterative approach to strategy and re-conceive strategy as being other than an approach based on formal planning.

In Section 27 the Rainforest metaphor is re-examined. It is explained that the rainforest metaphor connects Rainforests (the original object) to

. . . .

202   "Capitalizing on Complexity: Insights from the Global Chief Executive Officer Study," *IBM* (2010). Complexity was the 2010 theme of IBM's annual survey.

companies (the object for which the symbol now stands): "A company that seeks to manufacture cheaper, better, more profitable products would run operations like an agricultural farm. However, the community (such as an innovation ecosystem) that seeks to generate high levels of innovation throughout the whole system would do the opposite.... not controlling the specific processes but instead helping to set the right environmental variables that foster the unpredictable creation of new weeds."

Since the Rainforest symbolism was introduced, we have learned and described in this book that Rainforest ecosystems not only have much in common with complex adaptive systems but that Rainforest innovation ecosystems *are* complex adaptive systems. The Rainforest symbolism has acquired a new and different interpretation as a complex adaptive system. This realization opened up the large volume of research on complex adaptive systems to be used not only to understand but to analyze and anticipate the behavior of innovation ecosystems. This Section demonstrates it's time to move beyond over-reliance on the metaphor (see Section 27).

Is strategic planning possible in complex adaptive systems?

First, we need to be clear about terminology: "Strategy is not planning – it is the making of an integrated set of choices that collectively position the firm in its industry so as to create sustainable advantage relative to competition and deliver superior financial returns." [203] When there is a need for an organization to engage in planning there are three questions to be answered:

1. How does strategic planning change when the environment is a mix of certainty and uncertainty, of the predictable and the unpredictable, [204] and the discontinuous, that is, when the environment is a mix of the complicated and the complex, of complex regions and attractor basins, or, in Rainforest language, a mix of farms and Rainforests?

....

203 Roger L. Martin, "Don't Let Strategy Become Planning," *Harvard Business Review* (February, 2013), p 5.

204 As noted in the Introduction to this book, if something is unpredictable it does not mean it is inexplicable.

2. By applying what is known about complex adaptive systems how can strategic planning and strategy development enable and sustain innovation in organizations or communities which are a mix of Rainforests and farms, and which may switch between these depending on circumstances? [205]

3. How might emergence and non-optimization of building blocks disrupt conventional strategic planning, but create new opportunities?

A good strategic planning process yields good strategies – that is the value of the planning process. Immanuel Kant put this perhaps somewhat too bluntly stating "Making plans is the occupation of an opulent and boastful mind, which thus obtains the reputation of creative genius, by demanding what itself cannot supply; by censuring, what it cannot improve; and by proposing, what it knows not where to find." [206] This Section will discuss the formation of strategies for developing innovation ecosystems in complex environments and avoid Kant's censorious opinions. Tactics will then follow.

The main conclusions of this Section are:

1. Strategic planning is not possible except in regions of linearity ('farms' in Rainforest language or 'attractors' in complex adaptive systems language).

2. Many traditional, hierarchical, sequential, strategic planning methods which were developed for *complicated* production environments cannot be applied for strategic planning and implementation in *complex* environments.

3. Planning must be incremental. Therefore planning strategies matter, not strategic planning which assumes a cause and effect linearity over time.

While this may be a new way of looking at innovation ecosystems it parallels some thinking about strategy in general. For example, In **Your**

· ·

205 Organizations may have several reasons for developing strategic plans, e.g. for a merger or de-merger, or to become more competitive. We will focus on plans to improve innovation and the capacity to innovative.

206 Immanuel Kant, "Prolegomena to Any Future Metaphysics," *Early Modern Texts Edition* (2007), p 5.

Strategy Needs a Strategy [207] the Boston Consulting Group (BCG) authors note that "the oil industry holds relatively few surprises for strategists." Changes occur but in relatively predictable ways. "The internet software industry would be a nightmare for an oil industry strategist. Innovations and new companies pop up frequently, seemingly out of nowhere, and the pace at which companies can build – or lose – volume and market share is head-spinning." New platforms or standards are introduced by the major players in the space, rapidly changing the competitive environment. "Clearly, the kinds of strategies that would work in the oil industry have practically no hope of working in the far less predictable and far less settled arena of internet software."

This means that "companies operating in such dissimilar competitive environments should be planning, developing, and deploying their strategies in markedly different ways. But all too often, our research shows, they are not." A BCG survey found, "in practice many rely instead on approaches that are better suited to predictable, stable environments, even when their own environments are known to be highly volatile or mutable… As a result, a lot of time is being wasted making untenable predictions when a faster, more iterative, and more experimental approach would be more effective. Executives are also closely attuned to quarterly and annual financial reporting, which heavily influences their strategic-planning cycles. Nearly 90% said they develop strategic plans on an annual basis, regardless of the actual pace of change in their business environments – or even what they perceive it to be."

Not strategic planning but planning strategies

The **Rainforest Master Plan** (**RaMP**) deployment mentioned earlier (see later in this Section for details); also see this Section for more on moving from decisions to actions).

The RaMP process can be applied where the operating environment ('unit of analysis') is either a non-linear complex adaptive system or a linear attractor. In Rainforest language: a Rainforest or a farm. This means that

207   Martin Reeves, Claire Love, and Philipp Tillmanns, "Your Strategy Needs a Strategy," *Harvard Business Review* (September 2012) https://hbr.org/2012/09/your-strategy-needs-a-strategy

RaMP is an effective process in both. Yet another way to express this is that RaMP can be deployed in system states where there is a high degree of causality and a low level of uncertainty as well as in system states where causality is weak and uncertainty is high.

In order to initiate some program, such as strategic planning for example, the term "let's pick the low hanging fruit first" is often heard. While this choice makes sense to gain quick wins there is a downside of encouraging a risk-averse approach that needs to be recognized and evaluated. Making this choice may require assuming that a problem which is actually a complex one is not complex, leading to invalid strategic planning methods being used. Ignoring complexities and uncertainties in a situation can produce an impression of clear cause and effect and validity of *ex-ante* assumptions where none exists (assumptions made at the starting point of a plan are called *ex-ante* assumptions).

To generalize, complex or partially complex situations require complex or partially complex responses. This means letting go of structurally familiar and accepting messiness [208] including uncertainty and unpredictability which may be difficult for many. Messiness doesn't preclude analysis or, as the historian Jacques Barzun put it: "Wisdom lies not in choosing between [intuition and analysis] but in knowing their place and limits." [209] Remember also the work of Daniel Kahneman and Amos Tversky (Section 24).

This simple tool can be used to assess an organization's environment and make decisions on whether a Rainforest-like strategy development or farm-like strategic planning is the better option. It is necessary to understand your environments before making decisions so as to not oversimplify the complex or overcomplicate the simple.

---

208 Messiness celebrates the benefits that messiness has in our lives and why it should be embraced. Tim Harford, "Messy: How to be creative and resilient in a tidy-minded world," *Little, Brown* (2016).

209 Quoted in Kenneth R. Hammond, "Beyond Rationality: The Search for Wisdom in a Troubled Time," *Oxford University Press* (2007), p 166.

About the organization or project	Organization's operating environment	Recommended choices
1. Does the organization want to enable, support, and/or maintain innovation in products or services?	High uncertainty and low predictability.	Path (1) Rainforest-like strategy development is the appropriate option. High uncertainty and low predictability suggests a high degree of complexity rather than clear causality.
	High certainty and high predictability.	Path (2) Farm-like strategic planning is the better option. High certainty and high predictability suggests a low degree of complexity
2. Is the organization's focus on becoming more innovative within its industry rather than internal reorganization?	Focus is on becoming more innovative within its industry.	Path (1) Rainforest-like incremental strategy development should be chosen.
3. Is the organization's focus on its internal performance rather than competitiveness within its industry?	Focus is on internal performance.	Path 2) Farm-like strategic planning should be chosen. If internal performance improvement which goes beyond organizational management is the objective and a more innovative internal structure is sought, then Path (1) Rainforest-like incremental strategy development should be chosen.
4. What are existing assumptions about the organization's external environment and about what the organization can control?	Competitive environment and/or low control over its environment. Little competition and/or substantial control over its environment.	Path (1) Rainforest-like incremental strategy development should be chosen. Path (2) Farm-like strategic planning is the better option.
5. What assumptions have been made prior to the proposed project (ex-ante assumptions)? These may be either explicit or hidden.	Causal assumptions are not possible or uncertain due to the complexity of the project. Cause and effect assumptions have been made and it is expected will hold for the duration.	Path (1) Rainforest-like strategy development is the appropriate option. Path (2) Farm-like strategic planning which assumes linearity is the better option.

Table 9. Tool to assess an organization's environment.

It was noted in Section 8 that it is the intangibles of human relationships (trust, loyalty, misgivings, etc.) that cause the uncertainties in the reality in which we live. "[Policy makers] explicitly or unconsciously outline a limited number of policy alternatives which are familiar from past experience. When comparing these alternatives, policymakers tend to rely on previous records or their own experience rather than general theories because the former are often more available and less demanding in data collection and analysis." [210]

As expressed in Section 4: We can imagine an ideal world where everyone has all information needed to make rational decisions, where we are all perfectly rational beings thinking deductively and where causes have logical and linear connections to their effects..... or, we can try and deal with the world as it is, messy, confusing, unpredictable where we behave as real people subject to the stresses of existence and who make illogical, irrational, decisions, influenced by emotions and the culture and norms in which we live our lives. The latter choice means engineering innovation ecosystems under such real-world conditions. When the wicked problem description was introduced (Section 15) on discovering that many, possibly most, challenges in innovation ecosystems are indeed wicked we asked: "So what should we do? Throw up our hands and admit defeat, or try to make these wicked problems if not tame then at least a little less wicked?" The same could be asked about uncertainty. Instead, we will follow what we do in our frequently unpredictable everyday lives by making plans.

Answers will first be addressed in general terms and then the results applied to building an innovation ecosystem. In both cases, **RaMP**, of which the Rainforest Scorecard is the first step, will be the foundation.

How can we know if, as Peter Drucker noted, the methodologies we are using are not obsolete but are inappropriate for the environment where their use is planned? Problems begin and multiply when we attempt to shoe-horn the world as it is into the world as we would like it to be, or into a model with which we are familiar (see false models, Section 8). Such an action may not be deliberate, after all conventional modern strategic

210 Kevin C. Desouza, Yuan Lin "Towards Evidence-Driven Policy Design: Complex Adaptive Systems and Computational Modeling," *The Innovation Journal: The Public Sector Innovation Journal*, Volume 16(1), (2011) article 7.

planning has been with us since the 1920's and we have become familiar with its widespread and successful use. [211]

In most cases, knowledge of the behavior of complex systems cannot somehow be embedded, baked in, or bolted onto a conventional linear strategic planning framework. Planning in complex systems cannot begin with a model and then the environment and its conditions and needs fitted to the model. The reverse process is required; fit the model to the environment and its conditions and needs. This model can be constructed from all that is known from Rainforest science.

The effectiveness of conventional strategic planning designed for a mostly linear and predictable environment is not being disputed; an alternative view believed to be better suited to the world in which we live (Figure 1) is being offered.

We begin to provide answers by asking: what is the purpose of plans and planning? Definitions of planning are legion but for our purpose that given in a 2013 ODI report is appropriate. "The key function of plans is not to elaborate details of a situation expected in the future, but to provide a basis and guide for decision-making throughout the course of the intervention. Plans should not, therefore, lay tracks towards a desired future that must be rigidly followed. They should, instead, be sufficiently adaptive to incorporate new developments, challenges, and opportunities. The task for a team responsible for planning is to provide the necessary guidance and leadership, communicating a vision of change around which responses can emerge." [212] We are about to see that this definition is never truer than for environments where uncertainty and unpredictability rule. It has often been stated that no (conventional) strategic plan survives contact with reality, and that as soon as a strategic plan is completed (often in multi-page binders) it is obsolete. Contexts change in unpredictable ways.

. . . .

211 The word 'strategy' is from the Greek *'strategos,'* meaning 'general of the army.' A strategos headed an army regiment. During the battle of Marathon in 490 BC, the *strategoi* provided high level strategies for defeating the Persian invaders – the hoped for outcome – leaving others to figure out tactics. It's much the same in modern strategic planning.

212 This definition and many of the following ideas are from a more detailed explanation in Richard Hummelbrunner and Harry Jones "A guide for planning and strategy complexity development in the face of Complexity," *ODI Background Note* (March 2013), p 4.

For companies which are supported within innovation ecosystems, economic analysis of the structure of industries at odds with complexity identifies "(a) there is an assumption that industry boundaries are definable, (b) that industries can be defined around a set of firms producing the same or competitive products, and (c) that competitive forces move the industry to equilibrium." [213]

Strategic planning in any environment must be *for* something – meaning actions have to take place in order the reach an agreed set of objectives. For example, within an innovation ecosystem action planning may be to support effective communication among building blocks, attracting and retaining talent, improving university-industry relations, support for start-up companies or existing small and medium enterprises (SMEs), stimulating technology commercialization, improving access to financing, and so forth, depending on specific goals and objectives of the innovation ecosystem.

There are challenges for planning in (non-linear) complex adaptive systems and in systems which are a mix of linear (complicated) and non-linear (complex) sub-systems. Uncertainty and unpredictability in these environments produce problems – some of which may be wicked, that is, not susceptible to logical analysis (Section 15) – which lead to an alternative *problem solving* approach to planning and decision making (Section 24).

The ubiquity of wicked problems, non-linearity, and the properties of complex systems generally, raises questions about the applicability of conventional strategic planning methods. Traditional methods may not be appropriate for these environments. If conventional strategic planning is to be applied in complex systems it will be necessary to at least (i) inspect the system's underpinning cause and effect assumptions to see if they model the real world in which plans are to be created, and (ii) focus on applying traditional strategic planning methodology within regions of quasi or dynamic stability where linear cause-and-effect relationships are more likely to hold, at least while housekeeping heat is present (Section 20).

The above should not imply that complexity in planning is a negative factor. Quite the reverse, without the characteristics of complexity little or no

· ·

213   Jean G Boulton, Peter M Allen, Cliff Bowman, "Embracing Complexity: Strategic Perspectives for an Age of Turbulence," *Oxford University Press* (2015), p 139.

innovation would ever emerge. It is a question of how to conduct planning in complex environments. [214]

Strategy Development Methodologies

A Rainforest Strategy Development Methodology (SDM) should have the properties or traits which make it appropriate for complex environments. Questions to ask about a methodology include:

1. Is the SDM flexible enough to fit a wide variety of users' needs and sufficiently flexible to use in all environments?

2. Is the SDM flexible enough to allow frequent changes or modifications of strategies and performance measures within cost or other constraints?

3. Will the SDM allow for achievement of key objectives that are milestones of actual progress, so that gridlock will not take hold as a result of too many proposed changes?

4. How reliable or fallible are key leading indicators?

5. Are there indications that the SDM may create a static organization [215] and what are signs that this is the case?

6. How does the SDM develop innovation capacity [216] within an organization or community?

7. Does the SDM focus on both the organization's internal processes and the organization's context, environment, and external linkages?

8. What is the SDM's logic model: complicated or complex, linear or non-linear, strong or weak causal relationships? How much is

214 Parts of this Section draw on the Overseas Development Institute Report, Harry Jones, "Taking Responsibility for Complexity," *Overseas Development Institute (ODI) Report Notes, Working Paper 330* (June 2011).

215 The Balanced Scorecard (see Section 15) has been criticized as risking the creation of a static organization. Managers may align organization activities towards the achievement of Balanced Scorecard performance measures. The result may be too much focus on achieving these to the exclusion of other targets, creating unutilized potential.

216 Another criticism is that the Balanced Scorecard hampers a firm's innovation capacity. Because of its strong focus on an organization's internal processes and performance, the external networked environment and open innovation are not sufficiently taken into account.

it a mix of both? Can it handle embeddedness, mutability, and switching?

9. Does the SDM take into account factors such as distributed innovation, open innovation, and mobility of knowledge workers?

10. How much data has to be collected for the SDM? Can data collection overload be avoided?

Question 2 is of especial importance. In what we have discussed so far it is clear that fixed *ex ante* assumptions are simply not valid in Rainforest environments. There is a need to keep checking to see what has and hasn't happened and re-set assumptions regularly.

Other alternative planning tools such as Conditional Planning may be effective in uncertain or dynamic environments. Conditional Planning links the assumptions, conditions, and outcomes of previous activities or contextual factors to the actions of a plan in a three-part chain:

• Activity (what should be done?)

• Outcome (what should the activity achieve or contribute to?)

• Conditions (which factors should exist to implement the activity successfully?).

Non-traditional planning tools will benefit from experimentation and fast feedback to make changes before the program has gone too far. This approach is similar to the design thinking of "fail early and often" and rapid prototyping to deliver proof of concepts that resonate and encourage feedback from users (but see the possible paradox expressed earlier that designing lean and agile ecosystems might discourage adequate experimentation and learning from mistakes, thus defeating their very purpose?). This aspect, among others described here, is similar to the changes being made to traditional new product development methods in industry, such as the mostly linear StageGate™ procedure (Section 16); these changes are made upon the realization that new product development is non-linear and is embedded in a complex environment.

"Early research on new product development (NPD) has produced descriptive frameworks and models that view the process as a linear system with sequential and discrete stages. More recently, recursive and chaotic frameworks of NPD have been developed, both of which acknowledge that NPD progresses through a series of stages, but with overlaps, feedback loops, and resulting behaviors that resist reductionism and linear analysis." [217] Also, NPD processes may switch between linear and non-linear, that is, between farms and Rainforests.

Strategies for building innovation ecosystems

Critical questions to ask when preparing strategic plans include: how certain or uncertain is the environment? How predictable or unpredictable? Answers to these questions, which may not be easy to figure out, will determine what strategic planning and strategy development assumptions and tools are selected. Table10 provides an initial tool to assess an organization's environment.

Many traditional, hierarchical, sequential, strategic planning methods were developed for factory production environments which are complicated rather than complex (see comments on Logical Framework Analysis in Section 15). Implementing strategies will typically be a mix of traditional and non-traditional methods applied with care within their domains of farms and Rainforests with a single ecosystem, just as in agriculture.

Prediction is difficult in complex environments, and so is detailed or reliable forecasting, because there is not a clear causal chain. Consequently, it will be necessary to be flexible to allow for emergence instead of trying to completely pre-determine policies and actions in advance of events. New insights will emerge during the development path and through interventions resulting from these insights. By their nature, complex problems may produce several equally plausible conflicting goals. Typically these arise from different initial conditions (starting points) or assumptions, or both. Remember, complex systems are highly sensitive to initial conditions which may produce very different development paths. Efficient

217 Ian P. McCarthy, Christos Tsinopoulos, Peter Allen, and Christen Rose-Anderssen, "New
     Product Development as a Complex Adaptive System of Decisions," *Journal of Product
     Innovation Management* (2006; 23), p 437–456.

communication and continuing negotiated understanding and synthesis through planning and implementation of actions [218] is essential.

All the methodologies and tools covered in this book can be applied to strategy development for innovation ecosystems including: dealing with wicked problems, stimulating emergence among a system's components, determining the fallibility of indicators, assessing causality and functioning of system hierarchies, optimizing distributed non-deductive decision making, non-optimization of variable factors, determining the relevancy of context, learning from short term feedback loops, and building robustness, among others.

Let's see how these methodologies and tools may support strategy development and planning in environments where uncertainty prevails.

Capacity building

Capacity building among individuals, organizations, and communities is a frequently identified need, although not necessarily a clearly defined one. One example is an organization which supports entrepreneurs; capacity is a building block of such an organization.

Adaptive capacity can be defined as the property of a system to adjust its characteristics or behavior, in order to expand its range under existing or future conditions and contexts.

Capacity building to deliver results is difficult to include in a non-causal strategic plan from the results of an initial gap analysis of where we are and where we want to be. Instead, it should "be approached in an 'incremental' manner, combining a degree of formal strategic intent with a flexible design; taking an evolutionary approach to supporting programmes..." [219] This approach also helps to figure out if gaps, frequently a factor in

. . . .

218 One upside of the undoubted difficulties of strategic planning under uncertainty is that resulting action items will usually be fewer than in many more conventional strategic plans which benefit from clear causality. We have probably all seen strategic plans with hundreds of action items - resulting in similar confusion and paralysis to that which befell Buridan's donkey. Incidentally, the Rainforest Scorecard is designed to produce a restricted set of action items.

219 Harry Jones, "Taking Responsibility for Complexity," Overseas Development Institute (*ODI*) *Report Notes, Working Paper 330*, (June 2011), p 29.

strategic plans, are due to a lack of capacity or other reasons such as poor communications among building blocks. An incremental approach requires careful monitoring within a culture of trust.

In Section 23 decentralization was discussed. Decentralization will only function effectively if the decentralized units have sufficient capacity to carry out their tasks. If there is uncertainty whether decentralized units have the required capacity, a test is to first give them simple (a relative term) tasks. Again, such decentralization requires a culture of trust, cooperation, and sharing of power and responsibility – including the responsibility to intervene to resolve conflicts – and a facilitative leadership. This 'testing' is common when a corporation subcontracts R&D to other, usually smaller, domestic or foreign businesses, universities, or contract research organizations. There follows a testing period after which, if performance is satisfactory, more advanced work is then subcontracted. Innovation ecosystems are decentralized systems so the same testing applies to sub-system building blocks and their capacities. Viewing an innovation as a hierarchy (Section 16), different levels of the hierarchy have their own capacity requirements.

Decentralization is assisted by reducing barriers to self-organizing units (Section 5) and formal and informal networks of peers. Objectives, including learning objectives, can be set for decentralized systems. In fact, in complex systems learning objectives can be as equally important as development stage objectives. Once again, the reason is that not all decisions can be made at the starting point of a plan.

We already noted the benefits of building in short, cost-effective feedback loops as needed in *StageGate™ new product development to avoid expensive re-work*. As another example, many of us have experienced the need for quick, responsive, damage control following a product mal-function or inappropriate behavior by an organization's staff member.

Monitoring, measurement, and evaluation

What can we say about monitoring, measurement, and evaluation (MM&E) in unpredictable systems?

Turning again to the ODI report [220] reveals a situation which will be familiar to many readers. Monitoring and evaluation, which implies measurement, "must be used to revise understandings of how progress can be achieved, not to just record progress against predefined indicators." In traditional strategic planning applied in predictable ('farm' or 'attractor basin') environments it makes sense to apply MM&E methods to check progress against indicators and milestones established at the start (*ex-ante*). We are used to seeing these embedded in a logic model similar to a logframe (Section 15) where effects linearly follow causes and the possibility of emergence is absent or not considered.

MM&E is essential to any initiative – whether the environment is a farm or a Rainforest. The issue is that in Rainforests it should not be just a checking of boxes. If so there will always be the temptation to check as many boxes as possible, to show that a plan's objectives were met, even if milestones were perhaps not fully reached. Another way to express this is that accountability in complex systems can be assessed on whether there has been an improvement in how decisions are made when the task is complex.

Dane Stangler and Jordan Bell-Masterson [221] suggest some ways of measuring an entrepreneurial ecosystem through 'indicators of entrepreneurial vibrancy' to track over time such as:

Density

- Number of new and young companies in your defined geographic area per 1,000 people.
- Share of employment in new and young companies.
- High-tech (or other sectoral) startup density.

Fluidity

- Population flux.
- Labor market reallocation.

. . . .

220   Harry Jones, "Taking Responsibility for Complexity," Overseas Development Institute (*ODI*) *Report Notes, Working Paper 330*, (June 2011), p 31.

221   Dane Stangler, Jordan Bell-Masterson "Measuring an Entrepreneurial Ecosystem" Kauffman Foundation, (March 2015).

- High-growth firms – number and density.

Connectivity

- Connections between programs and resources.
- Spinoff company rate.
- Dealmaker networks.

Diversity

- Multiple economic specializations
- Immigrant share of population
- Economic mobility

A word of caution: these are a mix of outputs (number of new companies) and outcomes (changes in economic mobility).

Scanning the environment should identify what potential, or actual, innovation ecosystem building blocks are in place, or missing, especially core building blocks, and whether or not a culture of innovation exists. Tools such as the **Rainforest Scorecard** can help with these assessments. This activity should also begin to surface wicked problems.

Let's return to the three types of challenges present in uncertain or dynamic spaces introduced above.

What should the innovation ecosystem accomplish?

We must ask what innovations we want the innovation ecosystem to enable, support, and maintain. What outcomes are expected from an effectively functioning ecosystem?

If the environment is one of economic decline after a major company or entire industry has left the region, then a goal might be economic development through support for entrepreneurship and creation of new businesses, perhaps by capitalizing on skills of those previously employed in the departed sector. Universities in the region may want to leverage their resources in support of business development. Some rather selective cases of 'rust belt' renewal are described in **The Smartest Places on Earth.** [222]

What are the goals and objectives for the ecosystem? What short term and long term outcomes are sought? Remember what was said earlier about plans: "Plans should not, therefore, lay tracks towards a desired future that must be rigidly followed. They should, instead, be sufficiently adaptive to incorporate new developments, challenges and opportunities." This means it may only be possible to lay out the best expected outcomes but recognize these will be modified during the planning process in complex systems. Next, we apply the ODI recommendations.

Assess the level of uncertainty

Is there clear advance knowledge on how to achieve the desired outcomes in the given context? What works in one context will not necessarily work in another. Remember, contextual qualifiers are those pieces of knowledge that allow a user to assess whether a given policy or practice, either new or implemented elsewhere, is truly relevant or applicable to the user's environment (Section13). Can existing knowledge be used in the current context? Even if the level of uncertainty makes preparing initial detailed implementation plans difficult, is there a vision for the future? Is it possible to at least identify influencing factors and are these open to control?

Assess the level of agreement

Conditions and contexts may change over time together with how well they are understood. Therefore it is necessary to determine the level of agreement or disagreement about the problem as well as changing goals and strategies to reach them. This may require increased levels of cooperation and, consequently, of trust. Trust helps groups to self-organize. This may be especially the case where non-traditional planning methods are being used.

· ·

222   Antoine Van Agtmael and Fred Bakker, "The Smartest Places on Earth," *Public Affairs NY* (2016).

Assess the distribution of knowledge, capacities, and decision making

Top down planning which is too tightly controlled or rigidly structured may assume that all capacities, interventions, and decision making are also top down responsibilities. This approach clearly does not match spaces where knowledge, capacities, and decision making are not centralized. Distributed decision making is covered in more detail in Section 24.

Map the ecosystem.

Creating an inventory or map that indicates innovation ecosystem building blocks and how they are connected: strong, weak, and relevant links (Section 9) and knowledge flow among building blocks.

When examining the startup system in St. Louis, MO, USA, researchers from the Ewing Marion Kauffman Foundation and Washington University in St. Louis found that while much is known about the job-creating potential of new, young, and growing companies, not so much is known about the local ecosystems which support entrepreneurs, and how "players interact with one another and how the ecosystem evolves is likely to make both public and private-sector behavior more effective." [223]

Building the innovation ecosystem.

The methodology described here and the complex adaptive systems model which is its foundation will be familiar to anyone who has a knowledge of complex systems but unfamiliar to many of those who plan to build an innovation ecosystem. Both will have to invest time to understand each other's thinking. One way is to first model the proposed ecosystem (or improvements to an existing one) as simply as realities permit to seek joint understanding and acceptance, then gradually introduce additional acceptable features.

---

223   Yasuyuki Motoyama, Karren K. Watkins "Examining the Connections within the Startup Ecosystem: A Case Study of St. Louis," *Ewing Marion Kauffman Foundation* (2014), p 2.

The Rainforest Master Plan (RaMP)

The stages of building and innovation ecosystem fit into the **Rainforest Master Plan (RaMP)**, designed to assist communities and organizations in evaluating, understanding and developing the cultural and leadership conditions necessary for evaluating, designing and building effective innovation ecosystems. In many places in this book we have mentioned the importance of context. Every action must be evaluated within the context of the unit of analysis.

The RaMP process involves: (1) immersion of community and/or organizational leaders in Rainforest principles of innovation; (2) the creation of working teams to manage the strategic deployment of the assessment tool; (3) training and development of team members in both Rainforest principles and assessment management; (4) an internal communications strategy designed to educate, inform, and align the entire community and/or organization; (5) the assessment process, involving a wide-spread distribution of individuals; (6) the summary and aggregation of assessment results, and the reporting of those results to leaders; (7) the creation and leadership of design-based teams to develop solutions and approaches; (8) the deployment and management of solutions; and (9) the management and leadership of an iterative cycle of re-evaluation and creation of new and/or improved solutions.

Within the above basic RaMP stages are:

Stage 1. Assess the System State: The assessment part of the process institutionalizes language, terms, ideas, and thinking. The process also supports the creation of a baseline measurement that can be used for iterative measurements later.

Stage 2. Gaps & Opportunities: Gaps and/or high-return opportunities to implement cultural, leadership, frameworks, or resources changes are identified in this critical next step. Tools enable groups to undertake deliberation processes to increase local innovation and do so in a self-organized way.

Stage 3. Design & Build: This process focuses on the findings, insights, data, and information discovered during Stages 1 and 2. The basic procedure is to create and deploy work teams addressing specific opportunities or challenges that surface during an assessment.

Typically during RaMP Stage 3 Design and Build groups form, deliberate, and decide on actions to be taken, frequently using the small group patching process (Section 22). The process can be summed up as deliberate – decide – evaluate – act. This closes the gap between reasoning and actions, although there may be a time delay between these stages. To qualify the term 'act' – in some cases this may mean a plan for carrying out an action rather than an actual action.

If someone or some group is to carry out an action they must be motivated in some way to avoid too long a gap between accepting the conclusions of a deliberation, its evaluation, and acting on the conclusions. This may seem like an obvious statement but I suspect we have all seen plans that are supposed to result in actions to be taken but where actions never happen. Section 24 discussed different kinds of reasoning which can be used in the deliberation leading to the 'action being taken' process described here.

For example in two cities, one on each side of a US/Mexican border region, cross-border action planning teams are set up following application of the patching process, motivated by their agreed goal of improving the quality of life of its citizens through cross-border innovation. Because the teams were highly motivated there were only short time gaps in the deliberate – decide – evaluate – act sequence.

As Milligan notes, it may also "possible to have several explanations for the same action." [224] Take a typical case of the deliberation process in all phases of RaMP and especially in Stage 3 Design and Build. In each RaMP stage groups are formed to collect information and opinions, deliberate, and then making collective decisions on actions to be taken. The Rainforest Scorecard may be completed by individuals and also by groups by collecting information and opinions, and then making a group decision on scores to assign to the 6 Scorecard characteristics.

A vast amount has been written about how reasoning leads to action and people are motivated to act (much of it rather dense) so regard the description above as a minimal introduction to the topic.

A feature of RaMP is that both immediate and longer-term actions to resolve problems are identified during the process so that communities

. . . .

224   David Milligan, "Reasoning and the Explanations of Actions," *Harvester Press* (1980), pp 102-108.

can experience RaMP's impact. Significant results can emerge from quickly applied small changes, and accordingly the assessment process serves as both strategic background research and an immediate tactical call to action for improving innovation.

Stage 1 is especially significant as we have noted earlier (property #10, Section 5, of complex adaptive systems) namely, that complex adaptive systems are sensitive to *initial conditions*, and self-organizing networks are development path-dependent. Consequently, initial assumptions must be reviewed and their possible effects understood to the greatest degree possible. Therefore the initial immersion will guide further development paths.

Stage 4. Ongoing Re-Assessment & Continuous Improvement: Once deployed, the assessment process is repeated by the community or organization to judge the effectiveness of solutions, improvement in innovation, and changes to underlying conditions which are made.

RaMP is a procedure developed for use in a wide variety of cases. In Rainforest environments **Stage 3, Design & Build** is expanded as shown in Figure 20 and explained in more detail next.

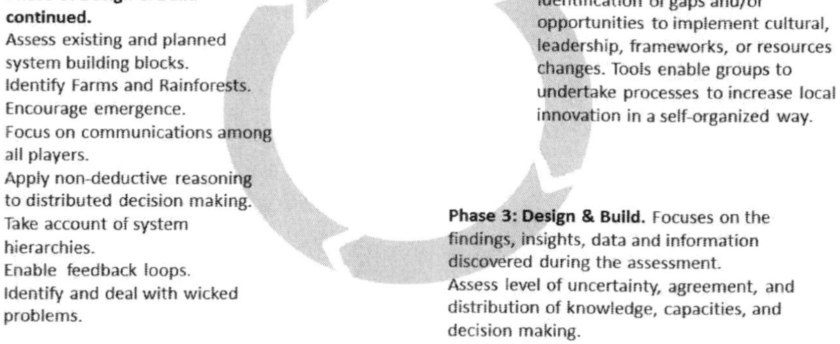

Phase 4: Ongoing Re-Assessment & Continuous Improvement The assessment process is repeated to judge the effectiveness of solutions, improvement in innovation, and changes to underlying conditions.

Phase 1: Assess the System State Institutionalizes language, terms, ideas, and thinking. Also supports the creation of a baseline measurement that can be used for iterative measurements later.

Phase 3: Design & Build continued. Assess existing and planned system building blocks. Identify Farms and Rainforests. Encourage emergence. Focus on communications among all players. Apply non-deductive reasoning to distributed decision making. Take account of system hierarchies. Enable feedback loops. Identify and deal with wicked problems.

Phase 2: Gaps & Opportunities Identification of gaps and/or opportunities to implement cultural, leadership, frameworks, or resources changes. Tools enable groups to undertake processes to increase local innovation in a self-organized way.

Phase 3: Design & Build. Focuses on the findings, insights, data and information discovered during the assessment. Assess level of uncertainty, agreement, and distribution of knowledge, capacities, and decision making.

Figure 20. Expanded Rainforest Master Plan (RaMP).

The Rainforest Scorecard provides base data for RaMP Stages 1 and 2. To adequately carry out RaMP **Stage 3, Design & Build,** needs more detailed guidance. It is important to know what to look for in building out an innovation ecosystem.

Based on this Expanded Rainforest Master Plan a typical Innovation Ecosystems Workbook can be created.

Stages are shown as a sequence for convenience. However, this does not necessarily imply that the sequence is always as illustrated. Initial stages may begin later and some may run in parallel depending on circumstances; remember we are dealing with non-linear systems.

We turn now to the practical development stages and actions in building an innovation ecosystem. The Table below shows how (table continues over several pages).

Innovation Ecosystem Development Stages	"How to" Strategies and Actions Outputs from the Rainforest Scorecard (or other assessments) are inputs to the development of strategies and actions.	Rainforest Science (Complex Adaptive Systems) Foundation for Actions
RaMP Phase 1		
Define the mission. Be clear about what the innovation ecosystem should accomplish in the short, medium, and long term.	A clearly expressed mission and mission statement should be agreed upon by all parties. Enable short corrective feedback to re-adjust goals and objectives if necessary. Ensure innovation ecosystems are directed by mission, goals, and objectives rather than methods. For example, a mission might be: Improve the quality of life of in a region through entrepreneurship.	The development path of a complex system is highly sensitivity to initial conditions. Therefore be sure the mission clearly sets the innovation ecosystem's starting point. An innovation ecosystem may be malfunctioning due to missing elements in its trajectory such as a lack of experience in a critical area. *Section 13 Contextual Qualifiers: One Size Doesn't Fit All* *Section 26 A Framework, Geometry, and Grammar for Rainforests*
Define the goals, and objectives to support the mission.	Within an innovation ecosystem there may be several goals – and multiple objectives under each goal. Typical Goals: Create new sustainable jobs, nurture and retaining talent in a region, or promote a region as a vibrant innovation hub. Typical Objectives: Improve communication among existing ecosystem building blocks, create support for start-up companies to grow, or develop university/industry R&D partnerships, and identify mentors for entrepreneurial ventures.	Because of sensitivity to initial conditions, initial goals and objectives should be defined for subsequent re-design. Objectives may include learning objectives for decentralized systems. In complex systems, learning objectives can be as equally important as development stage objectives. Recognize that not all decisions can be made at the starting point of a plan (*ex-ante*). *This Section.*

Research a deep knowledge of current conditions, existing plans, and the overall environment.	Before any substantial efforts are made, obtain and analyze documents such as existing strategic plans, identify feelings, concerns, possibilities, culture.	Context is critical to understanding complex adaptive systems.
	Conduct interviews or other assessments in addition to the Rainforest Scorecard, such as a technology assessment, where needed.	Enables questioning of pre-conceived mental models. Section 13 Contextual Qualifiers: One Size Doesn't Fit All
Conduct initial assessments.	Assess the system state. Use the short and long Rainforest Scorecards in assessing key factors describing the 'unit of analysis' in terms of key variables.	The assessment part of the process institutionalizes language, terms, ideas, and thinking.
	These variables are considered to be indicators to measure innovation potential in a unit of analysis.	Innovation variables and parameters or constraints are responsible for the evolution of complex systems into systems of greater innovation and adaptability.
	Supports the creation of a baseline measurement that can be used for iterative measurements later.	To understand possible causation in complex systems a process of analysis of variables is required because complex systems have emergent properties, and a change in one variable will probably affect all the other variables.
	Specialized assessments may also be needed such as technology assessments.	*This Section.* *Section 8 Systems, Models, and Attractors* *Section 22 Should Everything be Optimized?*

RaMP Phase 2, and repeat of Phase 1 elements where needed		
Assess the level of system uncertainty. Assess the level of system agreement.	Determine how certain or uncertain is the environment? How predictable or unpredictable? Is there clear knowledge on how to achieve the desired outcomes in the given context? Is there a vision for the future? Is it possible to at least identify influencing factors and are these open to intervention or control? Answers to these questions, which may not be easy to figure out, will determine what planning assumptions (both hidden and explicit) are made and what tools are selected.	What works in one context will not necessarily work in another. Even if the level of uncertainty makes preparing initial detailed implementation plans difficult Conditions and contexts may change over time together with how well they are understood. Therefore it is necessary to determine the level of agreement or disagreement about problems as well as changing goals and strategies to reach them. High levels of cooperation and self-organization and, consequently, of trust may be required, especially where non-traditional planning methods are used. *This Section.*
Assess the distribution of knowledge, capacities, and decision making.	Use group sessions to assess where decisions are made and the level of distributed decision making. Use group sessions to assess where knowledge resides in hierarchies.	Top down planning which is too tightly controlled or rigidly structured may assume that all capacities, interventions, and decision making are top down responsibilities. This approach does not match spaces where knowledge, capacities, and decision making are not centralized. *Section 16 Hierarchy and Necessity.*

Assess existing and planned building blocks.	Develop an innovation ecosystem map, validated by participants, as a tool to developing strategies and tactics. Revisit and re-draw regularly. Regularly review building blocks for possible re-arrangement to optimize innovation ecosystem fitness. Bring in those with diverse knowledge to enable solutions to emerge. Experiment with different ways in which building block components communicate and work with each other, bringing people together in new settings, and encourage unstructured events to positively change the culture in an innovation ecosystem. Develop 'response-able' components to support agility. Quickly identify communication breakdowns. Identify strong, weak, and relevant links.	In complex adaptive systems the re-arrangement of building blocks can create emergence of new ideas. A complex adaptive system cannot be decomposed into a set of independent non-interacting parts. However, some systems may be 'nearly decomposable.' Building blocks are not static; they may change over time, traits are added or removed, they coalesce or split, they generate new building blocks. Building blocks have to be assembled to optimize *overall* innovation ecosystem 'fitness' which may be defined to match the mission. Building blocks may be 'hardware' or 'software' and are more than just physical objects or organizations; they are attitudes, experience, feelings, and culture. Optimization requires hierarchical problem solving, where interface standards are defined first, followed by building block properties within the constraints of the interface standards. *Section 10 Building Blocks for Innovation Ecosystems.*

Identify where farms are located and where Rainforests are located.	Identify, or create, farms to take advantage of their stability and predictability which may be necessary for some ecosystem building blocks.	The Rainforest model explains that farms are regions of local dynamic equilibria (attractors) that complex systems may settle into.
	Use linear planning methods within farms – subject to contextual qualifiers.	Within farms, systems are predominantly linear and cause and effect relationships are predictable allowing conventional strategic planning methods to be used.
	Identify Rainforests, recognizing that innovation is more likely to occur in Rainforests.	
	Use non-linear planning methods within Rainforests – subject to contextual qualifiers.	*Section 7 The Rainforest Model Explained.*
		Section 15 Wicked Problems are Everywhere.
		Section 17 Cause, Effect, and Trying to Predict.
		Section 26 A Framework, Geography, and Grammar for Rainforests,
RaMP Phase 3		
Implement first actions.	Set up working groups to recommend first actions for review.	A complex ecosystem is full of conflicting constraints, and may be sub-divided into a number of non-overlapping but interacting self-optimizing parts called patches.
	Apply patching methods to optimize outcomes.	
	Incentives to focus on 'low hanging fruits' are frequently effective, but may discourage a risk-averse approach and/or mistakenly identify a complex problem as a non-complex one.	Enabling each patch to optimize its behavior enables all patches to co-evolve with one another. Patching may support decentralized leadership and decision making which are otherwise prevented by social barriers.
		Section 22 Should Everything be Optimized?

Encourage emergence.	Work with existing building blocks to re-arrange them to encourage emergence of innovation.	Emergence is a critical feature of complex ecosystems leading to invention and innovation occurring incrementally or in disruptive leaps.
	Develop new building blocks needed based on previous steps.	Emergence occurs through the interactions among group of agents – individuals, networks, and organizations – rather than behaviors of formal managers.
	Encourage self-organization of development teams.	
	Identify properties which can emerge only when system levels reach a high enough state of organization.	Emergent organizations are typically very robust and able to survive and self-repair damage from shocks.
		Re-arrangement of building blocks can create emergence of new ideas and actions.
		Emergence is an outcome of self-organization; a new level of order in the system that comes into being as novel structures which maintain themselves over a period of time.
		Innovation emerges aided by absorption of information and formation of knowledge structures. Structural changes tend to be followed by long periods of incremental variations.
		Newer signals and boundaries can then emerge from combinations of building blocks at this new level of organization. Some properties can emerge only when the system reaches a high enough level of organization.
		Section 10 and throughout the book.

Enable small changes to produce large impacts.	Watch for tipping and bifurcation points.	Take advantage of a feature of nonlinear complex systems, namely that small changes in certain parts may cause large changes in the system's overall behavior due to cross-coupling among building blocks. *Section 5 What is a Complex Adaptive System?*
Develop effective communications among all players and as far as possible optimize internal and external communications.	Set up standard interfaces between building blocks to improve communications and reduce transaction costs between innovation ecosystem building blocks. . Check for the most frequent reasons for communication difficulties: (1) lack of trust between partners, (2) wrong expectations, (3) preconceptions and stereotypes, (4) cultural misalignments, (5) lack of business communication skills, (6) language barriers – where applicable, and (7) fear of recriminations for open communication of bad news. Assess cultural alignment and matching, or mismatching, of communications.	Effective and efficient communication within building blocks of ecosystems and their external environments is the most important contributing factor to an ecosystem's success. Poor communications will lead to failure. *Section 10 Building Blocks for Innovation Ecosystems.*

Assess needs and wants.	Wants are not always the same as needs. Assess which are which in the mission, goals, and objectives. Decide what's critical and what's not (i.e. which issues need to be addressed up front and which can be delayed). Assess risks of both. Understand people's desires and wants and what excites them and spurs them to action. Find champions in potential partners.	
Create and support working groups and their decision making.	Divide the overall decision making system into smaller local decision making working groups or sub-systems. Make sure that knowledge of local conditions at sub-levels can be effectively incorporated into actions of higher level decision makers. To prevent initial enthusiasm from fading supply working groups and action teams with a constant input of energy in the form of new knowledge, new ideas, challenges, and encouragement of peers, mentors, and so forth, to keep them productive. Working groups should develop a small number of feasible action items, including, among others, timelines, milestones, and financing requirements for different stages of the innovation ecosystem's development.	The elements in the ecosystem are sub-divided into any number of non-overlapping but interacting self-optimizing parts called patches. To reach a high level of ecosystem fitness it can be helpful, if a problem is complex and full of conflicting constraints, to break it into patches, and let each patch try to optimize, such that all patches co-evolve with one another. Some form of energy (known as housekeeping heat) is needed to prevent self-organizing complex innovation ecosystems from dropping into a dysfunctional, static, equilibrium state. *Section 20 Noise and Housekeeping.* *Section 22 Should Everything be Optimized?*

| Apply non-deductive reasoning to distributed decision making. | Apply non-deductive reasoning to deal with wicked problems – those problems having an unclear cause and effect connection. Avoid jumping to incorrect 'obvious solutions.' | If an action can be taken which transforms the present state to the desired one, then the problem has been solved

Many possible explanations may exist for wicked problems. Depending on the explanation, a solution takes on a different form.

Steps to addressing a problem are: (1) identifying the right problem, which might not be obvious, and its context unclear, (2) making a decision about what might be an effective solution in some context, and (3) taking actions to apply the solution.

Non-deductive reasoning is close to the real world where decision makers have biases and subconscious feelings and reasoning may be driven by non-rational motives.

Section 24 Practical Reasoning: Decision Making and Solving the Right Problem. |

Set up indicators.	Develop leading indicators for the development paths of innovation ecosystems. Developing leading indicators to measure the extent to which people organize to both acquire and use resources. Assess the degree of fallibility of an indicator, and guard against cognitive traps.	Knowledge of how complex adaptive systems behave enables some leading indicators to be developed. This knowledge supports Rainforest Scorecard indicators and leading indicators for disruptions in innovation ecosystems and resilience of innovation ecosystems. Indicators may be fallible. *Section19 Indicators and Fallibility.*
Enable adaptive capacity building.	Build in adaptive capacity – the property of a system to adjust its characteristics or behavior, in order to expand its range under existing or future conditions and contexts. Increase agility and self-organization through adaptive capacity among individuals, organizations, and communities. Ensure that decentralized units have the capacity to carry out their tasks	In complex adaptive systems capacity building to improve delivery of results should be approached in an incremental manner, combining a degree of formal strategic intent with a flexible design; taking an evolutionary approach to supporting programs. This approach also helps to figure out if gaps are due to a lack of capacity or other reasons such as poor communications. An incremental approach requires careful monitoring within a culture of trust. *This Section.*

Take account of hierarchies or levels in systems.	Be aware of system hierarchies. Enable hierarchical levels to stimulate emergence in the form of entrepreneurship. Within hierarchies make sure decisions made at whatever level knowledge resides. Where knowledge resides, be sure decisions are made by those who have the capacity to implement them. Use knowledge of hierarchies to recognize the need to create higher level supportive policies for lower level applications. Lower levels can sometimes address complex problems effectively because they often have a strong understanding of the local dynamics and tacit knowledge of the drivers of behavior.	Building blocks are typically arranged in a hierarchical structure as sets of boxes nesting within sets of boxes, or as a set of layers. Hierarchy does not imply one level is more important than another. Not being aware of hierarchies is a common cause of wasted time and money. Complexity science highlights how there is often untapped potential for change in lower-level decision-making units, and for groups not linked by formal hierarchies to self-organize and work coherently towards a common goal. *Section 16 Hierarchies and Necessity.*
Enable feedback loops.	Use positive feedback to encourage deviation from the existing state of affairs and adaptation to produce emergence of innovation. Use negative feedback as a stabilizing force to reduce deviations from an existing state, and to keep needed minor changes and adjustments from becoming too large by re-stabilizing the system post-changes. Build in long and short feedback and feed forward loops. Assess whether there are sufficient weak links in the system's network to provide new paths to recover from shocks.	If a new emergent order is creating value it will stabilize itself, finding variables and parameters that best increase its overall sustainability in an ecosystem. Feedback from a reality assessment of all the possibilities identified by working groups produces a decision to first work on those possibilities which are close to the ecosystem's existing experience and skills. *Section 14 Networks and Feedback.*

Decide what should be optimized.	Evaluate what functions of the ecosystem should be optimized and which should not. Make cost/benefit analyses to help decide which building block functions to optimize.	Why trying to optimize all the elements of an innovation ecosystem is not necessary, or always desirable to optimize the whole. *Section 22 Should Everything be Optimized?*
Match capabilities.	Match building block properties for efficient communication and reduction of social barriers. Look for a 'champion' or 'integrator' within organizations being matched who will support the project and help overcome internal barriers.	Matching of signals, **results expectations, and cultures**, between innovation system building blocks positively affects diffusion and learning *Section 10 Building Blocks for Innovation Ecosystems.*
Identify contextual qualifiers.	Understand the context of any situation or action. Determine the influence of contextual factors in making decisions and taking actions. If policies or other solutions for problems of economic development or building innovation are borrowed from other contexts, assess how critical was their context.	Contextual qualifiers are those pieces of knowledge that allow a user to assess whether a given policy or practice, either new or implemented elsewhere, is truly relevant or applicable to the user's environment. *Section 13 Contextual Qualifiers: One Size Doesn't Fit All.*
Analyze systems as Networks.	Picture the ecosystem as a network to obtain an alternate view and apply what is known about networks. Cultivate links within innovation ecosystems and with their environments to stabilize the ecosystem, improve transaction efficiency, optimize the use of resources, and open the innovation ecosystem up to new ideas and different ways of thinking.	It can be beneficial to view an innovation ecosystem as a network of nodes or points connected by links rather than a system of connected building blocks. *Section 14 Networks and Feedback.*

Re-use knowledge where possible.	Evaluate if and where existing knowledge may be used in the current context. Set up conditions for knowledge re-use to reduce re-invention.	Conditions for knowledge re-use include (1) motivating factors such as a culture within the project which encourages reuse, (2) work processes that optimize exposure to diverse knowledge sources, (3) availability of flexible ways to assess the credibility of potentially reusable knowledge, and (4) an ability to scan for fit. *Section 21 Reusing Knowledge: Create Early, Use Often.*
RaMP Phase 4		
Design for resilience and sustainability.	Engineer innovation ecosystems to be sustainable and resilient to internal and external perturbations. Plan to repair results of the perturbation to allow the system to recover.	Complex systems are intrinsically hazardous. It is the presence of these hazards that drives the creation of actions against failure. Such defenses might be a robust innovation culture, knowledge, trust, diversity and openness, and various forms of physical and intellectual resources and capacity. Emergent organizations are typically very robust and able to survive and self-repair substantial damage or perturbations. Distributed decision making systems are robust in absorbing shocks to the system. *Section18 Shocks to the System: Resilience, Sustainability, and Scalability.*
Monitor, measure, and evaluate.	Develop Monitoring, Measurement, and Evaluation (MM&E) tools for use under conditions of unpredictability. Recognize some results may take time. 'Fail fast' is not always the best policy. Use MM&E to revise understanding of how progress can be achieved, not to just record progress against predefined indicators.	Accountability in complex systems can be assessed by whether there has been an improvement in how decisions are made when the task is complex. In traditional strategic planning applied in predictable (farm) environments it makes sense to apply MM&E methods to check progress against indicators and milestones established at the start (*ex-ante*). *This Section.*

Table 10. Building an innovation ecosystem: development stages and actions.

The above Workbook table is only a guide which will need to be tailored to its application environment.

26

A Framework, Geometry, and Grammar for Rainforests

....

Section Summary: There is no complete theory of complex systems. However, it is helpful to have a framework or geometry, language, and grammar. A framework may provide a foundation for apparently disconnected or unrelated events. A framework may help us identify phenomena not previously understood. A trait is a generalized term for characteristics, attributes, qualities, or properties of a complex system. Contours and boundaries are defined. Language elements of this framework include: 'alescence' as a more encompassing term than emergence or growth. Augmentative alescence is when an existing complex system is extended. Spoliative alescence is when an existing complex system suffers a loss, for example because of failure or a change of policy. Coalescent alescence is a complex system arising from the intersection of novel configuration of complexes. For instance, if new capabilities to support entrepreneurship and new business creation are added.

"To pursue science is not to disparage the things of the spirit. In fact, to pursue science rightly is to furnish the framework on which the spirit may rise."

— Vannevar Bush, founder of the US National Science Foundation.

This Section is experimental or speculative in places. However, it may stimulate new ideas by providing a framework inside of which to think, and it contains some practical applications. Treat this Section as a reference to provide a basis for most of the concepts introduced in this book.

There is no complete theory of complex systems. To help understand how complex adaptive systems can explain reality and help us perhaps make some level of prediction at least within parts of a complex system, for example by creating leading indicators, it is helpful to have (1) a framework or geometry and (2) a language and grammar to build on this framework. A framework may provide a foundation for apparently disconnected or unrelated events. A framework may help us identify phenomena not previously understood.

Another key feature from Holland [225] is that complex adaptive systems include generators, and operators, i.e. a grammar or set of rules for assembling the generators. In other words, niche roles provide different results based on boundaries, niches, and sequences.

The framework or geometry is state space as introduced in Section 8. The structure of a complex adaptive system is as defined by the components of the system, the ways they interact, and the system's contextual constraints. New structures, such as new configurations of building blocks or new networks are formed by the creation, or elimination, of new sub-complexes and boundaries. More details later in this Section.

Language and grammar are all about how a system, with its associated properties, moves from one state to another. For example, an innovation ecosystem was expected to increase the level of entrepreneurship and new business creation in a community from its present level A to an improved level B. It has not done so; level B has not been attained. The same innovation ecosystem was also expected to attract business from outside the area. In this it succeeded and the system state changed. Naturally, methods to measure a system state are needed. Metrics can be tricky to devise. They should focus on outcomes not outputs, namely, real system changes not just number of programs delivered, for example. Much work remains to be done on metrics for innovation ecosystems.

Several times in other Sections the importance of emergence has been emphasized so the changes above can be summarized as (1) a new state emerges, (2) transitions occur between this state and another, and (3) additional new states are created. [226]

. . . .

225   John H. Holland, "Signals and Boundaries: Building Blocks for Complex Adaptive Systems," *MIT Press* (2012), p 50.

226   Emergence and transition phenomenon are also present in biological systems.

The language and grammar behind these transitions are what mathematicians call 'non-commuting' algebra. To illustrate this, suppose, again, we want to increase the level of entrepreneurship in a community and decide there are two possible actions we might take (see Sections 24 and 25 for decisions and actions). Action 1 (let's call it A1) is an action to provide more funding. Action 2 (call this A2) is an action to provide more mentoring by experienced entrepreneurs. Does the sequence in which these actions are taken matter? Will A1 followed by A2 be different from A2 followed by A1? Very likely. For example, available funding may be wasted if mentors are not in place to guide the best way to spend the funding. On the other hand, mentors may not have a sufficient number of entrepreneurs or entrepreneurial businesses to mentor if start-up funding has not been available. Therefore the sequence A1>A2 is 'not equal' to the sequence A2>A1 in the way that 2x3 = 3x2. [227]

All this may seem arcane, however many innovation ecosystems do not pay sufficient attention to the sequence in which actions should be carried out, resulting in unnecessary expenditures and disappointing outcomes.

A feature of all complex systems is that the emergence of such systems is typically based on a small set of axioms like the rules of a game. The game itself may have a multitude of different histories, because of different contexts, which may never be repeated.

Rainforests have Axioms (Section 7) but perhaps to be overly precise, not all these are Axioms according to the usual definition that Axioms cannot be proved or reduced to more basic ones.

Mathematics has been a valuable tool in economics and produced breakthrough results. However, it must be remembered that human behavior is not predictable or subject to a stable relationship between cause and effect in the ways that the fundamental laws of physics are for example. As the Nobel Physics Laureate Richard Feynman put it: "imagine how much harder physics would be if electrons had feelings!"

. . . .

227 To demonstrate a non-commuting algebra, do the following: take a closed book and note its
     position (e.g. normal reading position). Action 1 is rotating the book 90° about its vertical
     axis. Then, from this new position, Action A2 is rotating the book 90° about its horizontal
     axis. Note the book's final position. Then carry out these actions in reverse order. The final
     position of the book in the second action will not be the same as in the first case. Action 1
     and Action 2 are thus non-commuting (or non-commutative).

As, in general, mathematical equations cannot be used to describe complex adaptive systems, except in some cases around local equilibria – inside attractors – and in computer simulations, then we must be careful and precise in our use of written language. The language of culture is usually considered to be the language of narrative and stories. We can amplify narrative with clear definitions of words making up the narrative forming a geometry and grammar of innovation narrative. [228] In written and spoken languages words are the building blocks to assemble sentences which in turn enable communication within and between language complexes. Indeed, research in the cognitive sciences has demonstrated how language is acquired, used, and changes over time in interconnected processes 'tailored' to serve the communicative needs of its users. Language itself is a complex adaptive system with the following key features: [229]

1. The system consists of multiple agents (the speakers in the speech community) interacting with one another.

2. The system is adaptive, that is, speakers' behavior is based on their past interactions, and current and past interactions together feed forward into future behavior.

3. A speaker's behavior is the consequence of competing factors ranging from perceptual mechanics to social motivations.

4. The structures of language emerge from interrelated patterns of experience, social interaction, and cognitive processes.

Written language does not need too many building blocks to construct a large variety of systems (an alphabet to construct words placed in sequences of words). This complex model of language is fragile, as everyone who has misunderstood someone's conversation or has been misunderstood

. . . .

228 Paul Romer has pleaded us to "avoid mathiness" in economic writings "Like mathematical theory, mathiness uses a mixture of words and symbols, but instead of making tight links, it leaves ample room for slippage between statements in natural versus formal language and between statements with theoretical as opposed to empirical content." He asks us to "verify that the formal arguments are correct, that the connection between the symbols and the words is tight, and that the theoretical concepts have implications for measurement and observation" – that variables are observable and have units of measurement. Paul M. Romer, "Mathiness in the Theory of Economic Growth," *American Economic Review: Papers & Proceedings* 105(5) (2015), pp 89-93 http://dx.doi.org/10.1257/aer.p20151066

229 "Language is a Complex Adaptive System," *The Five Graces Group. Language Learning 59, Suppl. 1* (December 2009).

knows. Likewise, metaphors intended to enlighten may be misunderstood or extended beyond the realm of sensible applicability.

A huge stride in understanding the framework for complex systems was made by Justus Buchler the American philosopher widely recognized as the author of a new metaphysics, and frequently quoted in this book, although his contributions are rarely discussed these days. Writing in the 1960's before much was being said about complexity, Buchler came up with many prescient ideas which later translated into the language of complexity in a beautiful book **Metaphysics of Natural Complexes** [230] referenced earlier in this book but not often mentioned by writers about complexity. The reason may be, as a biographer succinctly put it, Buchler's writings "are notable for their elegantly spare style" meaning a tough read.

Buchler calls the ontology that determines his view of nature 'metaphysics of natural complexes.' Rather than seeing nature to be composed of substances, events, processes, matter, spirit, or any other specific type of entity or being, Buchler finds all such categories too narrow. Given the other categories and principles of his ontology, he maintains that there is nothing that cannot be accurately construed as a natural complex. The term is applied by him to attributes as well as entities, to ideas and terms of discourse as well as bodies, human individuals, and the constituents of human experience.

The principle of 'ordinality' that governs Buchler's system is inseparable from his concept of a natural complex, and is the fullest expression of what it means to be a natural complex. Buchler denies that complexes can be composed of ultimate 'simples' as proposed by some philosophers. Briefly, the principle of ordinality asserts that every complex must be constituted by other complexes, and also that every complex must be a constituent of some other complex or complexes. The term 'order' refers to a complex viewed as having constituents. For a complex viewed as a constituent of an order, Buchler uses the term 'trait', giving to this term a generalized sense which makes words that might be considered synonymous with it, such as 'characteristic' or 'attribute', only types of trait. [231]

. . . .

230 Justus Buchler, "Metaphysics of Natural Complexes," *Columbia University Press* (1966).

231 Adapted from: Beth J. Singer, "Ordinal Naturalism. An introduction to the philosophy of Justus Buchler," *Lewisburg, Bucknell University Press* (1983), pp. 11 and 21-22.

Because there are no equations we can write down using symbols and their relationships for complex systems we need to be very careful how words, which tend to be less precise than symbols, are used to avoid misunderstandings. Definitions will help.

In the following, I have gently and respectfully re-interpreted some of Buchler's definitions to make them more relevant to understanding innovation and innovation ecosystems.

Alescence

Alescence from the Latin *alascere*, meaning to grow up. It's a more encompassing term than emergence, or growth, but includes these under what might be called variation. Therefore we can say that alescence is a more basic foundation for what we see in actual systems as growth, emergence, and adaptation. Buchler identified three forms of alescence:

Augmentative – a prevailing (meaning an existing) complex is extended, increased or enhanced.

Example: An innovation ecosystem engineered to support technology commercialization from a university adds new capabilities to support entrepreneurship and new business creation not based on university research.

Spoliative – there is a loss or attenuation or expiration of a complex that has prevailed.

Example: An innovation ecosystem either because of failure or a change of policy discontinued early stage competitive funding for small businesses.

Coalescent – a complex arising from injunction or intersection of novel configurations of complexes.

Example: A university-based innovation ecosystem engineered to support local entrepreneurship merges with an innovation ecosystem established to support wider regional economic development. Section 10 demonstrates how a new rearrangement of existing building blocks (a coalescence) can lead to emergence. Coalescence can include cooperation, collaboration, partnerships, joint ventures, and so forth.

In all these examples it is necessary to keep in mind that any change in one part of an ecosystem will affect other system properties or indeed the whole system.

We use both the terms emergence and alescence in this book. As emergence is the more familiar term it is used in most cases. Alescence is used when it is important to identify one or more of the three forms of alescence. The three forms of alescence support a rich diversity of signals and boundaries (see Section 11).

Traits

A trait is a generalized term for characteristics, attributes, qualities, or properties of a complex. But, the complex or sub-complex should not be thought of as a 'container' of traits. The trait is 'of the complex' in Buchler's belief. To see how some traits are not contained in a complex, consider Buchler's example of the traits of a tree. A tree has traits of, for example, the color of leaves and texture of the bark. The tree has traits that are not seen as within it such as rain and sun which it needs to grow. Therefore, that a complex should not be thought of as a container of traits is very important for the study of innovation ecosystems and their wider environments. There cannot be a complex without traits or sub-complexes. Traits are 'of the complex' as sub-complexes.[232]

"[I]f we allow that the New York Stock Exchange and the specialized provisions of contract law are as much means to human purposes as our steel mills and textile machinery we can say that they too are in a wider sense technologies. If we include these 'arrangements' in the collective of technology, we begin to see the economy not as a container for its technologies, but as something constituted from its technologies. The economy is a set of activities and behaviors and flows of goods and services, mediated by – draped over it – its technologies. It follows that the methods, processes, and organizational forms. …. form the economy."[233]

. . . .

232 Buchler calls these 'subaltern complexes.' Sub-complex is a more current term used this book. 'Sub' does not imply any inferiority or secondary importance of the complex.

233 W Brian Arthur, "Complexity and the Economy," *Oxford University Press* (2015), p 136.

Throughout this book, context is a recurring theme. A solution which may work in one context may not work in another; causation is driven by context. This is obvious from our experience but sometimes overlooked or not sufficiently emphasized. Context should not be considered as external to a complex system in which the complex system is somehow embedded. Context is a trait. It is a trait in the same way that the rain and sun are traits for a tree. Realizing that context is a trait, and using Buchler's ideas enables us to fully understand the role or extreme significance of context. We saw in Section 16 that an upper level of a hierarchy can be the context for a lower level.

An alescent complex admits traits – new sub-complexes – into its contour. A prevalent (existing, enduring, or invariant) complex excludes traits into its contour. This can be done by setting entry and exit conditions. Traits help us understand how sub-complexes communicate.

A given trait is connected with numerous other traits

Alescence is also produced by re-arranging its sub-complexes or components.

Contour

The traits of a complex define or delineate its contour. Sub-complex traits which define or chart the 'prospect before it' are its possibilities. A possibility is a prefinition (meaning: previous limitation) on the relevant traits in the contour of a natural complex. The order, with its makeup of traits, is what basically prefines. Note that contour is not a boundary as the name might suggest but as a path or trajectory.

Boundary

Every complex adaptive system must be constituted by other complexes, and also every complex must be a constituent of some other complex or complexes (non-reducibility or non-decomposability introduced in Section 5). This implies complexes have boundaries. [234] Interactions with

234   Buchler calls this "integrity" but for our purposes "boundary" is a more descriptive term.

other complex adaptive systems and with its environment occur through signals passed across boundaries.

The boundary is the limit of a complex, the conditions under which these limits are formed, and where these limits are located. The limits of a complex, like every other aspect of it may be alescent.

In Section 11 we saw the importance of boundaries and how communication across boundaries and between building blocks (sub-complexes), and between complexes and the external environment occurs and can be increased or decreased.

"Identical conglomerates can have distinct individual histories because of conditional reactions to different local environments and agents. The agent's boundary encapsulates this history, so that propagation of the boundary propagates the effects of that history." [235] This statement recognizes the concept of path dependency. A path, or trajectory, is the movement from one state to another in time.

Conglomerates (coalescences) may reach the same state by different paths. If the development of an innovation ecosystem system appears to be following the same path as a previously known innovation ecosystem they can be said to be 'near neighbors' and similar path dependency may, in some cases, be used to make predictions from the history of the first one.

Self-organization is path dependent. When re-arranging building blocks we should consider how they came to be building blocks – what has been their path/history?

Relevant Links

If two complexes are related then each is relevant to the other in either of two ways: *strongly relevant* or *weakly relevant*. [236] See Section 9 for details.

. . . .

235   John H. Holland, "Signals and Boundaries: Building Blocks for Complex Adaptive Systems," *MIT Press* (2012), p 54.

236   This concept was introduced by Buchler writing in the 1960's before Mark Granovetter's famous research on weak and strong links in the 1970's.

27

Beyond Metaphor

....

Section Summary: The rainforest metaphor connects Rainforests (the original object) to innovation ecosystems and their building blocks (the object for which the symbol now stands). Metaphors are liberating; analogies can constrain. The Rainforest symbolism has acquired a new and richer interpretation as a complex adaptive system. This realization opens up the large volume of existing research on complex adaptive systems which can be used not only to understand but to analyze and predict the behavior of innovation ecosystems. Having grabbed our attention the metaphor remains as a comfort blanket as we enter the sometimes insecure world of complexity.

A Harvard business school alumnus responding to the intra-Harvard debate about theories of disruptive technologies is quoted as saying "We don't learn laws of business. We learned stories."

— John McDermott, Career Advice from Marina Keegan, Financial Times (US), June 26, 2014.

Much has been written about the effectiveness of stories in business. This will not be discussed here. However, the Rainforest concept introduced in the book by Victor H. Hwang and Greg Horowitt [237] opened up the idea of a Rainforest as a metaphor for expressing the innovation ecosystem concept. The Rainforest metaphor as described by Hwang and Horowitt connected Rainforests (the original object) to companies (the object for which the symbol now stands): "A company that seeks to manufacture cheaper, better, more profitable products would run operations like an

....

237   Victor W. Hwang and Greg Horowitt, "The Rainforest: The Secret to Building the Next Silicon Valley," *Los Altos Hills: Regenwald* (2012).

agricultural farm. However, the community that seeks to generate high levels of innovation throughout the whole system would do the opposite .... not controlling the specific processes but instead helping to set the right environmental variables that foster the unpredictable creation of new weeds." The metaphor is also a comparison of properties or traits.

This book has demonstrated that Rainforest symbolism has acquired a new and different interpretation as a complex adaptive system. It is no longer a descriptive metaphor but a dynamic metaphor which illustrates similarities in the underlying dynamics of both.

We have learned that Rainforest ecosystems not only have much in common with complex adaptive systems but that Rainforest innovation ecosystems *are* complex adaptive systems. The Rainforest symbol has acquired a new and different interpretation as a complex adaptive system. This realization opened up the large volume of research on complex adaptive systems to be used not only to understand but to analyze and anticipate the behavior of innovation ecosystems. Having grabbed our attention the metaphor remains as a comfort blanket as we enter the sometimes insecure world of complexity.

The philosopher Friedrich Nietzsche (1844 – 1900) identified the drive toward the formation of metaphors as the "fundamental human drive, which one cannot for a single instant dispense with in thought, for one would thereby dispense with man himself."

Without going into too much detail, and giving a quick version of the meaning of metaphor which might horrify a linguistic specialist, we can probably agree that language, prose or poetry, is used to communicate with others and therefore must be meaningful to others. Much of language is metaphor. It has been said that metaphor is the root of all transfer of meanings in speech. In metaphor or analogy, a word is detachable from its original meaning and transferred so that the meaning no longer adheres to the original object. By using words in new contexts, new meanings and aspects of the word may be revealed.

Metaphors use symbols, such as words or signs, which have intuitive meanings and are used within a universe of discourse. A universe of discourse is a context where the symbol has an understood meaning. Just as we would not describe a painting using terminology of chemistry, when using stories to communicate understanding we must not stray into universes of discourse having other accepted symbols. When I started working in international development I was confused by colleagues using the term 'actor' – with a meaning familiar to a sociologist but to a physicist (me) had me wondering how thespians came into the picture.

We may talk about adequacy or coherence and correspondence to facts. A bad image or symbol is that which contains internal contradictions, which conflict with facts or which leave facts un-illuminated. Conversely, a good symbol is internally consistent and does not conflict with facts.

Metaphors are liberating; analogies can constrain. If we use a rainforest *analogy* we would have to say the trees are like this and the weeds are like that, and so forth and the poetic symbolism would be lost. If I reminisce about my youth and inexperienced using the metaphor of being 'apple green,' an implied metaphor from Dylan Thomas's poem **Fern Hill**, this metaphor has more poetic power that the analogy that I was '*like* a green apple.' Metaphor opens up our imaginations and helps us build shared mental models.

Francis Thompson in his poem **Contemplation** uses the metaphor which nudges us into a sense of contemplation:

"This morning so I, fled in the shower,

The earth reclining in a lull of power"

Much has been written by philosophers about how the hearer decides to seek a nonliteral meaning in a metaphor, makes us attend to some likeness between two things, conveying an idea to open different frames of mind beyond the more straightjacketed analogy (A is like B, freshness after a rain shower *is like* the earth resting).

The linguistic philosopher Wilbur Urban in analyzing metaphor wrote: "it is the nature of the symbol to take the primary and natural meaning of both objects and words and modify them in certain ways so that they acquire a meaning relation of a different kind." [238] Thus, according to Urban a symbol has (1) reference to the original object – a rainforest in our

238   Warren A Shibles, "Analysis of Metaphor in the Light of W. M. Urban's Theories," *Mouton, Paris* (1971).

case – and (2) reference to the object for which the symbol now stands – a complex adaptive innovation ecosystem in our case.

Rick Dove expressed the concern of many of us: "I don't like using words like ecology to explain in shorthand a rich and useful organizational concept for business. For one, these soft edged metaphors turn off a lot of hard edged business people who occupy a large portion of the organizational power structures, especially in operations and manufacturing. For another, nature has the patience and resilience to absorb a lot of failed or marginal experiments that would terminate a business enterprise.... Simply referencing the metaphorical links and then postulating a new business paradigm doesn't appear successful in communicating with most people who have operational concerns." [239] Rick Dove's studies on agile manufacturing and 'Response-Able' systems appeared in Section 10. Great care must be taken in using the metaphor, especially, for example, within corporations. In Section 8 it was noted that the farm part of the Rainforest metaphor fails us; it does not distinguish between a static equilibrium and a dynamic equilibrium.

The Rainforest metaphor expands our thinking. Philosophers have postulated that "even a quite definite speaker intention does not finally determine the meaning of a metaphor" and that "the interpretation of the light the metaphor sheds on its subject may outrun anything the speaker is thought explicitly to have in mind." [240] In the Rainforest case, the metaphor, in fact, preceded the more detailed analysis of the complex adaptive systems model. The metaphor worked as antecedent to innovation ecosystem science.

In Molière's play **Le Bourgeois Gentilhomme**, produced in 1670, Monsieur Jourdain asks something to be written in neither verse nor prose. He is told, "Sir, there is no other way to express oneself than with prose or verse." Jourdain replies, "By my faith! For more than forty years I have been speaking prose without knowing it." To parallel Monsieur Jourdain, we may be surprised we've been talking about complex adaptive systems without knowing it.

. . . .

239   Rick Dove, "Response Ability: The Language, Structure, and Culture of the Agile Enterprise," *John Wiley and Sons, Inc.* (2001), p 134.

240   "An Irenic Idea about Metaphor," *Philosophy*, Vol.88, No. 343 (Jan 2013), p 25.

28
What Next?

. . . .

"If a man will begin with certainties, he shall in [be] doubts; but if he will be content to begin with doubts, he shall end in certainties."

— Francis Bacon, The Advancement of Learning 1605.

This book began with the statement that every innovation ecosystem is a complex adaptive system with shifting regions of non-complexity embedded within it. I hope this starting hypothesis has been validated by the cumulative findings in this book's Sections.

Our sometimes winding journey has taken us through the central message of this book: that the concept of emergence is a fundamental feature of complex adaptive systems as a precursor to innovation; and how arrangements of building blocks of innovation ecosystems can produce emergence and innovation.

On the way, many other concepts have been added. We should always remember that, although occasionally complex systems may appear to be mysterious, we are dealing with social systems, individuals or groups of *people* just like us.

So, what next, what needs to be investigated, what new knowledge do we need to acquire? Here are a few suggestions:

- Better methods for measuring monitoring and evaluating (MM&E) innovation ecosystems and ecosystem properties. Management thinker Peter Drucker is often quoted as saying that "you can't manage what you can't measure." Better metrics need to be developed. These will be novel metrics which apply to uncertain or unpredictable environments.

- Much more empirical evidence gained through pilot applications and experiments to support or falsify theories.

- Some of what is in Section 25 will be challenged. This feedback will be welcomed and addressed.

- More and better tools for building, repairing, and sustaining innovation ecosystems.

- More firmly based leading indicators.

- More knowledge on strategies, strategic planning, and roadmapping in complex adaptive systems under conditions of uncertainty, as well as decentralized policy-making and implementation.

- How Rainforest thinking might contribute to scenario creation in planning.

- The relation between complexity and entrepreneurship has not been sufficiently researched.

- Leadership in complex systems needs more study.

- The value of hierarchies in complex innovation systems has not been fully explored.

- There is more to be investigated in comparisons with the building block and network views such as cohesion (detection of sub-groups and their density and paths which link them), and network shape (overall distribution of links, core-peripherness, and clumping).

- The model of 'fluid' flow in networks has been suggested but not adequately studied.

- Complex adaptive systems as platforms should be investigated.

- More extensive translation of complexity research into applications for economic development, innovation, and entrepreneurial growth is needed.

- To help people to better understand complex systems a pictorial language of some kind could help.

These are just a few ideas. I'm sure, dear reader, you can think of many others which I hope you will earnestly pursue.

Acknowledgements

For their guidance, insights, encouragement, and honest critiques of several versions of this book I'm most grateful to: Harry Red, Tom Guevara, Victor Hwang, Scott Gillespie, David Winkelman, Deborah Jackson, Greg Horowitt, Patsy Kahoe, Al Watkins, Brad Rendle, Cathy Swain, and Gavin Peacock. I also thank the authors of over 200 articles and books which were sources for the research behind this book. Errors are, naturally, the author's responsibility.

About "Admired Disorder"

The word "admired" is used by Francis Bacon, statesman and philosopher, in his brief 1623 Essay titled **Of Innovations**.

"It is true that what is settled by custom, though it be not good, yet at least it is fit ... whereas new things piece not so well, but, though they help by their utility, yet they trouble by their conformity: besides, they are like strangers, more admired and less favored." Bacon argued that scientific knowledge should be based on observation of nature – a radical idea in his age.

In Shakespeare's Macbeth, Lady Macbeth chastises her husband:

"You have displaced the mirth, broke the good meeting,
With most *admired disorder.*"

In old English *admired disorder* means a wonderful or extraordinary state of disorder; very similar to what we see in this book. These events often include key, yet often overlooked, traits: unexpected emergence of innovation, self-organizing systems, wicked problems, lack of logical connections, insights from dissent, order coexisting with disorder, among others. Complex adaptive systems describes these collective traits.

Most admired disorder indeed.

About the Author

Alistair M. Brett has over 30 years of international consulting experience in some 15 developed and developing countries around the globe, specializing in commercializing science and technology, and developing support mechanisms for technology commercialization from universities and research centers.

Alistair focuses on how understanding innovation ecosystems as complex adaptive systems not only opens up the large volume of research on such systems but also help to analyze, design, create, and maintain, support for innovation in businesses, organizations, regions, and countries.

He is the co-founder of the Center for Technology Commercialization and the Center's graduate technology management degree programs at the Academy of National Economy in Moscow, Russia. He has some 20 years of experience in higher education administration. Alistair is also a senior consultant to The World Bank. He holds a B.Sc. in Physics from the University of London, and a Ph.D. in Theoretical Physics, from the University of St. Andrews (Scotland), and Drexel University (USA).

Contact: alistair@infyrno.com